Oracle8 Database Administration on Windows NT

Lynnwood Brown

Prentice Hall PTR
Upper Saddle River
New Jersey 07458
http://www.phptr.com

ISBN 0-13-927443-X
90000>

9 780139 274435

Library of Congress Cataloging-in-Publication Data

Brown, Lynnwood
   Oracle8 database administration on Windows NT / Lynnwood Brown.
     p.   cm.
   Includes index.
   ISBN: 0-13-927443-X
   1. Relational databases. 2. Oracle (Computer file) 3. Microsoft Windows NT. I. Title.
QA76.9.D3B7827   1998
005.75'85--dc21   98-11705
                                                    CIP

Editorial/Production Supervision/Design: *Joanne Anzalone*
Acquisitions Editor: *Mark L. Taub*
Cover Design Director: *Jerry Votta*
Cover Art: *Talar Agasyan*
Manufacturing Manager: *Alexis R. Heydt*
Marketing Manager: *Dan Rush*
Editorial Assistant: *Audri Bazlan*

© 1999 Prentice Hall PTR

Prentice-Hall, Inc.

Upper Saddle River, New Jersey 07458

Printed in the United States of America
10 9 8 7 6 5 4 3

ISBN 0-13-927443-X

Prentice-Hall International (UK) Limited, *London*
Prentice-Hall of Australia Pty. Limited, *Sydney*
Prentice-Hall Canada Inc., *Toronto*
Prentice-Hall Hispanoamericana, S.A., *Mexico*
Prentice-Hall of India Private Limited, *New Delhi*
Prentice-Hall of Japan, Inc., *Tokyo*
Prentice-Hall Asia Pte. Ltd., *Singapore*
Editora Prentice-Hall do Brasil, Ltda., *Rio de Janeiro*

CONTENTS

LIST OF FIGURES

LIST OF TABLES

FOREWORD

The past ten years have been an incredible adventure for me. It started on a day when as a college graduate, I stood in Union Square with my friend Lynnwood Brown and poured over the description of an Oracle training book with companion CD. As we excitedly discussed about the first true handbook for Oracle on the NT platform, Lynnwood and I didn't know exactly how it would be used or sold, but we were sure it would change us and the world of database training.

We are all beginning another journey. We aren't sure where this one will lead us either, but again I am sure this revolution will touch even more lives and take us all farther. The major changes coming will be in the way people communicate with each other. The benefits and problems arising from this upcoming communication revolution will be much greater than those brought about by the Internet revolution. There is never a reliable map for unexplored territory, but we can learn important lessons from the creation and evolution of the multi-billion dollar industry. The internet—its evolving hardware and software business applications, on-line education systems, Internet connections, electronic mail, multimedia titles, and authoring tools—is the foundation for the next revolution.

During the Internet's infancy, the mass media paid little attention to what was going on in the brand new business. Those of us who were enthralled by computers and the possibilities they promised were unnoticed outside our own circles and definitely not considered trendy.

The process of thinking about and writing *Oracle8 for NT* took Lynnwood longer than he expected. Indeed, estimating the time it would take proved to be as difficult as projecting the development schedule of a major software project.

I hope this book stimulates understanding, debate, and creative ideas about how we can take advantage of all that's sure to be happening in the database world ahead.

John W. Boone

Director Infrastructure Architecture And Standards
GTE Internetworking

PREFACE

This book is intended for people who have a basic understanding of computers and programming. The reader should be familiar with Windows NT, but does not have to be an expert. There are several appendices with helpful tips on the various utilities that are used to install, manage and tune the Oracle relational database management system. The Windows NT operating system will be covered at a level intended to show the integration of Windows NT and Oracle8. The book is written for those people that may have experience with mainframe, UNIX or Windows/DOS computing and need to understand how Oracle's RDBMS functions on the Windows NT platform.

The audience that this book is intended for includes:

❑ Working professionals who need to understand Oracle8 on the Windows NT platform and are not enrolled in a college or extension course. These are people that work for companies that are considering or have decided to invest in Oracle as a solution to their data processing needs.

❑ Working professionals that are taking a course in computer systems through a college or a computer training school.

❑ College students taking a course in computer science or information systems.

The book is compiled from my experience teaching Oracle database administration at the University of California at Berkeley Extension and teaching and consulting and at various corporations including DHL, MCI, Wells Fargo Bank, GTE, InfoWorld and Clarify Inc. I have also drawn on my experience working for the Oracle Corporation in the worldwide technical support group. Many of my students are working professionals who have many years of experience using various other RDBMS products and need to learn Oracle to advance their careers. One of my goals in writing this book is to consolidate relevant information on Oracle database administration into one easy to understand book and use this information in training other database administrators. I can be contacted at **www.ldbrown.com** if additional or specific training or consulting is required.

The intent of the book is not to teach database design or be a guide to SQL programming. The focus of the book is to show a person who has some basic programming skills what is Oracle8 and how can they use it. At various parts in the book the reader will be pointed to reference material that comes from Oracle. Therefore the reader will be able to gain an understanding of Oracle and how to use the system. Should they require further information into the theory behind how Oracle operates they will be pointed to the various Oracle reference manuals. It is my feeling that the Oracle manuals are the best place to get detailed information on Oracle. The problem is that the manuals are usually written for someone that already understands the product and the information is spread out among many manuals.

Some of the material for the book came from my first book on Oracle database administration on the UNIX operating system. This book is an expansion of the first book in that it describes the activities that a DBA performs while administering an Oracle8 database on the Windows NT operating system platform. The job of the database administrator (DBA) can be divided into the various tasks that the DBA may be required to perform during a normal day. These task include:

❏ Database installation and customization

❏ Database performance monitoring/analysis

❏ Database backup and recovery

❏ Database tuning

❏ Application tuning

❏ End user creation and management

❏ Client server application implementation

❏ Database capacity planning

❏ Implementing database security

❏ Database auditing

This book will demystify Oracle database administration by using real world examples of the various tasks that a DBA will be required to perform on a daily basis. The problem with a lot of the documentation that comes from Oracle concerning it's RDBMS and tools are that it is spread out among too many books. This book seeks to consolidate this information into one text. The book focuses on the following database administration topics:

❑ Introduction to the Oracle relational database management system and the various products that are offered by the Oracle Corporation. The reader will be introduced to the reasons why the Oracle relational database management system running on the Windows NT platform has become a very popular environment for client server computing.

❑ The Oracle8 RDBMS architecture. The architectural discussion provides the foundation that will be required in the latter sections on installation considerations and performance and tuning for the Windows NT operating system.

❑ Installation and configuration of the Oracle relational database management system software. Various tips will be given to help demystify the installation of Oracle on the Windows NT platform. The chapter will show the tight integration between Oracle8 and the Windows NT operating system.

❑ Client server implementation using Oracle's SQL*NET. The topics include SQL*NET's integration with the Window NT's networking strategy. In addition to defining what is a protocol and what are some of the more popular communications techniques/protocols (SPX/IPX, SNA, TCP/IP etc....) the configuration and debug of SQL*NET is covered.

❑ End user management and system security.

The reader is introduced to the various SQL commands that must be used to accomplish basic DBA task. The purpose of the book is not to teach SQL but an appendix on SQL programming is included. The language reference also includes examples of Oracle's procedural language PL/SQL. The reader is introduced to the SQL commands that are required for the DBA to manage the database. The reader will be introduced to the various graphical user interface (GUI) tools that are part of Oracle8 offering. The relationship between the various GUI tools and the SQL commands that they generate will be covered in detail.

Easy to understand performance guidelines will be covered. The reader is stepped through what system information should be collected from the Windows NT operating system as well as the Oracle kernel. The reader will be guided through how to tune the system based on the performance data.

The book includes sections covering application development and the management of very large databases. The reader will be introduced to table partitioning and how it is used to manage large tables. The reader is also introduced to entity relationship modeling and its role in application development. The goal is to introduce the reader to data modeling as it relates to the DBA.

The book is organized into the following chapters:

Chapter 1—INTRODUCTION

❏ Introduce the reader to RDBMS from a historical perspective.

❏ Introduce the Oracle RDBMS and the various tools that make up the Oracle offering. A brief explanation will be given for the various Oracle tools and applications.

Chapter 2—THE ORACLE8 RDBMS ARCHITECTURE

❏ Introduce the reader to the Oracle RDBMS architecture. The various Oracle services and data structures will be described. The relationship between the data structures and the various Windows NT services will be described both pictorially and in writing.

❏ Introduce various commands and terminology that will be used in the latter sections of the book.

Chapter 3—SYSTEM INSTALLATION

❏ Explain the installation process is integrated with the Windows NT registry.

❏ Explain the various Windows NT system administration tasks that need to be performed to set up the correct environment for the installation and give examples on how to perform them.

Chapter 4—CLIENT/SERVER IMPLEMENTATION

❏ Introduce the reader to data communications. Various types of data communications architectures will be briefly covered. The OSI model will be described and related to the implementation of client server systems using Oracle's SQL*NET.

❏ Cover various installation and debug issues using SQL*NET v2.

❏ Cover the use of SQL*NET in implementing client server and distributed database environments.

Chapter 5—DATABASE ACCESS AND SECURITY

❏ Introduce the reader to the basic DBA task. The topics will include how to add users, controlling access (security), starting and stopping the database. Various examples will be given. The examples will show how the operations are performed using one of the new GUI tools (such as Data Manager) and it's command line equivalent.

❏ Sow the relationship between performing the various end user management tasks using the new Oracle GUI's (User Manager, Data Manager etc.) and using the command line utility Server Manager.

Chapter 6—DATABASE BACKUP/RECOVERY

❑ Backup and recovery techniques will be covered through various examples. The reader will be advised as to how to determine the best backup strategy for their environment.

❑ Database backup and recovery using the Oracle Backup and Recovery utility and using the command line utility Server Manager.

Chapter 7—DATABASE PERFORMANCE AND TUNING

❑ Show the reader how collect and interpret the database performance statistics.

❑ Show the reader how to tune the system (this includes the RDBMS and how it relates to the Windows NT operating system).

❑ Show the reader how use the utilities database analysis product DBAware.

Chapter 8—DATABASE CAPACITY PLANNING

❑ Estimating disk storage requirements.

❑ Estimating table, index and rollback segment requirements.

❑ Monitoring disk storage utilization.

Chapter 9—Application Development

❑ Entity Relationship modeling and its relationship to application development

❑ Defining database constraints related to the ER model.

Chapter 10—VLDB

❑ Managing large tables using table stripping

❑ Managing large tables using table partitioning

SQL is introduced as the programming language that is used to access the Oracle relational database system. The language reference that is provided contains various examples that the readers can use to familiarize themselves with the SQL language. The SQL language reference has also been expanded to include object oriented SQL and PL/SQL examples.

A project of this size cannot be accomplished without the help of other people. I want to thank my former students Sujata Raju for her assistance in writing the Oracle product summary and Robert Briley (now with Oracle Worldwide Technical Support) for his review and comments. I want to thank Fifi W. Agenhu of the

University of California at Berkeley Extension's Computer and Information Systems department for her comments on Windows NT system administration. Thank you Paul Osborn of MenloSoftware for providing the database analysis tool DBAware and the section on using DBAware for Oracle database analysis and tuning. I also want to thank Paul for being a good friend who kept me laughing as we discussed topics related and unrelated to database administration. I want to thank the publishing staff of Prentice Hall especially Mark Taub for believing in me and Joanne Anzalone for not giving up on me. I want to thank Barbara Brown for being my mom. As always I want to thank my sister Stephanie Brown for indexing the manuscript, tolerating all of my last minute changes and being my best friend.

## Chapter 1

INTRODUCTION TO DATABASE MANAGEMENT SYSTEMS

WHAT AND WHY

Before we explore the Oracle Relational DataBase Management System (RDBMS) let's establish what a database management system is and consider some of the reasons why we choose to use it to store information. In the IBM Dictionary of Computing a database is defined as:

❏ A collection of data with a given structure for accepting, storing and providing, on demand data for multiple users.

❏ A collection of interrelated data organized to serve one or more applications.

❏ A collection of data fundamental to a system or enterprise.

A database management system is defined as:

❏ A computer-based system for defining, creating, manipulating, controlling and managing a database.

❑ An integrated set of computer programs that collectively provide all of the capabilities required for the centralized management, organization and control of access to a database that is shared by many users.

❑ A computer-based system that may be invoked by nonprogrammers or by application programs to define, create, revise, retire, interrogate, and process transactions; and to update, backup, recover, validate, secure and monitor the database.

All organizations have data to manage. Data can include information that allows an organization to track customer invoices/orders, warehouse inventory or number of employees. For organizations that have a significant number of employees or customers, there will be large quantities of data. Being able to access the data is often critical to the success of the organization. Ease of access to the data can be accomplished by placing the data in a common repository and by using a standard, easy to use language. To answer the question "Why Use A Database," we can safely say that we use a database to help ease access to information and to manage it.

WHAT IS A DATABASE MANAGEMENT SYSTEM?

Now we have a definition of what a database is and why we should use one. Next we'll define a DataBase Management System. A DBMS can be defined as a software system that:

❑ Provides and controls access to the database.

❑ Supports multiple/concurrent users.

❑ Protects the integrity and security of the database.

❑ Recovers from system failure.

❑ Supports multiple tools and applications (e.g., forms generators, report writers, etc.).

❑ Supports several databases on different machines networked together to ensure consistency among all databases to form a distributed database.

We now have a complete set of definitions for what a database is, why we may choose to use a database and what does a database management system.

TYPICAL DATABASE APPLICATIONS

Almost any application can be a database application. Some typical database applications include:

- ❑ On-line Transaction Processing (OLTP). OLTP applications include order entry, inventory, personnel, airline reservations, and banking.
- ❑ Decision Support. Decision Support applications include market research, management information systems, manufacturing, engineering and scientific data analysis.

There are many types of applications that can (and do) use a database.

WHAT IS A DATA MODEL?

The are several types of architectural models for databases. These architectural models are also referred to as data models. A data model can be defined as a set of structures, operations, and integrity rules that define how the data is organized and manipulated. The three most popular data models are:

- ❑ Hierarchical: Tree-structured database used for top down and rapid data access.
- ❑ Network: Uses a collection or set of pointers to access records.
- ❑ Relational: Tables consisting of rows of data accessed by their value and their relation to other data.

Oracle uses the relational data model. The relational model was developed in 1970 by Dr. Ted Codd. At that time Codd was working in the area of database modeling and design as a mathematician for IBM.

The relational model developed by Dr. Codd offers the following advantages for accessing stored information:

- ❑ Simple data structures and data language.
- ❑ All relationship types easily represented.
- ❑ High degree of data independence.
- ❑ Increased accessibility for ad hoc access.

Some of the disadvantages of the relational data model are:

❏ Performance may be slow.

❏ Poorly models complex objects.

In spite of the disadvantages the relational model provides a solid foundation for growth. The maintenance of relational databases is simpler (and cheaper) than the various other data models.

❏ Data independence helps to reduce database maintenance.

❏ Ad hoc queries/OLTP reduce the need for reporting tools.

❏ Modern development tools reduce the time that it takes to create end user applications.

Some attributes of hierarchical and network databases include:

❏ Proprietary platforms (Wang, Hewlett-Packard, etc.).

❏ Extremely high performance systems.

RELATIONAL DATABASE TERMS

The SQL programming language provides the Database Administration (DBA) with a tool for performing several different operations on the table data. The types of operations that are supported and the terminology used to describe the operations are included in Table 1.1.

TABLE 1.1   Database Operations and Their Functions

Database Operation	Function Performed
Manipulation	Insert, Update, Delete
Selection	Choose a subset of rows
Projection	Choose a subset of columns
Join	Match two or more tables by row

WHAT IS ORACLE?

Now that we have an idea of what a database is and what it can be used for the next question to answer (at least in this introduction) is: "What is Oracle?"

The answer to the question "What is Oracle?" is that when most people say Oracle they are referring to a family of software products made by the Oracle Corporation. The central product of the Oracle offering is the relational database. There are several other products that Oracle manufactures besides the database. Oracle Corporation makes application development tools. These applications development tools can be used to create the data entry screens or reports that make up an end user application. Oracle Corporation also makes end-user applications. These applications can include such things as Order Entry, and Inventory Management as shown in Figure 1.1.

OPERATING SYSTEMS AND THE ORACLE RDBMS

The Oracle RDBMS is an application that can be run under many different operating systems. An operating system is a computer program that provides an environment for other computer programs that are often referred to as application programs. The computer's operating system is responsible for controlling the main processor, all I/O devices such as disk drives, and provides the interface to the computers hardware for the end user.

There are many different operating systems on the market today. They range from the operating systems such as MVS which is used to run large mainframe computers to operating systems like QUNX which is used for small embedded computer systems. A list of the various operating systems in use today would include:

- ❏ A/UX
- ❏ Amiga
- ❏ BeOS
- ❏ BIOS
- ❏ CP/M
- ❏ DOS
- ❏ Mach
- ❏ Macintosh
- ❏ Microsoft Windows

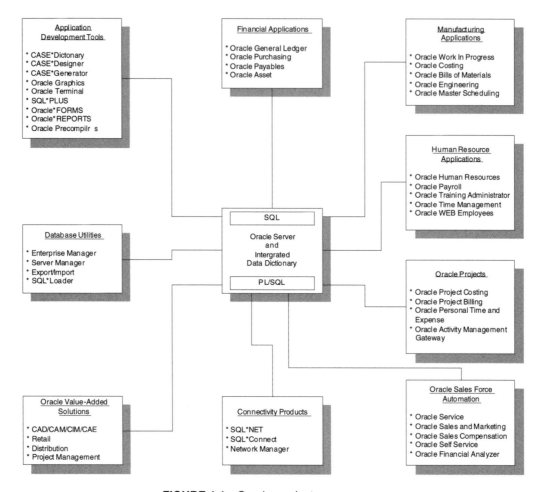

FIGURE 1.1 Oracle product summary

- ❏ Minix
- ❏ Multics
- ❏ NetWare
- ❏ OS/2
- ❏ OSF DCE
- ❏ OSF/1
- ❏ UNIX
- ❏ VMS

The operating systems that support the Oracle RDBMS include:

❑ **MVS/VS**: This is an operating system that runs on IBM or IBM compatible mainframes.

❑ **VAX/VMS**: This operating system was made popular by the Digital Equipment Corporation.

❑ **UNIX**: There are various versions of this operating system. It runs on many hardware platforms including SUN/Solaris, IBM/AIX, and Hewlett-Packard/HPUX to name a few.

❑ **Windows NT**: This multitasking operating system from Microsoft Corporation runs on computers that are based on the Intel microprocessor.

❑ **OS/2**: This multitasking operating system from IBM runs on computers that are based on the Intel microprocessor.

❑ **Windows 95**: This is a single-user operating system from Microsoft Corporation. It allows a user to have their own local version of the Oracle RDBMS along with their other desktop applications.

INTRODUCING WINDOWS NT

The movement of a processor through a set program of instructions that are stored in memory is called a thread of execution. Threads can be run in one of the various privilege levels of the processor. Code running at a high privilege level can access data at lower privilege levels, but code running at a low privilege level cannot access data in memory marked with higher privilege levels. The NT Executive runs in kernel mode, which is the highest privilege level that the processor offers. On Intel x86 processors, which support four privilege levels referred to as rings 0 through 3, kernel mode is synonymous with ring 0. Applications run in user mode (ring 3 on the Intel central processing unit), so the protection mechanisms built into the processor protect the NT Executive from application programs.

Each application hosted by Windows NT constitutes one process, and each process must consist of at least one thread running in a separate address space where it is physically isolated from other processes. Before transferring control from one process to another, the operating system alters the processor's page tables so that each process sees only its own code and data. It's not possible for one process to access code or data belonging to another process.

One of the aspects of the Windows NT architecture is that portions of the operating system and subsystems run in user-mode processes alongside application processes. The subsystems provide the environments in which applications run. The Win32 subsystem provides the application program interface (API) services that Win32 applications call to do useful things such as create windows and open files. The POSIX and OS/2 subsystems provide similar API services to character-mode POSIX and OS/2 applications.

Much of Windows NT's stability is a direct result of the operating system's architecture. Applications cannot interfere with one another because they run in separate address spaces. Operating system code and data in the subsystems is protected from applications because subsystems, too, reside in their own address spaces. The Windows NT Executive shares address space with running processes, but it's protected by the wall between kernel mode and user mode. It's impossible for an application to corrupt code or data stored in the Windows NT Executive because the processor notifies the operating system of, or prevents, invalid memory accesses before they occur.

Ultimately, an operating system's reliability and resistance to application-induced crashes is a function of how effectively it guards itself and the processes it hosts from other processes. Windows NT excels in this regard because of the high level of protection it provides both to the operating system and to its application programs.

However reliability doesn't come for free. When a Windows application calls an API function in the Win32 subsystem (as might happen several hundred times per second), the operating system has to perform a context switch from the calling process to the subsystem process and then back again. Context switches are costly in terms of performance. So are the ring transitions—shifts from one privilege level to another—that are incurred when ring 3 code calls code in ring 0. Ring transitions occur because applications running in user mode use the Windows NT Executive's kernel-mode Local Procedure Call (LPC) facility to communicate with the subsystems, and also because the subsystems must call into kernel mode to invoke services in the Windows NT Executive.

To boost performance and reduce memory requirements, the designers of Windows NT 4.0 decided to move many of the operating system's API services out of the Win32 subsystem and into the operating system kernel. The new Win32K Executive houses three important elements of the operating system: the window manager, the Graphics Device Interface (GDI), and the graphics device drivers that render GDI output on screens and printers. In Windows NT 3.x, these components were part of the Win32 subsystem. In Windows NT 4.0, they're part of the Windows NT Executive, where, like other kernel-mode services, they can be accessed in the context of calling processes.

The new architecture promises to deliver dramatic increases in performance, particularly in the execution of graphics. All output to the screen is performed through function calls to the GDI. Now that the GDI is part of the kernel, applications can call GDI functions directly and avoid costly context switches, video drivers can get to the hardware more quickly, and Win32 API services can call services in the Windows NT Executive without incurring ring transitions.

Performance in other areas is also improved. Moving the window manager to the kernel eliminated a key bottleneck that limited bandwidth between the window manager and application programs that call window manager services.

And what about memory? Now that the bulk of the code and data implementing the operating system's Win32 API services are mapped into the address of every process, there's no longer a need for server threads and shared memory buffers. Consequently, the system's appetite for memory is reduced. The savings are roughly offset, however, by the enlarged footprint of the user interface shell. So while it's true that Windows NT 4.0 uses memory more efficiently than did Version 3.x, it's also true that you'll still need at least 16MB of RAM to achieve minimally acceptable performance.

INTRODUCING ORACLE8

Oracle8 for Windows NT extends the tradition of the industry-leading Oracle RDBMS. With enhancements in performance, scalability, functionality, manageability, and reliability, Oracle8 for Windows NT represents an advance in database technology. The combined strength of Oracle8 and the tight integration with Windows NT brings ease of use and power to the RDBMS community.

Oracle8 for Windows NT offers tight integration with the Windows NT Registry, Windows NT Performance Monitor, Windows NT Event Viewer, Windows NT Service, and Windows NT Security Login. In addition, Oracle8 for Windows NT has been optimized to take full advantage of NT's multitasking and I/O capabilities. OLTP applications take advantage of Oracle8 for Windows NT's parallel architecture by distributing tasks or worker threads across multiple processors or machines, such as in a clustered environment, improving individual transaction response times and overall system throughput. Oracle8 for Windows NT efficiently prioritizes the threads to achieve maximum performance. The Windows NT operating system automatically balances processing workload evenly across allocated hardware and operating system resources.

Oracle8 for Windows NT includes support for Oracle's Multithreaded Server (MTS) architecture. This architecture coordinates thousands of simultaneous user requests. Individual requests are queued and serviced by a minimum of server threads. This allows for efficient memory utilization.

Sophisticated caching of database blocks, SQL execution plans, and executable stored procedures take advantage of available server memory. Available system resources can be allocated with a high degree of control, optimizing performance to the capabilities of the system and to the system workload on a dynamic basis. I/O operations are similarly specialized, utilizing different techniques such as asynchronous and multi-block reads and writes to improve response times and overall system throughput for all users and all requests. Stored procedures and database triggers are stored in compiled form, allowing them to be executed directly without recompilation or parsing, resulting in optimum run-time performance.

Oracle8 and the Oracle networking solution Net8 efficiently utilize operating system and networking resources, allowing tens of thousands of concurrent users to connect over multiple network protocols. Connection pooling temporarily drops the physical connection for idle users (and transparently reestablishes the connection when needed), increasing the number of users that can be supported. The Connection Manager multiplexes several user sessions over one network connection, reducing resource requirements especially for multitier applications.

Oracle8 for Windows NT provides XA support for Transaction Processing (TP) monitors. Dynamic XA support provides high performance for multitier applications with industry-standard, XA-compliant, transaction, processing monitors. This offers a robust way to bring Oracle8 for Windows NT into a heterogeneous environment, supporting mission-critical applications that use distributed transactions across multiple platforms and databases.

Oracle8 for Windows NT supports databases up to hundreds of terabytes in size. Partitioned tables and indexes divide large tables and indexes into pieces which can be separately managed, rather than managing the entire table as one large monolithic object. Partitioning is a technique that provides scalable performance for OLTP applications that have large amounts of data. Partitioning decreases the time required to perform many administrative operations by applying the operations to smaller units of storage, which improves performance through increased parallelism, and improves availability by containing the impact of failures.

Oracle8 extends Oracle's parallelism to insert, update, and delete operations, as well as queries. In addition, all queries can now be run in parallel, including those based on an index scan and a single partition scan, as well as full-table scans.

Oracle8 for Windows NT provides an object-relational paradigm for complex applications. This improved way of defining data structures allows developers to directly define their business documents, such as purchase orders, inventory items, and data warehouse information, within Oracle8. This allows developers of mainstream commercial applications to better manage their business documents.

Oracle8 for Windows NT incorporates easy to use features that make installation and setup simple. The install procedure provides all that is needed to get a pretuned and preconfigured Oracle8 database up and running. This installation allows users to focus more on their database applications rather than on the database itself. A preconfigured and pretuned database allows for quick deployment of the database and the applications that it supports.

Enterprise Manager provides a single integrated management console for central administration of multiple remote servers, enabling the kind of management that is vital in large, distributed environments. The fully integrated, graphical Oracle Enterprise Manager (shown in Figure 1.2) allows administrators to perform complex management tasks with point-and-click ease. The combined power and simplicity allows any administrator, at any level of expertise, to manage the Oracle8 database, freeing up time for other tasks. They can schedule and automate jobs and events on both specific objects or groups of objects, greatly simplifying management operations.

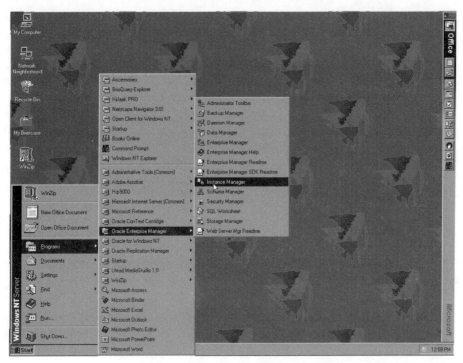

FIGURE 1.2 Oracle Enterprise Manager

❏ Oracle8 for Windows NT includes improvements in manageability through the use of several new Wizards. The task of managing a robust, powerful database engine can now be done easily and efficiently with these Wizards.

❏ Wizards such as the Oracle Database Assistant help you quickly create databases. The task of creating a database can now be done automatically and easily.

❏ Oracle Migration Assistant for Microsoft Access provides complete and easy migration of schema or data, or both, from your Microsoft Access database to Oracle8 for Windows NT. The wizard walks you through several simple tasks and in just seconds you're up and running.

❏ The Oracle INTYPE File Assistant provides an easy and intuitive GUI to generate input files necessary for the Object Type Translator. This tool is used in conjunction with Oracle development environments to build rapid object-based applications.

❏ Oracle Net8 Assistant provides fast and simple configuration of networking for Oracle8. Configuring your network environment is easier than ever.

Oracle8 for Windows NT includes several other management enhancements to provide greater flexibility and simplicity.

❏ Customer sites supporting Microsoft SMS for software distribution and asset management may now distribute Oracle8 client software and Oracle8 for Windows NT. Predefined Oracle packages have been added to allow for simple software distribution through SMS.

❏ You can now start or shut down the Oracle8 for Windows NT instance by simply going to the Windows NT Service Control Panel and selecting the appropriate service action.

❏ Oracle8 for Windows NT employs a more integrated security log in model. Administrators can grant access to Oracle8 for Windows NT via secured access to NT domains.

SUMMARY

There are many applications that can and do benefit by including a database. The database provides a centralized repository and a standard interface to critical information. The Oracle8 database running on the Windows NT is an attractive solution. The ease of use and popularity of Windows NT when combined with the many features of Oracle8 will satisfy the need to access and store critical information. The remainder of this book focuses on the various topics that are part of Oracle database administration. The SQL commands that the various Oracle wizards are executing will be shown. We will cover the Oracle RDBMS architecture and its integration with the Windows NT operating system. In the communications chapter we discuss client/server implementation using Oracle's Net8. How end-user management and object management is implemented is covered in Chapter 5. System performance analysis and tuning are covered in Chapter 7, with an emphasis on interrupting the performance data that is collected.

THE ARCHITECTURE

The Oracle RDBMS consist of various files and programs that interact with the Windows NT operating system. To understand the Oracle RDBMS we must first develop an understanding of the interaction between the files and programs that make up the RDBMS. We should also have an understanding of how the programs that make up the RDBMS interact with the Windows NT operating system. In this chapter we will explore the functionality of the programs and files that make up the architecture for the Oracle RDBMS and how the programs interact with the Windows NT operating system.

ORACLE8 AND THE WINDOWS NT OPERATING SYSTEM

The Oracle8 RDBMS for NT is written using Microsoft's 32-bit API. By using the Microsoft 32-bit API the Oracle8 RDBMS has been tightly integrated with the underlying hardware. Oracle8's architecture for Microsoft Windows NT has been implemented as a single multithreaded process to conform with the Windows NT memory model.

Under the Windows NT operating system a process represents a logical unit of work or job that the operating system is to perform. A thread is one of many sub-tasks that are required to accomplish the job. The various components of a process are shown in the Figure 2.1 and explained in Table 2.1.

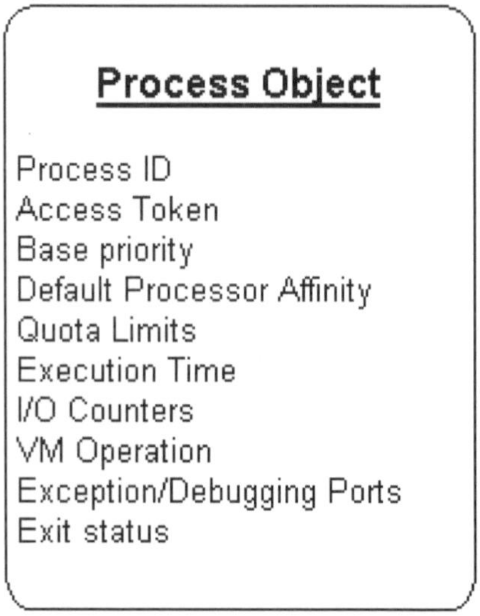

```
Process Object

Process ID
Access Token
Base priority
Default Processor Affinity
Quota Limits
Execution Time
I/O Counters
VM Operation
Exception/Debugging Ports
Exit status
```

FIGURE 2.1   Various components of a process

Where the various components have the following meanings:

TABLE 2.1   Components of a process

Process Identifier	Unique value identifying the process to the operating system
Access Token	Object containing security information about the user that is represented by the process.
Base Priority	Baseline execution priority for all the process's threads.
Default Processor Affinity	The default set of processors that the process can run.

The components of a thread include:

❑ A unique identifier called a client ID.

❑ The content of a set of registers that represent the state of the processor.

❑ A stack for when the thread is running in user mode and a stack for when the thread is running in kernel mode.

The thread resides within the process's virtual address space. When more then one thread exists in the same process, the threads share the address space of all the process's resources. The NT kernel schedules processes thread(s) for execution. All processes running under Windows NT must have at least one thread before the process can be executed.

Unlike Oracle8 for UNIX, Oracle8 for NT uses a single process with multiple threads, thereby sharing memory in a single address space. The database uses the operating system facility for preemptive scheduling and load balancing across multiple CPUs.

The Oracle instance on Windows NT consists of a memory segment and a number of background threads. By default, the Oracle8 server and its associated background threads run in the Normal Priority class. In this class, the scheduler can dynamically vary the priority between 1 and 15, but it cannot raise the dynamic priority to the real-time priority class. The real-time priority class ranges from 16 to 31 and cannot vary in priority based on behavior.

The Windows NT GUI and its associated utilities can be used to observe various portions of the Oracle8 RDBMS. To observe the services that are running on a Windows NT based machine. In Figure 2.2 the Windows menu is used to access the Windows NT control panel.

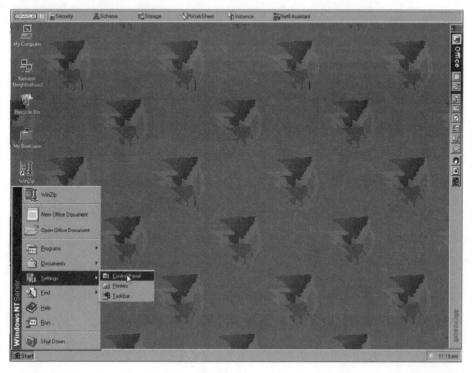

FIGURE 2.2   The Windows menu is used to access the Windows NT control panel

By accessing the Windows NT *CONTROL PANEL* the administrator can perform various task (see Figure 2.3).

FIGURE 2.3 Control Panel

One such task may be to observe, start, or stop any of the various services that are running on the machine. The various services associated with the Oracle RDBMS are shown in Figure 2.4.

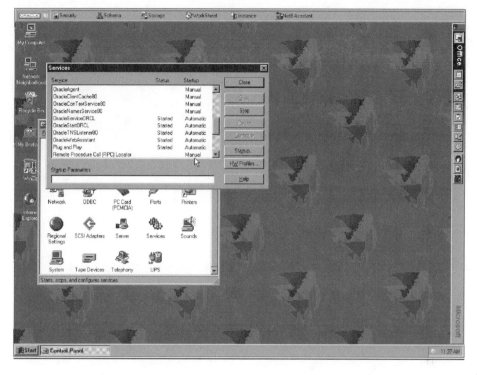

FIGURE 2.4   Services associated with the Oracle RDBMS

The remainder of this chapter is used to investigate the various components of the Oracle8 RDBMS architecture. Where possible the GUI utilities provided by the Windows NT operating system are used to observe the various components of the RDBMS. The same utilities will also help develop our understanding of how the Oracle8 RDBMS is integrated with the Windows NT operating system.

ORACLE8 RDBMS ARCHITECTURE

The architecture of the Oracle RDBMS is divided into two distinct parts. One part is called the Oracle database the other part is called the Oracle instance (see Figure 2.5).

The Oracle database is defined as:

❏ A logical collection of data to be treated as a unit (tables).

❏ Operating system files called data files, redo log files, initialization files and control files.

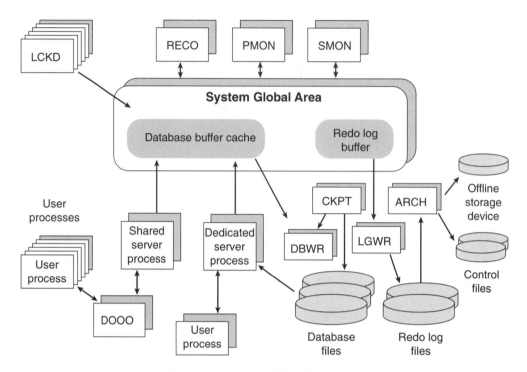

FIGURE 2.5   Oracle8 RDBMS architecture

The Oracle instance is defined as:

❑ The software mechanism used for accessing and controlling the database.
❑ Having at least four background threads called PMON, SMON, DBWR and LGWR.
❑ Including memory structures called the SGA and the PGA.
❑ Each Oracle instance is identified by a System Identifier (SID).

Instances and databases are independent of each other, but neither is of any use without the other. For the end user to access the database the Oracle instance must be started (the four background threads must be running) and the database must be mounted (by the instance) and opened. In the simple model a database can be mounted by only one instance. The exception to this is the Oracle parallel server, where a database can be mounted by more then one Oracle instance.

ORACLE DATABASE STRUCTURE

Our discussion of the Oracle RDBMS architecture will first focus on that part that makes up the Oracle database. The Oracle database has both a physical and a logical structure. The physical structure consists of the operating system files that make up the database. The logical structure is determined by the number of tablespaces and the databases's schema objects.

TABLESPACES

All Oracle databases must consist of at least one logical entity called a tablespace. The characteristics of a tablespace are:

❑ One or more per database. The database must have at least one tablespace called "SYSTEM." The SYSTEM tablespace holds the Oracle Data Dictionary. The Data Dictionary holds the various system tables and views such as the Oracle performance tables, information about the users of the database, and how much space is left in the various tablespaces that make up the database. There are usually more tablespaces other than the SYSTEM tablespace. Most Oracle databases also include additional tablespaces. These tablespaces are used to hold user data for sorting, and indexes that are used to speed up data access. Additional tablespaces should be created to hold data that is being sorted and another tablespace to hold data that is required for read consistency.

❑ The physical representation of the tablespace is called a data file (a tablespace may consist of more then one data file).

❑ Can be taken off line (due to media failure or maintenance purposes) leaving the database running. The exception to this rule is that the SYSTEM tablespace cannot be taken off line if the database is to remain running.

❑ Unit of space for object storage. Objects are tables, indexes synonyms, and clusters.

❑ Contains default storage parameters for database objects.

❑ When an end-user's Oracle user ID is created the user is given access to a default tablespace and a temporary tablespace (where the sorting of data is performed).

❑ Can be dropped (removed from the database).

As stated previously tablespaces are logical entities. Tablespaces are physically represented by files that are called data files.

Data files have the following attributes:

❏ Are operating system files.

❏ There is one or more per tablespace.

❏ The finest granularity of the data file is called the data block.

❏ A collection of data blocks is called an extent.

❏ A segment (by definition) consists of one or more extents (therefore to make a segment larger, extents are added to the segment).

❏ A data file consists of segments.

❏ Contain transaction System Change Numbers (SCNs).

DATA FILE CONTENTS AND TYPES OF SEGMENTS

A data file can consist of several types of segments and a segment can consist of one of more extents. The four different types of segments are rollback segments, temporary segments, index segments and data segments.

Rollback segments have the following attributes:

❏ Records old data.

❏ Provides for rollback of uncommitted transactions.

❏ Provides information for read consistency.

❏ Used during database recovery from media or processor failure.

❏ Wrap-around/reuseable.

❏ Can be dynamically created or dropped.

Rollback segments contain the following information:

❏ Transaction ID.

❏ File ID.

❏ Block number

❏ Row number

❏ Column number

❏ Row/column data.

Temporary segments have the following attributes:

❏ Used by the Oracle RDBMS as a work area for sorting data.

❏ The DBA defines which tablespace will contain temporary segments and therefore the tablespace where sorting will occur.

Index segments have the following attributes:

❑ Allows for faster data retrieval by providing an index for the data in a table, thus eliminating a full table scan during the execution of a query (similar to how a reader would use the index in a book rather then scanning through the entire book to find a particular topic).

Data segments have the following attributes:

❑ One per table/snapshot.
❑ Contains all table data.

Data segments contain the following information:

❑ Transaction ID.
❑ File ID.
❑ Block number
❑ Row number
❑ Column number
❑ Row/column data.

Besides data files there are also files called redo log files. Redo log files record changes made to the database by various transactions. All changes made to the database will first be written to the redo log file. These files can also be written to an off-line log file (archived). Redo logs are used during database recovery to recover the database to the last physical backup or to the point in time of failure (for this type of recovery the database must be running in ARCHIVELOG mode). Redo log files have the following attributes:

❑ Records new data.
❑ Ensures permanence of data transactions.
❑ Provides for roll forward recovery during database startup and after a media failure.

Redo log files contain:

❑ Transaction IDs
❑ Contents of redo log buffers.
❑ Transaction SCN.

THE CONTROL FILE

Each database has one or more control files. The control file is used to store information about the database. The information in the control file includes:

❏ Transaction System Change Number (SCN)

❏ Location of all datafiles.

❏ Names and locations of the redo log files.

❏ Time stamp when database was created.

❏ Database name.

❏ Database size.

For database recovery purposes it is best to have multiple copies of the control file. Without the control file the Oracle RDBMS cannot find the pointers to the rest of the files that make up the database (data files and redo log files).

THE INIT<SID>.ORA FILE

The init<SID>.ora file is the database initialization parameter file. It is only read at database start-up time. Every Oracle instance that is running will have its own init<SID>.ora file (the user should substitute <SID> with the Oracle System IDentifier for their instance). This file contains various initialization and tuning parameters that are needed by the RDBMS. Some of the parameters in the init<SID>.ora file are:

❏ The maximum number of processes that the Oracle instance will use (PROCESSES=).

❏ The name of the database (DB_NAME=).

❏ Various parameters for tuning memory management (DB_BLOCK_BUFFERS, SORT_AREA_SIZE...)

❏ The location of the control file(s).

How these parameters affect the starting and running of the database are covered in the chapters on Oracle RDBMS installation and performance analysis and tuning.

THE MEMORY STRUCTURES

The Oracle RDBMS creates and uses storage on the computer hard disk and in random access memory (RAM). The portion in the computer's RAM is called memory structure. Oracle has two memory structures in the computer's RAM. The two structures are the Program Global Area (PGA) and the System Global Area (SGA).

The PGA contains data and control information for a single, user process. The SGA is the memory segment that stores data that the user has retrieved from the database or data that the user wants to place into the database.

The SGA contains the following structures:

❏ Fixed part containing internal Oracle structures.

❏ Variable part containing the Oracle data dictionary and the shared and private SQL areas. The shared SQL area contains the parsed SQL statement and its execution plan (example: whether an index will be used). The private SQL area contains run-time buffers that are used by the session that issued the SQL statement.

❏ Database buffer cache. This part contains the data buffers. The data buffers contain data blocks, index blocks, rollback segment blocks and temporary segment blocks. In the illustration (see Figue 2.6), the Database buffer cache contains a buffer for the data and a buffer for the rollback after the data manipulation language (DML) statements UPDATE and COMMIT are issued. The data in the database buffer cache will be written to the data files by the Oracle DataBase WRiter thread (DBWR). The number of buffers in the cache is specified by the init<SID>.ora parameter DB_BLOCK_BUFFERS. The size of an individual buffer is specified by the init<SID>.ora parameter DB_BLOCK_SIZE. Both of these parameters are specified in bytes.

❏ Redo log buffer. This is a circular buffer used to record changes to the database and whether the changes have been committed. The changes made to the database are made by the end user issuing any of the various DML statements (INSERT, UPDATE, DELETE...). This buffer is written to when the Oracle server thread moves data from the user's memory space to the buffer. In Figure 2.6, the new value (after the UPDATE) and the old value are stored. There is also a flag that indicates whether the data has been committed. The data in the redo log buffers will be written to the redo log files by the LoG WRiter thread (LGWR). The size of the buffer is specified by the init<SID>.ora parameter LOG_BUFFER.

DATABASE BUFFER AND REDO LOG BUFFER STRUCTURE

How end user-data is moved from memory to disk is best explained by example (refer to Figure 2.6). Assume that the current entry in the employee table shows that the employee with the ID (emp#) number 9999 is Chris. We then run the following statement to change the name of the person with ID number 9999 from Chris to Dave (refer to Display 1-1):

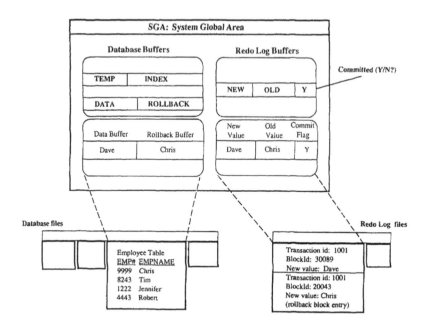

FIGURE 2.6   End user data is moved from memory to disk

```
SQLPLUS> update employee_table
SQLPLUS> set empname = 'Dave'
SQLPLUS> where emp# = 9999;
SQLPLUS> COMMIT;
```

DISPLAY 2.1

The contents of the data buffer are changed from Chris to Dave. The contents of the rollback buffer reflect the original state of the data buffer prior to the update command being issued. In this case the contents is the name Chris. The modified database buffer will be written to the data file on the disk using a least recently used algorithm.

The contents of the redo log buffer reflect the state of both the old and the new data. In addition, the contents of the redo log buffer contains a flag that indicates whether the data has been committed. Upon the issuing of the commit, the flag will be changed to indicate that the commit has been issued and the data will be written to the redo log file on the disk.

The size of the SGA is controlled by parameters in the database initialization file called "init<SID>.ora." The controlling of the size of the SGA will be covered in the tuning memory management chapter.

The PGA is a fixed-size memory structure that is created when a user thread (such as SQL*PLUS or any another tool) connects to the database. The PGA contains the following information:

❏ Stack Space. This space holds the contents of the variables and arrays that the session is using.

❏ Session Information. If the RDBMS is not using the multithreaded server the PGA will also contain the private SQL area. The private SQL area contains the run-time buffers that are used when a SQL statement is executed.

The SGA also contains another area (not shown) called the shared pool. The shared pool is divided into two areas. One area is called the library cache, the other area is called the data-dictionary cache. When a SQL statement is executed, parsed representation of the statement will be placed into the library cache. If a similar SQL statement is being issued by another user the RDBMS will keep the parsed representation of the SQL statement in the part of the shared pool called the library cache. This eliminates the need to parse the statement as its parsed representation is already in memory.

The data-dictionary cache contains information from the Oracle system tables. The system tables are updated by the RDBMS. The updates reflect the changes that have been made to the database. An example of a system table is the table DBA_USERS. This table contains all the users that are defined in the database. The RDBMS updates this table each time a new user is added to the system.

THE ORACLE PROCESS AND THREAD STRUCTURE

Under the Windows NT operating system a running program is referred to as a process. The running program associated with the Oracle RDBMS process is "oracle80.exe" and can be observed using the Windows NT utility *TASK MANAGER* (see Figure 2.7).

Starting the Oracle RDBMS starts the process oracle80.exe. A process must have at least one thread associated with it. The oracle process oracle80.exe has several threads associated with it. This section will describe four threads that must be running for the Oracle RDBMS to be operational.

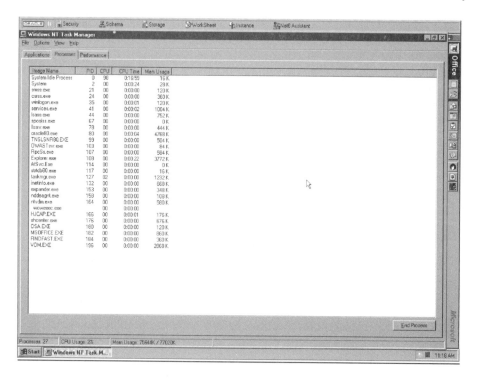

FIGURE 2.7   Windows NT utility Task manager

PMON: The Process Monitor performs the following functions:

❏ Performs thread recovery by releasing system resources (locks on tables, etc.)
when a user thread fails.

❏ Restarts dispatcher and shared server threads that have died.

❏ Rollback of aborted transactions.

❏ Can be called by any Oracle thread that detects a need for PMON thread to
be run.

SMON: The System Monitor performs the following functions:

❏ Performs instance recovery.

❏ Releases temporary segments.

❏ Coalesces contiguous free extents to make larger blocks of free space.

❏ Can be called by any Oracle thread.

DBWR: Database Writer performs the following functions:

❏ Writes modified database buffers from the database buffer cache into the data files on the disk every three seconds.

❏ Uses a least recently used (LRU) algorithm to keep data blocks that are accessed frequently from being written to disk, therefore reducing disk I/O during a query. When a server thread modifies a database buffer that database buffer is moved to the "dirty list." If the number of entries in the dirty list grows past the threshold set by the init<SID>.ora parameter DB_BLOCK_WRITE_BATCH, the DBWR thread will write the buffers in the dirty list to disk. If a server thread scans the list of free buffers in the LRU list and the number of buffers scanned is greater then the init<SID>.ora parameter DB_BLOCK_MAX_SCAN_CNT, then the DBWR thread will be instructed to write database buffers to disk so that room can be made for a new cache entry.

❏ Performs checkpoint processing (the process of writing modified buffers to a data file is called a checkpoint).

LGWR: The Log Writer thread performs the following functions:

❏ Writes redo log buffers to the redo log files.

❏ Determines when a checkpoint should be taken (the writing of the data will be done by the DBWR thread). This occurs when the number of data blocks needed to write a checkpoint is exceeded. The threshold is set by the init<SID>.ora parameter LOG_CHECKPOINT_INTERVAL. If the init<SID>.ora parameter CHECKPOINT_PROCESS is set then the thread called CKPT performs this function.

❏ Writes redo log data when a commit is issued, every three seconds or when the redo log buffer is one-third full.

PMON, DBWR, LGWR and SMON represent the four main threads associated with the Oracle RDBMS. There are two other Oracle background threads that are also part of the Oracle RDBMS, they are the recover (RECO) thread and the checkpoint (CKPT) thread.

A checkpoint is defined as the process of writing a list of modified database buffers (including committed and uncommitted data) to disk. With respect to the Oracle RDBMS the Oracle background thread LGWR signals the DBWR thread to write the buffers to the data files on the disk. The CKPT thread updates the headers of all control files and data files indicating that a checkpoint has occurred. In the absence of the CKPT process the updating of the header files is done by the LGWR thread. In systems with significant database activity it is often best to relieve the LGWR thread of performing the extra activity of writing the checkpoint.

Checkpoints ensure that data segment blocks that change frequently are written to disk. Because of Oracle's LRU algorithm data blocks that are frequently modified may never be written to disk if checkpoints did not occur.

Checkpoints occur automatically under the following situations:

- ❏ A log switch occurs.
- ❏ When set by database initialization parameters.
- ❏ When beginning an on-line backup
- ❏ When a tablespace is taken offl ine.
- ❏ When the database is shut down
- ❏ Until a checkpoint completes all redo log files written since the last checkpoint are needed in case database recovery is needed.

The RECO thread performs the following functions:

The RECO thread is part of the distributed option. It is used to handle failures in distributed transactions. The RECO thread automatically connects to databases that are involved in an in-doubt transaction. The RECO thread establishes a connection with the involved databases and resolves all in-doubt transactions. All rows involved in the in-doubt transaction are removed from the databases involved in the transaction.

The various threads associated with the Oracle process oracle80.exe can be observed using the Microsoft C++ process viewer. Using the Oracle *ADMINISTRATION TOOLBAR* the utility *INSTANCE MANAGER* can be started (see Figure 2.8).

The utility INSTANCE MANAGER can be used to verify that the Oracle RDBMS is not running (see Figure 2.9).

Prior to starting the Oracle RDBMS the process oracle80.exe has only three threads associated with it (see Figure 2.10).

To start the Oracle process and its associated threads the Oracle instance is started (in Figure 2.11, the instance is started and the database is opened for end-user access).

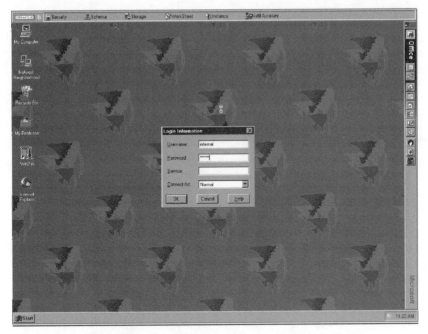

FIGURE 2.8   Microsoft C++ process viewer

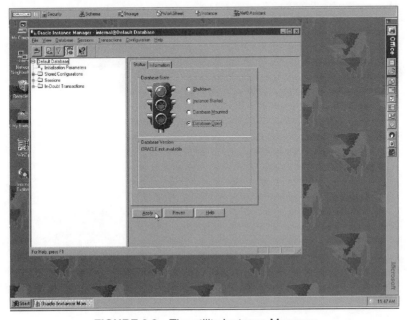

FIGURE 2.9   The utility Instance Manager

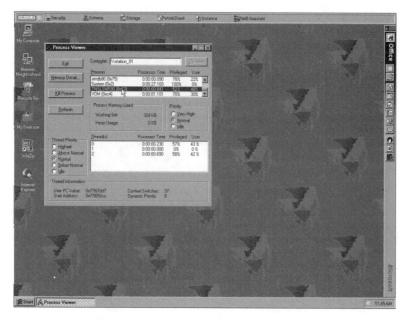

FIGURE 2.10   The three threads of oracle80.exe

Starting the Oracle instance will start the threads PMON, SMON, DBWR, LGWR and other threads associated with the Oracle RDBMS as shown in Figure 2.12.

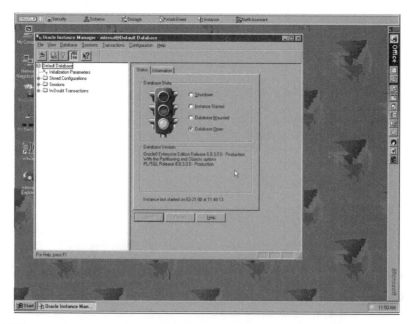

FIGURE 2.11   The instance is started and the database is opened for end-user access

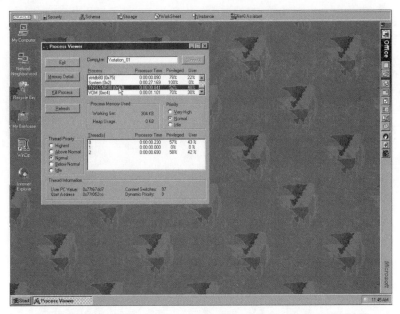

FIGURE 2.12   Other threads associated with the Oracle RDBMS

An end user can log into the Oracle database using an end-user utility such as SQL*PLUS (see Figure 2.13).

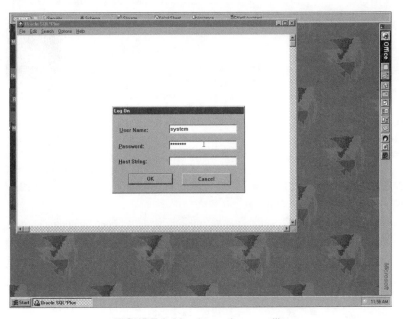

FIGURE 2.13   An end-user utility

Each time a user logs into the database a new Oracle thread is created to handle the end-user's session.

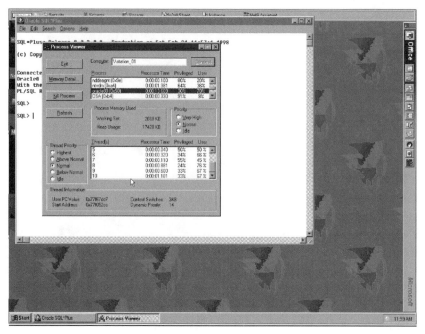

FIGURE 2.14   Oracle thread is created to handle the end-user's session

SUMMARY

The architecture of the Oracle RDBMS (shown in Figure 2.15) is implemented using various programs and files. The Oracle instance consists of the various threads and memory. The RDBMS processes threads reside in the computer's RAM. The four main threads associated with the Oracle process oracle80.exe are PMON, SMON, LGWR and DBWR. The process threads interact with the RDBMS memory structures called the SGA and the PGA.

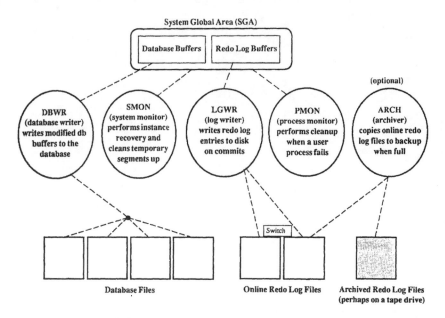

FIGURE 2.15   Oracle's process/thread structure

The next part of the RDBMS is the database. The database is made up of data-files (used to store system and end-user data), database initialization files and log-files.

In the remaining chapters we will take a closer look at the Oracle RDBMS. We will also cover the various tasks that an Oracle DBA is expected to perform.

SYSTEM INSTALLATION

BACKGROUND

In the previous chapter the architecture of the Oracle RDBMS was presented. This chapter will focus on the various installation issues that must be addressed when installing the Oracle RDBMS on the Windows NT platform. There is a version of the Oracle RDBMS for most operating system platforms. The operating system platforms include mainframe operating systems such as VM or MVS, and operating systems for mid-departmental systems such as OS/2, UNIX and Windows NT. Those issues that are relevant to installing the Oracle RDBMS on the MS Windows NT platform will be addressed here.

Oracle8 is mostly additions made to Oracle7, at least from a compatibility viewpoint. For those that are familiar with installing Oracle7 the procedure for installing Oracle8 is the same. There are a few more reserved words, the headers on data files are different so you cannot go downward, but going up can be just a migration utility away. Some internal things are different such as row identifier (ROWID), and executables are larger, control files are also larger. A lot of the internal changes have to do with the MTS, parallel server, distributed locks, backups and caching. However, the installation technique is the same for both Oracle7 and Oracle8.

Prior to installing Oracle8 RDBMS the DBA should first check for the required software prerequisites. The prerequisites are shown in Table 3.1. A CD-ROM is required for installation.

TABLE 3.1   Required Software Prerequisites

Hardware	Intel 486 or higher	DEC ALPHA	RAM	Disk
Software	MS Windows NT 4.0	MS Windows NT 4.0	48 MB	200 MB

These prerequisites should be satisfied prior to installing the Oracle RDBMS. A list of prerequisites can be obtained from:

❏ Oracle's support web site (WWW.ORACLE.COM/SUPPORT).

❏ Getting Started—Oracle8 Server for MS Windows NT (published by The Oracle Corporation).

A user that has administrator privileges must install the software. This is done using the NT utility user manager (see Figure 3.1):

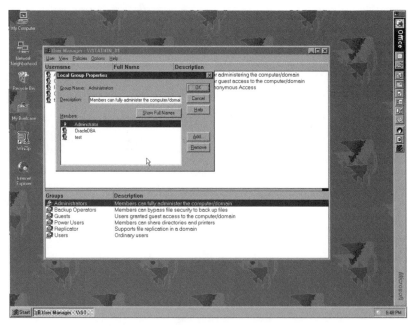

FIGURE 3.1   The NT utility User Manager

The utility that is used to install all Oracle products on the Apple, OS/2, Windows/Windows NT and UNIX operating system platforms is called ORAINST. The utility has a menu driven interface that the DBA can use to select the installation or maintenance operation that is to be performed. The installation utility ORAINST will copy the selected Oracle products from the CD to the target disk drive. On the Windows NT platform the RDBMS and its utilities such as IMPORT, EXPORT, SQL*LOADER, and SVRMGR and all server executables are loaded from the installation CD using the ORAINST utility.

The ORAINST utility can be invoked by:

Loading the installation CD into the PC's CD-ROM drive will start the installer ORAINST as shown in Figure 3.2.

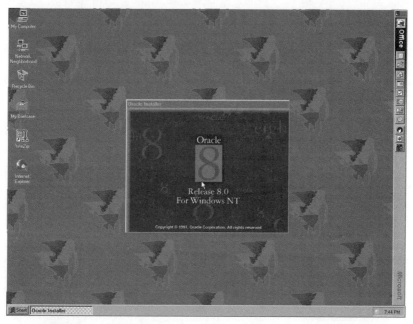

FIGURE 3.2   CD-ROM drive will start the installer ORAINST

If the RDBMS has been installed previously the installer can also be invoked from the MS Windows NT GUI as shown in Figure 3.3.

Oracle8 for Windows NT incorporates many ease-of-use features that make installation and setup simple. The GUI installation procedure provides an easy-to-use interface that will install a pretuned and preconfigured Oracle8 database. The GUI presents the DBA with a list of products that can be installed. The DBA has to choose which products they want to install on their computer system. At the very least the DBA should choose to install:

❏ **Oracle Server**: The RDBMS and the various server utilities such as IMPORT, EXPORT, and SQL*LOADER.

❏ **Distributed Option**: Required for implementing database links. Such links are used in the creation of transactions across multiple databases.

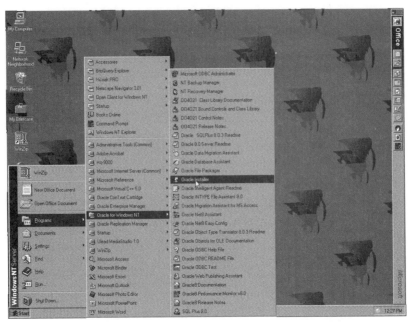

FIGURE 3.3 The MS Windows NT GUI

❏ **Oracle Common Libraries and Utilities**: Oracle libraries that are referenced by other Oracle products.

❏ **SQL*NET8**: Oracle's client/server communications subsystem.

❏ **SQL*PLUS**: Oracle's end-user tool for submitting SQL to the database server.

❏ **PL/SQL**: Oracle procedural extension to SQL*PLUS.

If disk space is not a limitation then installing all of the products on the CD (as shown in Figure 3.4) is as simple as installing only a few selected products. The DBA can install a product (or products) by highlighting the product that the user wants to install and then pressing the INSTALL button.

The ORAINST utility can also be used to remove or de-install products. This can be done by starting the ORAINST utility. The utility the DBA can remove a product (or products) by highlighting the product that the user wants to de-install and then pressing the remove button (see Figure 3.5).

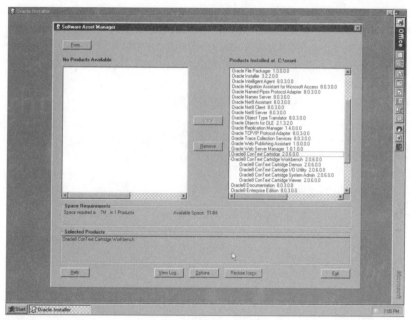

FIGURE 3.4 Installing all of the products on the CD is as simple as installing only a few selected products.

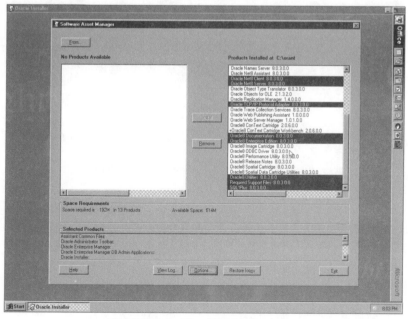

FIGURE 3.5 The ORAINST utility

After the software is installed the instance will be automatically started and the database mounted. When the instance is started the Oracle server executable will allocate space for the SGA and start the various Oracle background threads (PMON, etc.).

THE ORACLE DIRECTORY STRUCTURE

One of the functions of the ORAINST utility is to create the various directories in the NT file system. These directories are where ORAINST will load the product executables. Under the root directory, the directory ORANT is created. This directory is the directory that is used as the ORACLE_HOME location for the RDBMS. All product executables will be loaded under the ORACLE_HOME location (see Figure 3.6).

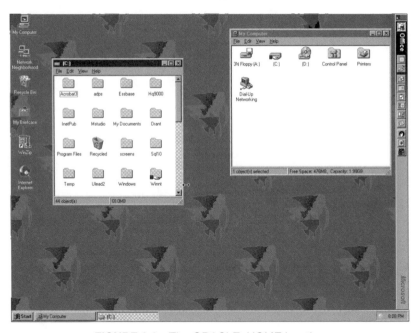

FIGURE 3.6   The ORACLE_HOME location

The installer ORAINST will create product directories under the C:\ORANT (ORACLE_HOME) directory. Each of the various products will have their own product directory under the ORACLE_HOME directory (Figure 3.7).

The database initialization file init<ORACLE_SID>.ora file is located in the ORACLE_HOME\database directory. The executables for the products are loaded into the ORACLE_HOME\bin directory. These executables include the executables for SQL*PLUS and the various server utilities such as IMPORT, SQL*LOADER, and SVRMGR as shown in Figure 3.8.

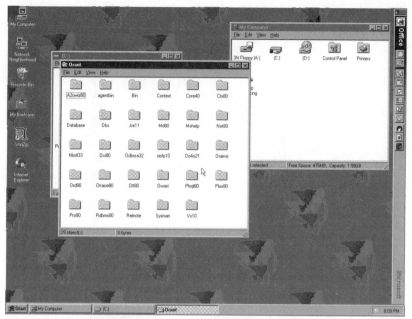

FIGURE 3.7 The ORACLE_HOME directory

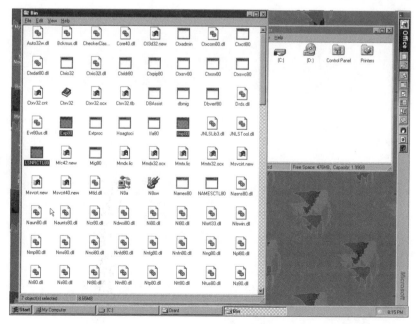

FIGURE 3.8 The IMPORT, SQL*LOADER, and SVRMGR

CHECKING THE DATABASE

After the RDBMS is installed the DBA can use the following Oracle utilities to verify that the database has been installed correctly. These utilities include:

❏ Instance Manager: Used to start and stop the Oracle instance, and mount or dismount the Oracle database.

❏ Schema Manager: Used to verify that the various database objects have been created. This utility can also be used to create database objects such as tables, views, synonyms, and indexes.

❏ Storage Manager: Used to manage the data files associated with the various Oracle tablespaces.

Oracle has provided an *ADMINISTRATIVE TOOL BAR* that can be used to invoke the various utilities (INSTANCE MANAGER, SCHEMA MANAGER, etc.). The *ADMINISTRATIVE TOOL BAR* can be invoked from the Windows NT menu bar as shown in Figure 3.9:

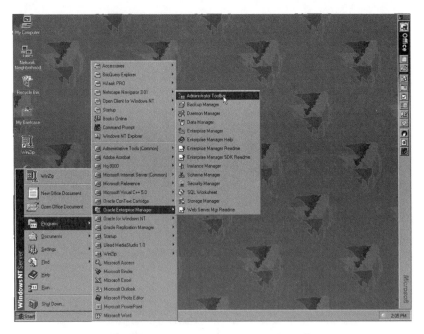

FIGURE 3.9   The Administrative Tool Bar

Here we see that the Oracle INSTANCE MANAGER can be started from the *ADMINISTRATIVE TOOL BAR*. The DBA can use INSTANCE MANAGER to:

❏ Start and stop the Oracle instance.

❏ Mount and dismount the Oracle database.

❏ Create and Modify the Oracle initialization file init<ORACLE_SID>.ora.

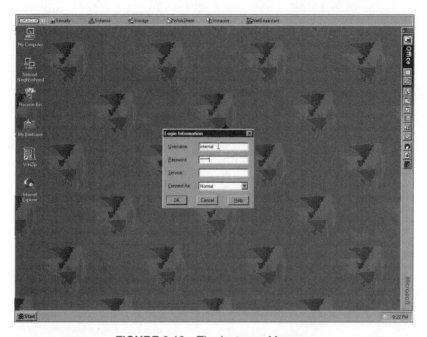

FIGURE 3.10   The Instance Manager

As part of the installation, three Oracle user accounts are created. The three user accounts are:

1. SYS (userid = SYS) with default password CHANGE_ON_INSTALL. This is the highest user in the Oracle RDBMS. Most of the tables and views in the Oracle data dictionary are owned by this user. This userid should only be used for maintenance purposes such as installs, upgrades and migrations. This is done to avoid accidental corruption of the data dictionary.

2. SYSTEM (userid = SYSTEM) with default password MANAGER. This user account is normally used to perform most routine database maintenance activities. The activities normally performed by the SYSTEM user are database backup, creating new users, monitoring user sessions, and controlling database access.

3. INTERNAL (userid = INTERNAL) with default password ORACLE. This userid is used to start and stop the database.

The typical starter database also includes the users CTXSYS and DRSYS. Their passwords are CTXSYS and DRSYS respectively and are required when using the Oracle8 ConText Cartridge.

In Figure 3.11 we see that the database can be started and stopped from the INSTANCE MANAGER utility. Keep in mind that the user INTERNAL is the user that starts and mounts the instance and database respectively.

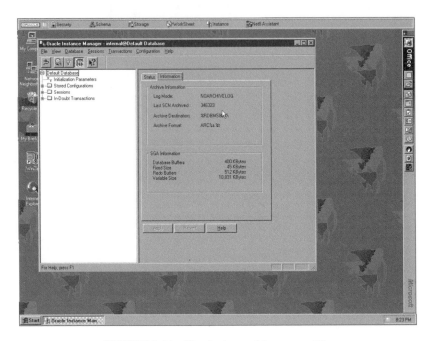

FIGURE 3.11   The Instance Manager utility

In Figure 3.12 we see that the databases tuning parameters can be modified using the INSTANCE MANAGER utility.

In Figure 3.13 we see that the databases initialization parameters can also be modified using the INSTANCE MANAGER utility.

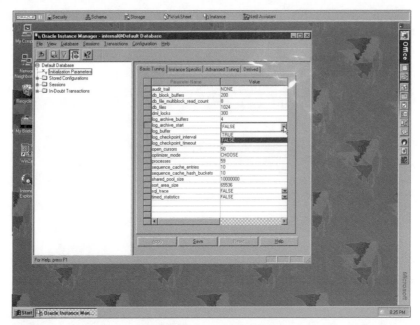

FIGURE 3.12 Tuning parameters can be modified using the Instance Manager utility

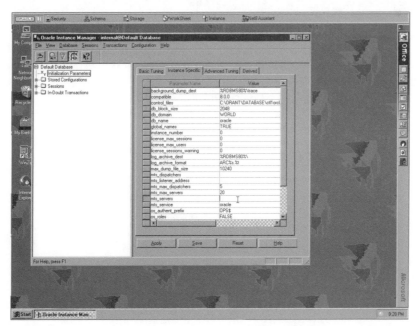

FIGURE 3.13 The database initialization parameters can also be modified

The INSTANCE MANAGER utility can also be used to see which user sessions have been started. In Figure 3.14 we see that the user INTERNAL has a session. In this case the user INTERNAL is known to the RDBMS as the user SYS.

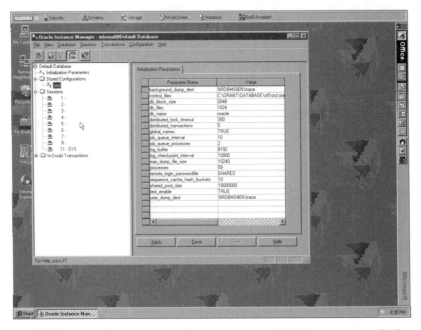

FIGURE 3.14   The user Internal is known to the RDBMS as the user SYS.

The information about the database can also be obtained by using the Oracle command-line utility SVRMGR. The utility is the command-line equivalent of INSTANCE MANAGER. The utility can be invoked from the MS Windows NT DOS prompt as shown in Figure 3.15.

Here we see (Display 3.1) that the name of the database can be obtained by querying the data dictionary view V$DATABASE. We can also determine which users have a session with the database by querying the view V$SESSION. Therefore we have several alternatives for obtaining information about the database.

```
SVRMGR> select username from v$session;
```

DISPLAY 3.1

FIGURE 3.15 The SVRMGR utility can be invoked from the MS Windows NT DOS prompt

A schema is a collection of database objects. A schema includes such database objects as tables, views, indexes, and synonyms. A schema can also contain program objects. Program objects are routines that are written in PL/SQL. They include database triggers, functions, procedures, and packages, where a package is a group of procedures in one source listing.

Oracle's SCHEMA MANAGER gives the DBA or application programmer a graphical interface for managing their schema objects or the schema objects of other users of the database. SCHEMA MANAGER can also be accessed from the *ADMINISTRATION TOOL BAR*. In Figure 3.16 we see the various users that are defined to the database and the collection of objects in each user's schema.

The utility STORAGE MANAGER (Figure 3.17) can also be accessed from the *ADMINISTRATION TOOL BAR*. Storage manager gives the DBA a graphical interface to:

❑ Create and manage tablespaces that are associated with the database.

❑ Create and manage data files associated with a tablespace.

❑ Create and manage the database rollback segments.

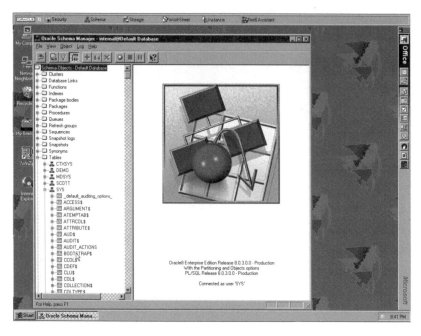

FIGURE 3.16 Various users that are defined to the database and the collection of objects in each user's schema

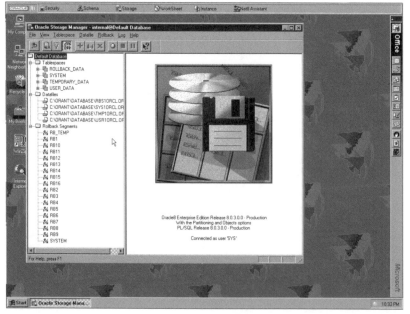

FIGURE 3.17 The utility Storage Manager can also be accessed from the Administration Tool Bar.

In Figure 3.18 we see that the DBA has the ability to get detailed information about the SYSTEM tablespace. This information includes:

❏ The location of the data files associated with the database tablespaces.

❏ The size of the data files.

❏ The tablespaces accessibility (off line or on line).

The DBA can also control access to the various data files and tablespaces. This can be done by taking the tablespace off line. Taking a tablespace off line is usually necessary for database recovery (more about this when we cover database backup and recovery.

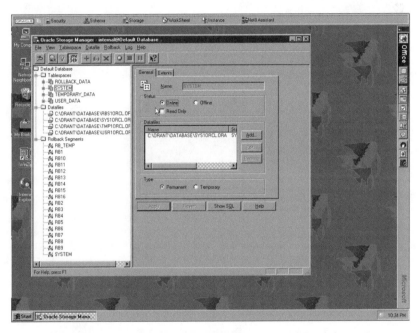

FIGURE 3.18   The DBA has the ability to get detailed information

In our discussion we have relied on using the GUI that is supplied to gain information about the database. These GUIs provide a convenient way to access information that is in the various tables and views that are in the database. GUIs provide this ease of use by allowing the DBA to gain information about the database without the DBA writing any SQL. In this case the GUI will generate the SQL and display the results from executing it. Oracle also provides two command-line interfaces that can be used to access information about the database and its users. One is called SERVER MANAGER the other is the tool SQL*PLUS.

Earlier we saw that SVRMGR can be accessed from the DOS prompt. The SQL*PLUS utility can be accessed from the MS WINDOWS application tool bar as shown in Figure 3.19.

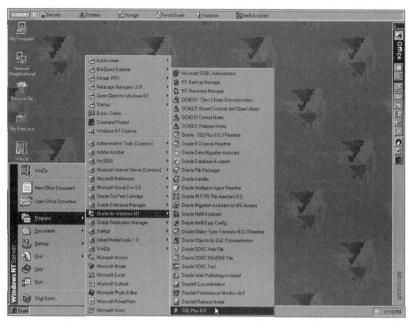

FIGURE 3.19   The SQL*PLUS utility can be accessed from the MS Windows application tool bar

In Figure 3.20 we see that we can get the same information about the various tablespaces by querying the data dictionary view DBA_DATA_FILES rather then using the STORAGE MANAGER utility. This alternative to using the supplied GUIs allows the DBA to write batch SQL scripts that they can be customized to investigate the database.

Most database administration tasks can be performed using SQL*PLUS. SQL*PLUS has additional data formatting features that are not present with SVRMGR. SQL*PLUS cannot be used for starting up or shutting down the database.

The Oracle's *ADMINISTRATION TOOL BAR* can also be customized. The applications such as INSTANCE MANAGER, STORAGE MANAGER and other applications can be removed from the tool bar. Other applications can be added to the tool bar. Clicking on the tool bar's ORACLE logo as shown in Figure 3.21 does this.

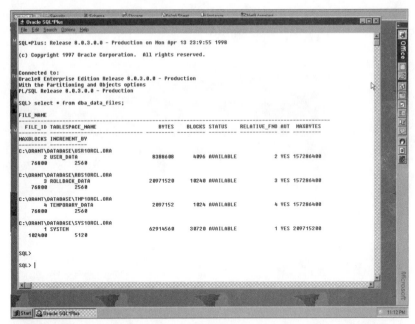

FIGURE 3.20 Various tablespaces by querying the data dictionary view DBA_DATA_FILES

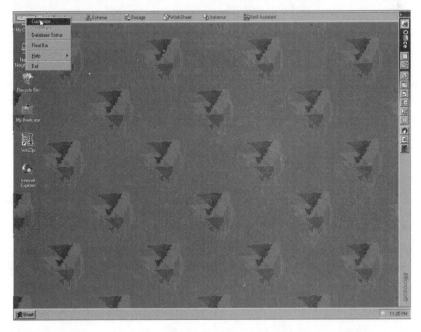

FIGURE 3.21 Applications Instance Manager, Storage Manager and other applications can be removed from the tool bar

The DBA can remove applications that they do not want to give end users access to (Figure 3.22). Applications can also be added to the tool bar.

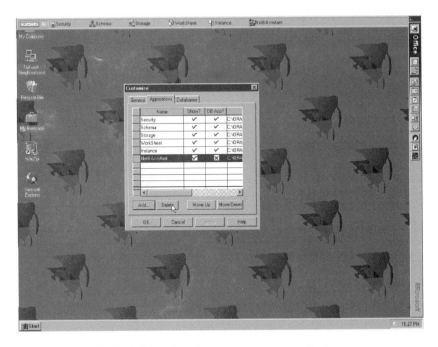

FIGURE 3.22   The DBA can remove applications

FREQUENTLY REFERENCED DATA DICTIONARY TABLES AND VIEWS

The data dictionary is a group of tables and views that contain descriptive information about system performance, user access and privileges, and descriptions of all database objects. The DBA should verify that the Oracle Data Dictionary tables and views exist.

Table 3.2 is a list of frequently used data dictionary tables and views. A complete listing can be found in Appendix A.

LICENSING

Oracle licenses its RDBMS to the end user. There are two methods of licensing.

❑ Named users - Total number of users defined in the database.

TABLE 3.2 Frequently Used Data Dictionary Tables and Views

View Name	Description
DBA_CATALOG	List of all database tables, views and sequences.
DBA_CONSTRAINTS	List of all constraint definitions on all tables in the database.
DBA_INDEXES	List of all indexes in the database.
DBA_SEQUENCES	List of all sequences in the database.
DBA_SYNONYMS	List of all synonyms in the database.
DBA_TABLES	List of all tables in the database.
DBA_USERS	Information on all users of the database.
DBA_VIEWS	List of all views in the database.
DBA_DATA_FILES	List and location of all database tablespaces and data files.
DBA_EXTENTS	List of extents for all segments in the database.
DBA_FREE_SPACE	List of free extents in all tablespaces.
DBA_SYS_PRIVS	List of system privileges that have been granted.
V$SESSION	Information on all current sessions.
V$DATABASE	Database information obtained from the control file.
V$LOCK	Information on all locks on system resources.
V$PARAMETER	Information about database initialization/tuning parameter settings.
V$NLS_PARAMETER	Information on the database character set.
V$LOGFILE	Information on the redo log files.
V$LIBRARYCACHE	Statistics on library cache management.
V$VERSION	Version numbers for core library components.

❏ Concurrent users—Total number of users having an active session at one time.

To stay within the licensing agreement the DBA can set the parameters:

❏ LICENSE_MAX_SESSIONS—This will set the maximum number of concurrent sessions. When this limit is reached, only users with the RESTRICTED SESSION privilege can connect to the server. If LICENSE_MAX_SESSIONS is set, the parameter LICENSE_SESSIONS_WARNING can also be set so that a warning message is issued before all the sessions have been allocated.

❏ LICENSE_MAX_USERS—This will set the maximum number of users that can be defined in the database.

SUMMARY

In this chapter we have covered the various topics relevant to installing Oracle8 on the Windows NT platform. Some of the features of Oracle's installation strategy include various "ease of management tools." These tools include:

❏ Oracle Database Assistant
❏ Oracle Data Migration Assistant
❏ Oracle Web Publishing Assistant
❏ Oracle Migration Assistant for Microsoft Access
❏ Oracle Net Assistant
❏ NT Backup/Recovery Manager
❏ Start/Stop Oracle Instance from NT Service

These tools allow for easy installation of the Oracle RDBMS. In the remaining chapters we will show how Oracle's GUI tools make system management as easy as system installation.

CLIENT/SERVER COMMUNICATIONS AND SQL*NET

BACKGROUND

In the previous chapters the architecture of the Oracle RDBMS and various installation issues were described. In this chapter we will see how the Oracle's communication software SQL*NET ties into the Oracle architecture. We will also show how installing and configuring Oracle's communication software SQL*NET allows us to implement client/server environments.

The installation of an Oracle communication subsystem requires that SQL*NET (NET8) and the SQL*NET Protocol Adapter be installed. This is shown in Figure 4.1.

In this chapter we will see that the combination of SQL*NET and it's protocol adapter is used to link the Oracle RDBMS to the underlying network hardware and software on the server. We will also show that the combination of SQL*NET and it's protocol adapter is used to link client application software to its underlying network and machine hardware and software.

The data communications architecture that the Oracle RDBMS participates in is based on the communications model defined by the International Standards Organization (ISO). The communications model that is used is the Open Systems

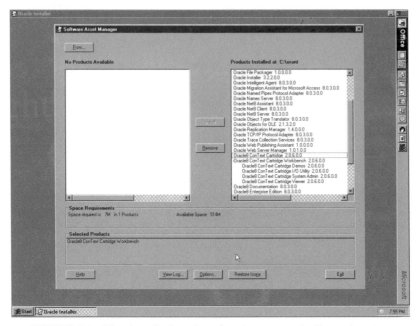

FIGURE 4.1   The installation of an Oracle communication subsystem

Interface (OSI) model. The OSI model is a seven-layer structure that consists of various programs. The various programs are used to pass information between the seven OSI layers. When information is requested from the server by the client the client request moves through the client OSI layers across the transmission media and then through the servers OSI layers. The application layer (RDBMS) of the server will satisfy the request and send the reply back to the client, thus starting the reverse leg of the round trip.

OSI DATA COMMUNICATION MODEL

Each layer of the OSI model performs a specific function before it passes the information onto the next layer. The various functions performed by the various layers consist of:

LAYER 7: APPLICATION LAYER

The application layer is the OSI layer closest to the user. It differs from the other layers in that it does not provide services to any other OSI layer, but rather to application threads lying outside the scope of the OSI model. Examples of such application threads include spreadsheet programs, word-processing programs, banking terminal programs, and so on.

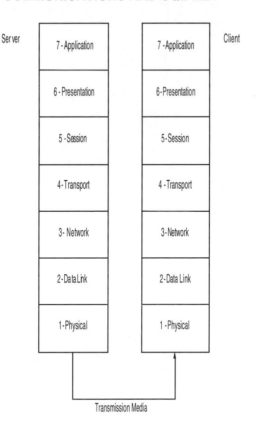

The application layer identifies and establishes the availability of intended communication partners, synchronizes cooperating applications, and establishes agreement on procedures for error recovery and control of data integrity. Also, the application layer determines whether sufficient resources for the intended communications exist.

LAYER 6: PRESENTATION LAYER

The presentation layer ensures that information sent by the application layer of one system will be readable by the application layer of another system. If necessary, the presentation layer translates between multiple data-representation formats by using a common data-representation format.

The presentation layer concerns itself not only with the format and representation of actual user data, but also with data structures used by programs. Therefore, in addition to actual data format transformation (if necessary), the presentation layer negotiates data transfer syntax for the application layer.

LAYER 5: SESSION LAYER

As its name implies, the session layer establishes, manages, and terminates sessions between applications. Sessions consist of dialogue between two or more presentation entities (recall that the session layer provides its services to the presentation layer).The session layer synchronizes dialogue between presentation layer entities and manages their data exchange. In addition to basic regulation of conversations (sessions), the session layer offers provisions for data expedition, class of service, and exception reporting of session-layer, presentation-layer, and application-layer problems.

LAYER 4: TRANSPORT LAYER

The boundary between the session layer and the transport layer can be thought of as the boundary between application-layer protocols and lower-layer protocols. Whereas the application, presentation, and session layers are concerned with application issues, the lower four layers are concerned with data transport issues.

The transport layer attempts to provide a data transport that shields the upper layers from transport implementation details. Specifically, issues such as how reliable transport over an internetwork is accomplished are the concern of the transport layer. In providing reliable service, the transport layer provides mechanisms for the establishment, maintenance, and orderly termination of virtual circuits, transport fault detection and recovery, and information flow control (to prevent one system from overrunning another with data).

LAYER 3: NETWORK LAYER

The network layer is a complex layer that provides connectivity and path selection between two end systems that may be located on geographically diverse subnetworks. A subnetwork, in this instance, is essentially a single network cable (sometimes called a segment).

Because a substantial geographic distance and many subnetworks can separate two end systems desiring communication, the network layer is the domain of routing. Routing protocols select optimal paths through the series of interconnected subnetworks. Traditional network-layer protocols then move information along these paths.

LAYER 2: LINK LAYER

The link layer (formally referred to as the data link layer) provides reliable transmission of data across a physical link. In so doing, the link layer is concerned with physical (as opposed to network, or logical) addressing, network topology, line discipline (how end systems will use the network link), error notification, ordered delivery of frames, and flow control.

LAYER 1: PHYSICAL LAYER

The physical layer defines the electrical, mechanical, procedural, and functional specifications for activating, maintaining, and deactivating the physical link between end systems. Such characteristics as voltage levels, timing of voltage changes, physical data rates, maximum transmission distances, physical connectors, and other similar attributes, are defined by physical layer specifications.

PROTOCOL STACKS

OSI layers 3 and 4 are often referred to as the protocol stack. Several different protocol stacks are available for data communications. Some of the more popular protocols are listed below:

- ❑ TCP/IP
- ❑ DecNet
- ❑ IPX/SPX (Novell NetWare)
- ❑ Banyon VINES
- ❑ SNA (LU6.2/APPC)
- ❑ AppleTalk
- ❑ XNS
- ❑ X.25
- ❑ ASYNC

NETWORK DEVICES

Various types of hardware devices may be needed to construct a communications network. The following is a list of the various types of communications devices and the function they provide.

❏ Modems: MODulator DEModulator

Computers can only understand data sent in a digital format. The digital signal must be converted into an analog signal if it is to be transferred across a telephone line. The modem takes the digital signal from the computer and converts it into an analog signal. The modem then sends the analog signal to the telephone line. On the other side of the telephone another modem takes the analog signal and converts it into a digital signal so that it can be understood by the receiving computer system.

❏ Routers

Allow for the transmission of data across dissimilar protocols (OSI layer 3)

❏ Bridges (OSI layer 2)

Allow for the transmission of data between networks that are using the same protocol

❏ Transmission Lines/Media

Transmission lines allow for data communications between network devices. There are several types of transmission lines. For data communications we are interested in the speed of the transmission line. Transmission lines come in various speeds. Some typical speeds are 1200 BitsPerSecond (bps), 4800 bps, and 256 bps. There are also several types of high speed transmission lines such as T1 and T3.

❏ Network Interface Card (NIC)

The NIC is the electronic device that is usually installed in the computer. It provides the hardware (and some software) interface between the computer and the communications network. There are several types of NICs. The two most popular are Token-Ring and Ethernet. The NIC plus the transmission line/media make up the Physical Layer of the OSI model.

CLIENT/SERVER COMMUNICATIONS AND ORACLE'S SQL*NET

In the OSI model the RDBMS occupies the application layer on the server machine. The end-user application resides in the application layer on the client machine. In order to implement the client server architecture we need something to link the application layer to the protocol stack layers. The Oracle software that makes that connection between the application layer and the protocol stack is called SQL*NET. Several attributes of SQL*NET are:

❏ Removes end-user application-program processing from the server, therefore distributing application-program processing.

❏ Occupies OSI Layers 5 and 6.

❏ Must be installed on both the client and the server machine.

❏ Requires that the protocol stack be installed first.

❏ Supports various types of protocols.

❏ Implemented as a service on the MS Windows NT platform. The service's name is OracleTNSListener80.

SQL*NET must be installed on both the server machine and on the client machine when implementing a client/server environment using the Oracle RDBMS as the server. The server must also have an IP address and a port number. The combination of the IP address and the port number define the socket connection between the Oracle listener service OracleTNSListener80 on the server machine and the client application (as shown in Figure 4.2).

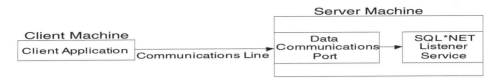

FIGURE 4.2 The Oracle listener service OracleTNSListener80

On the server machine starting the SQL*NET communications subsystem means starting the SQL*NET listener service OracleTNSListener80. Starting the service can be done from the MS Windows NT control panel as shown in Figure 4.3.

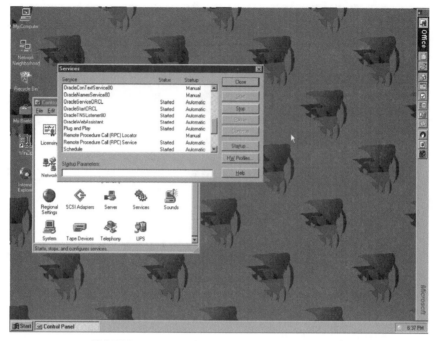

FIGURE 4.3   The MS Windows NT control panel

The service OracleTNSListener80 can also be started from the DOS command-line prompt. This is done using the command-line utility LSNRCTL80. The various options for the command LSNRCTL80 are shown in Figure 4.4.

By issuing the appropriate argument with the LSNRCTL80 command the DBA can control and interrogate the state of the listener service OracleTNSListener80. To get the status of the listener the command shown in Display 4.1 is issued.

C:\> LSNRCTL80 STAT

DISPLAY 4.1

The result of issuing the instruction is shown in Figure 4.5.

FIGURE 4.4 The various options for the command LSNRCTL80

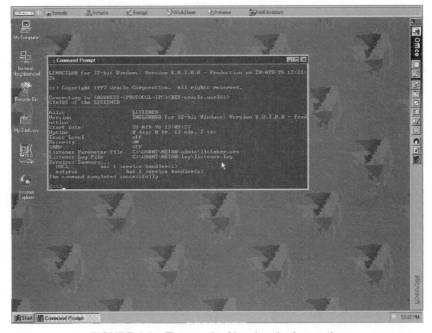

FIGURE 4.5 The result of issuing the instruction

CONFIGURING SQL*NET (NET8)

There are several configuration files that reside on the database server machine. The files are:

❏ LISTENER.ORA: Contains service names (or database aliases) and addresses of all listeners on the machine, the Oracle system IDs (ORACLE_SID) for the databases they listen for and various control parameters used by the listener. This file is created during the installation of SQL*NET. All machines that will act as a server must have a LISTENER.ORA file.

❏ NAMES.ORA: Contains control parameters for the Oracle Names Server.

❏ SQLNET.ORA: Includes optional diagnostic parameters, client information about Oracle Names Server, and can contain other optional parameters for logging or tracing. This file is created during the installation of SQL*NET. This file can be modified using either *SQL*Net Easy Configuration Tool* or the Oracle Network Manager.

A client machine may also have several configuration files. The client configuration files are:

❏ TNSNAMES.ORA: Contains a list of service names (or databases aliases) of network databases mapped to connect descriptors. This file is created on both clients and servers. It is modified using either *SQL*Net Easy Configuration Tool* or the Oracle Network Manager.

❏ SQLNET.ORA: Includes optional diagnostic parameters, client information about Oracle Names Server, and can contain other optional parameters for logging or tracing. This file is created during the installation of SQL*NET. This file can be modified using either *SQL*Net Easy Configuration Tool* or the Oracle Network Manager.

❏ TNSNAV.ORA: Lists the local communities of the client profile or node. This file is not needed and used for single-community networks (single protocol). This file is required when using the Multi Protocol Interchange. This file is created using the Oracle Network Manager.

The utility *SQLNet Easy Configuration* is used to create and modify the TNSNAMES.ORA file. The utility *SQLNet Easy Configuration* is used to:

❏ Modify a database alias.

❏ Deleting a database alias.

❏ Viewing database alias configuration information.

The *Easy Configuration* utility is started from the Windows NT menu as shown in Figure 4.6.

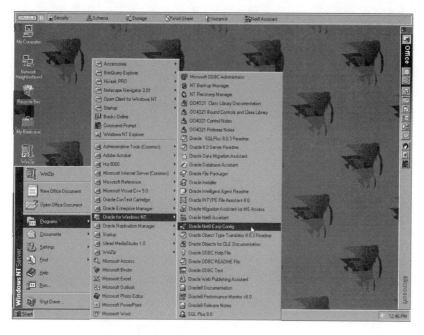

FIGURE 4.6 The Easy Configuration utility

When the utility is started the user is prompted for an alias name (Figure 4.7). This alias name is used when the client application wants to connect to the database.

Next the user is prompted for the protocol that will be used as shown in Figure 4.8.

Next the server name or its internet protocol (IP) address is entered with the communications port number that the Oracle server's listener service OracleTNSListener80 is listening on. This is shown in Figure 4.9

Next the ORACLE_SID that this alias is to connect to is entered as shown in Figure 4.10.

With the ORACLE_SID, host name, port number, and protocol defined, a complete connection between the client machine and the server machine can be tested using the configuration GUI as shown in Figure 4.11.

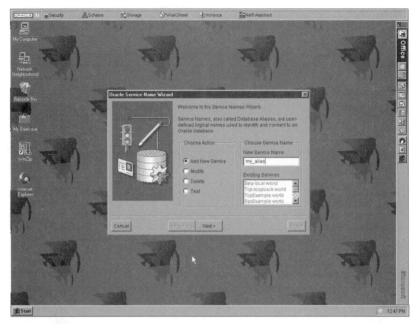

FIGURE 4.7 When the utility is started the user is prompted for an alias name

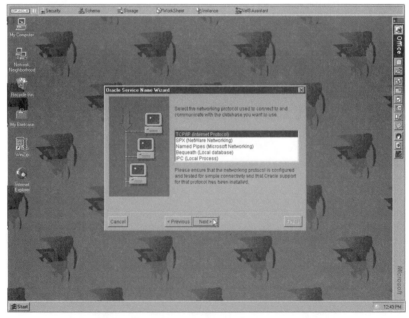

FIGURE 4.8 The user is prompted for the protocol

FIGURE 4.9 Enter server name or Internet protocol address

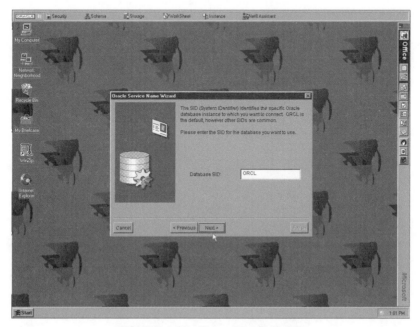

FIGURE 4.10 Enter ORACLE_SID

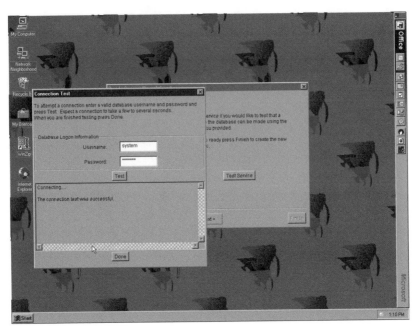

FIGURE 4.11   Client machine and the server machine can be tested using the configuration GUI

To test that the communications software is functioning the DBA should first start the SQL*NET listener thread. After the listener has been started the DBA should test that the server OSI layers are all functioning correctly. This is done by performing a loop-back test. A loop-back test will test the database servers ability to establish a session using SQL*NET. This same technique can be used to eliminate the server as the point of failure when testing for communications between a client machine and its database server machine.

The DBA can use SQL*PLUS or SV MGR to perform the loop-back test. In Figure 4.12 the SQLPLUS command is issued to start the utility SQL*PLUS. In the example that follows, the user ID and password are followed by the "@" sign and the name of the database alias. The database alias contains (contents of the TNSNAMES.ORA file) all the information to make the connection to the database on the host machine.

USING THE NET8 ASSISTANT

Oracle8 network management software includes the tool called NET8 Assistant (shown in Figure 4.13).

FIGURE 4.12   The SQLPLUS command is issued to start the utility SQL*PLUS

FIGURE 4.13   The tool called NET8 Assistant

The network utility (shown in Figure 4.14) can be used to:

❏ Modify attributes of the client alias. The client alias is stored in the TNSNAMES.ORA file. This file can also be modified using the utility *SQLNet Easy Configurator*.

❏ Turn on logging or tracing for either a client or a server connection. Tracing allows the user to see the information that is flowing between the network's transport layer (TCP Layer 4) to the session layer (SQL*NET protocol adapter at Layer 5).

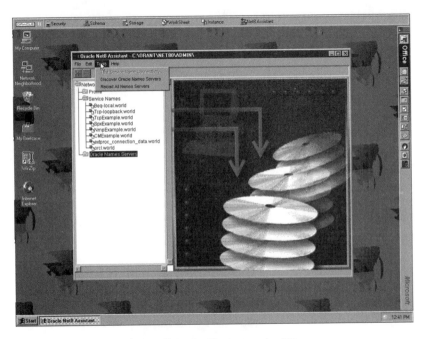

FIGURE 4.14   The network utility

We can use the NET8 Assistant to modify the connection aliases' attributes (shown in Figure 4.15). The NET8 Assistant can be accessed from the MS Windows NT menu or the Oracle supplied *ADMINISTRATION TOOL BAR*.

SOL*NET LOGGING AND TRACING

Both SQLNET.ORA and LISTENER.ORA log files and trace files are available to use in trouble-shooting network problems. Log files are located in the directory:

```
ORACLE_HOME\NETWORK\ADMIN \LOG
```

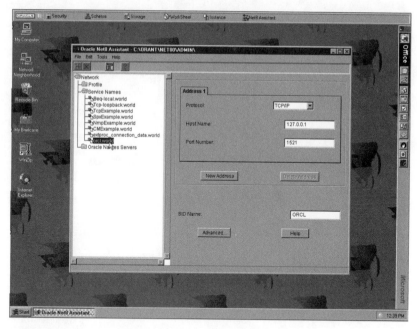

FIGURE 4.15 The NET8 Assistant

trace files are located in the directory:

```
ORACLE_HOME\NETWORK\ADMIN \TRACE
```

All errors encountered in Oracle network products are logged to a log file for evaluation by a network or database administrator. The log file provides additional information for an administrator when the error message on the screen is inadequate to understand the failure. The log file, by way of the error stack, shows the state of the software at various layers.

SQL*NET tracing is used to track and examine application connections across the network. Tracing can be used to examine and diagnose application connections across the network and can be activated using the NET8 Assistant as shown in Figure 4.16. The trace facility allows a network or database administrator to obtain more information on the internal operations of the components of an Oracle application network than is provided in a log file. Tracing an operation produces a detailed sequence of statements that describe the events as they are executed. All trace output is directed to trace-output files that can be evaluated to identify the event that led to an error (see Figure 4.17).

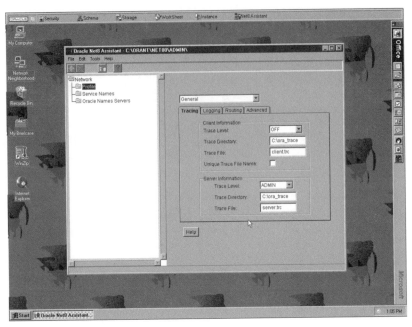

FIGURE 4.16 Tracing can be used to examine and diagnose application connections

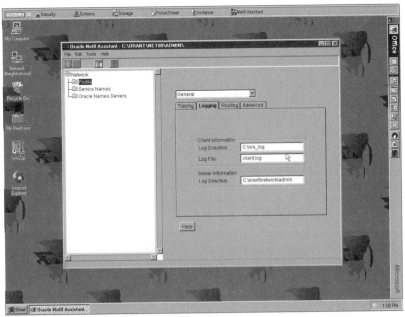

FIGURE 4.17 Trace output is directed to trace-output files

Logging reveals the state of the Oracle components at the time when an error occurs. Errors are logged to the log file. However, tracing describes all software events as they occur; that is, even when an error is not occurring, information is posted into the trace file to show what is happening in the software. Thus, tracing provides additional information about events whether or not there is an error.

WINDOWS95 CLIENTS

The Oracle installer for Windows 95 (also called ORAINST) is used to install SQL*NET. When installing SQL*NET the directory structure shown in Figure 4.18 will be created on the PC client (in this case the ORACLE_HOME directory is c:\ORAWIN)

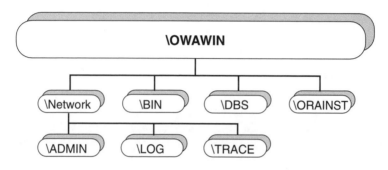

FIGURE 4.18   SQL*NET directory structure

\ORAWIN	Oracle home directory, also referred to as ORACLE_HOME
BIN	Holds executable programs and batch files for ORACLE tools and the dynamic link libraries (dll) used by SQL*NET Protocol Adapter
DBS	Holds the SQL*NET message files
ORAINST	Contains the Oracle Installer ORAINST.
NETWORK	Created when SQL*NET v2 is installed.
NETWORK\ADMIN	Holds all of the *.ORA files used by SQL*Net v2\
NETWORK\LOG	Holds SQL*NET log files.
NETWORK\TRACE	Holds SQL*NET trace files.

TRACING FOR WINDOWS 95 CLIENTS

Tracing can also be turned on for client sessions. When this is done the trace file stores all communications between the transport layer (TCP) and SQL*NET at the presentation layer. Because this is a client level trace the trace information is stored on the client machine. For Windows 95 client, the following additions must be made to the SQLNET.ORA file prior to starting the client application:

```
TRACE_LEVEL_CLIENT=16
TRACE_FILE_CLIENT= CLIENT
TRACE_DIRECTORY_CLIENT = C:\TRACE
```

In this case the trace file will be written to the directory C:\TRACE. The file will be called CLIENT.TRC.

CREATING AND USING DATABASE LINKS

It is often desirable that an application be able to access data that is distributed across several Oracle database servers. To accomplish this the DBA can create a database link between the database servers. An example is the best way to illustrate how a database link can be set up and used. Picture the following:

1. You're logged into the database named "ARNOLD" on the machine named "SERVER1."
2. There is another database called "ELMER" that holds a table called "EMP." This database resides on the machine called "SERVER2."
3. The two machines are both running SQL*NET.

By creating a database link between ARNOLD and ELMER the DBA (or application) can access both databases from SERVER1. To create a database link the following instruction is issued at either the SQL* PLUS or server manager (SVRMGR) prompt (refer to Display 4.2):

```
SQLPLUS> CREATE DATABASE
SQLPLUS> LINK ELMER EMP
SQLPLUS> CONNECT TO SCOTT
SQLPLUS> IDENTIFIED BY TIGER
SQLPLUS> USING 'ALIAS_NAME';
```

DISPLAY 4.2

Where the parameter ALIAS_NAME is defined in the TNSNAMES.ORA file

To access the table EMP that is in the database ELMER when we are currently logged into the database ARNOLD on SERVER1 we would use the following statement (refer to Display 4.3).

```
SQLPLUS > select*
SQLPLUS>from EMP@ELMER_EMP;
```

DISPLAY 4.3

Notice that in the example we used the table name with the name of the database link. Keep in mind the following:

1. The link is only in one direction (from ARNOLD to ELMER).
2. The user must have a valid user name on the machine that they are linking to (ELMER)

MTS

One feature of Oracle7 and SQL*NET v2 is MTS. In the pass (Oracle6 or Oracle7 with SQL*NET v1) when a client application wanted to make a connection to the database a dedicated server thread was required. The dedicated thread was created by the SQL*NET v2 thread TNSLSNR. The server thread remained active until the user logged off.

The architecture for MTS is shown in Figure 4.19. In this case we have two new threads. One is called the Dispatcher (DISP) thread. The other thread is called the SHARED-SERVER thread.

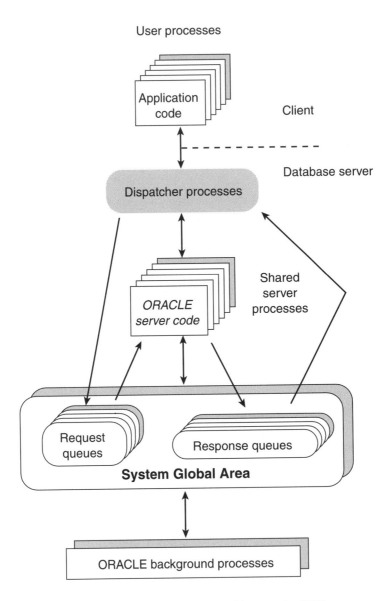

User processes

Application
code

Client

Database server

Dispatcher processes

Shared
server
processes

ORACLE
server code

Request
queues

Response queues

System Global Area

ORACLE background processes

FIGURE 4.19 The architecture for MTS

To satisfy an end-user request, the Oracle MTS performs the following functions:

1. The user thread is connected to a dispatcher thread by the SQL*NET v2 listener thread TNSLSNR.

2. When the user thread executes an SQL statement the dispatcher thread places the request into the input queue of the dispatcher.

3. A server thread (also called a shared-server thread) takes the request off the dispatcher input queue and looks to see if the data is in the SGA's database buffer cache (the input queue is also part of the SGA). If the data is not in the SGA the server thread will get the data from the disk (database).

4. The server thread will then place the results into the dispatcher's output queue.

5. The dispatcher then moves the data to the user thread.

The number of dispatchers is controlled by the following INIT.ORA parameters:

1. MTS_DISPATCHERS: Initial number of dispatcher thread.
2. MTS_MAX_DISPATCHERS: Maximum number of dispatcher threads that can be created.
3. MTS_SERVERS: Initial number of shared server threads.
4. MTS_MAX_SERVERS: Maximum number of server threads that can be created.

The two tuning issues that we are faced with are:

1. How many dispatchers do we need?
2. How many shared servers do we need?

The answer to the first question is that we need approximately one dispatcher for every 29 to 30 users. The second question is answered by asking the question how long does it take to satisfy a request. The Oracle RDBMS will create a new server thread automatically. Therefore, when more work comes in, new server threads are created (they are killed when they complete their work). Because the Oracle RDBMS controls when new server threads are created and the INIT.ORA parameter MTS_MAX_SERVERS controls the maximum number of dispatcher threads we therefore need to know how many server threads have been created and we are at the maximum number. This is done by issuing the query (refer to Display 4.4):

```
SVRMGR > select count(*)
SVRMGR> from v$shared_servers where
SVRMGR> status != 'QUIT';
```

DISPLAY 4.4

The result should always be less then MTS_MAX_SERVERS. If it is not increase the init<ORACLE_SID>.ora parameter MTS_MAX_SERVERS.

MTS INIT.ORA EXAMPLE

The following is a section from an INIT<sid>.ORA file. The sample section shows how the MTS settings should be coded.

```
mts_dispatchers="ipc,1"
mts_dispatchers="tcp,1"
mts_max_dispatchers=10
mts_servers=1
mts_max_servers=10
mts_service=YOUR_ORACLE_SID
mts_listener_address="(ADDRESS=(PROTO-
     COL=ipc)(KEY=YOUR_ORACLE_SID))"
mts_listener_address=
  "(ADDRESS=(PROTOCOL=tcp)(HOST=YOUR_HOST_NAME)(PORT=1521))"
```

DEAD CONNECTION DETECTION

If the network connection between the client computer and the database server is broken it is possible that the server will not release the system that the client application was using. This can lead to table locking problems because database resources are not released when the client application exits before the SQL COMMIT command can be issued.

The dead-connection detection feature of SQL*NET v2 allows the RDBMS to release locked resources and remove threads associated with remote sessions. This is done by:

1. The SQL*NET server thread sends probe packets to the client.
2. RDBMS removes the end-user session if no reply is received from the client. The removing of the end-user session will free all locks. The RDBMS will also remove threads associated with the sessions therefore freeing system memory.

The SQLNET.ORA file should be created by the DBA and placed in the $ORACLE_HOME/network/admin directory. Dead connection detection is activated by coding the following parameter in the SQLNET.ORA file:

```
SQLNET.TIME_EXPIRED = 1 (where the number is in minutes)
```

This will cause a probe packet to be sent to the client workstation at one-minute intervals. If the server does not get a reply from the probe packet the end-user session will be terminated.

SAMPLE LISTENER.ORA FILE

```
################
# Filename......: listener.ora
# Node..........: local.world
# Date..........: 24-MAY-98 13:23:20
################
LISTENER =
   (ADDRESS_LIST =
        (ADDRESS=
          (PROTOCOL= IPC)
          (KEY= oracle.world)
        )
        (ADDRESS=
          (PROTOCOL= IPC)
          (KEY= ORCL)
        )
        (ADDRESS=
          (COMMUNITY= NMP.world)
          (PROTOCOL= NMP)
          (SERVER= STATION_01)
          (PIPE= ORAPIPE)
        )
        (ADDRESS=
          (PROTOCOL= TCP)
          (Host= station_01)
          (Port= 1521)
        )
        (ADDRESS=
          (PROTOCOL= TCP)
          (Host= station_01)
          (Port= 1526)
        )
        (ADDRESS=
          (PROTOCOL= TCP)
          (Host= 127.0.0.1)
          (Port= 1521)
        )
    )
STARTUP_WAIT_TIME_LISTENER = 0
CONNECT_TIMEOUT_LISTENER = 10
TRACE_LEVEL_LISTENER = 0
SID_LIST_LISTENER =
   (SID_LIST =
     (SID_DESC =
```

```
       (GLOBAL_DBNAME = station_01)
       (SID_NAME = ORCL)
     )
     (SID_DESC =
       (SID_NAME = extproc)
       (PROGRAM=extproc)
     )
   )
PASSWORDS_LISTENER = (oracle)


SAMPLE TNSNAMES.ORA FILE:

# TNSNAMES.ORA Configuration file:
    C:\ORANT\NET80\ADMIN\tnsnames.ora
# Generated by Oracle Net8 Assistant

Beq-local.world =
  (DESCRIPTION =
    (ADDRESS =
          (PROTOCOL = BEQ)
          (PROGRAM = oracle80)
          (ARGV0 = oracle80ORCL)
          (ARGS = '(DESCRIPTION=(LOCAL=YES)(ADDRESS=
                  (PROTOCOL=beq)))')
    )
    (CONNECT_DATA = (SID = ORCL)
    )
  )
TcpExample.world =
  (DESCRIPTION =
    (ADDRESS =
          (PROTOCOL = TCP)
          (Host = Production1)
          (Port = 1521)
    )
    (CONNECT_DATA = (SID = SID1)
    )
  )
SpxExample.world =
  (DESCRIPTION =
    (ADDRESS =
          (PROTOCOL = SPX)
          (Service = Server_lsnr)
    )
```

DATABASE OBJECTS, ACCESS AND SECURITY

There are several types of objects that can exist in a database. The various objects that are owned by an end user exist in what is called the end-user's schema. Each user that is defined in the database has their own schema. For example, the Oracle database user with the userid of JONES has a corresponding schema called JONES. There are several different types of schema objects. The different types of schema objects include:

❑ Table—A database object used to store data in row/column format. Each row is also referred to as a record.

❑ View—A database object that shows a customized presentation of a table (or group of tables).

❑ Synonym—A database object that is an alias for another database object such as a table or view.

❑ Index—A database object used to speed access to table data.

In general a schema is a collection of objects.

CREATING DATABASE OBJECTS

The various types of database objects can be created using SQL*PLUS or the Oracle utility SCHEMA MANAGER. The following examples will show how database objects are created.

CREATING A TABLE

The SQL command to create a table is shown in Display 5.1:

```
SQLPLUS> create table new_emp
SQLPLUS> (empno        number (4),
SQLPLUS> ename         varchar2(l 0),
SQLPLUS> job           varchar2 (9),
SQLPLUS> mgr_no        number(4),
SQLPLUS> hire_date     date,
SQLPLUS> sal           number (7,2),
SQLPLUS> comm          number (7,2),
SQLPLUS> deptno        number (2));
```

DISPLAY 5.1

In this example we have created a table called "emp." The table will contain information about the employees that work for the company. The information will be arranged into records. Each record will contain information about an employee. The records that will make up the table have eight columns as shown in Table 5.1.

TABLE 5.1   Emp Table Record Format

empno	ename	job	mgr_number	hire_date	sal	comm	deptno

Oracle8 contains many helpful "WIZARDS" for assisting the DBA in creating tables and other database objects. In the example, the "TABLE WIZARD" feature of the SCHEMA MANAGER utility is used to create the same table that was created using SQL*PLUS as shown in Figure 5.1.

The GUI allows for the definition of the various data types that are supported by the Oracle RDBMS (see Figure 5.2).

Number data types are easily defined and initialized using the "TABLE WIZARD". In this example two types of number fields are created. The employee number (EMP_NO) is defined as a number with zero precession. The number field that will contain the employee's salary is defined to have two positions to the right of the decimal point to signify the "cents" portion of the salary (see Figure 5.3).

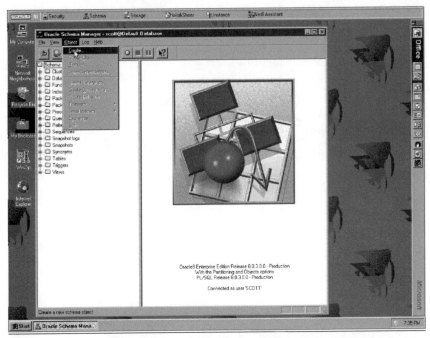

FIGURE 5.1 The Schema Manager utility

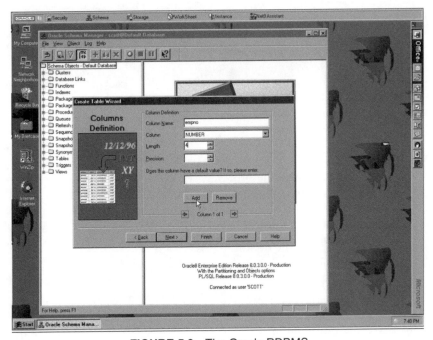

FIGURE 5.2 The Oracle RDBMS

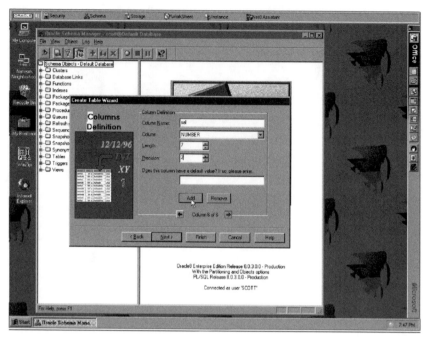

FIGURE 5.3 The Table Wizard

Variable length character fields can be created and modified using the TABLE WIZARD (see Figure 5.4).

Date fields are added to our table so that we can keep track of when employee's were hired (see Figure 5.5).

The "TABLE WIZARD" lets us create the table "NEW_EMP" without writing any SQL as in Figure 5.6.

SCHEMA MANAGER can also be used to create database objects in any schema that the end user or DBA has access to (refer to Figure 5.7).

To compute the size of a record we would use the following technique:

❏ Number fields are computed using the formula: *number of bytes = precession/ 2 + 1*. In our example we would compute the number of bytes used by the fields empno, mgr_number, sal, comm and deptno. This would result in the following computation: number of bytes = (4/2+1) + (4/2+1) + (7/2+1) + (7/2+1) + (2/2+1) = 17 bytes.

❏ One character requires one byte. Therefore the fields denoted by varchar2 will result in the following computation: number of bytes = 10 + 9 = 19 bytes.

❏ Date fields require 7 bytes.

Therefore, the maximum size of a record would be 43 bytes.

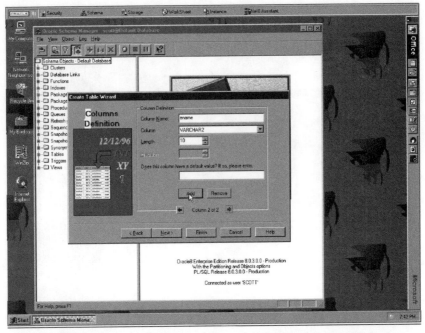

FIGURE 5.4 Variable length character fields can be created

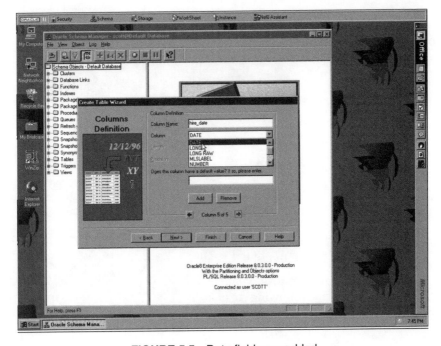

FIGURE 5.5 Date fields are added

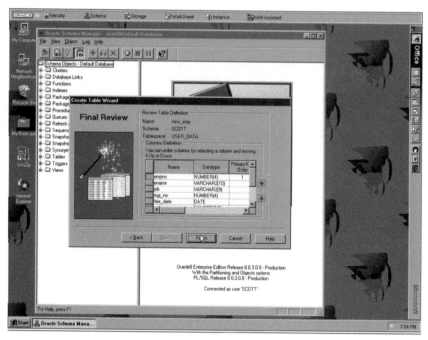

FIGURE 5.6 The table NEW_EMP

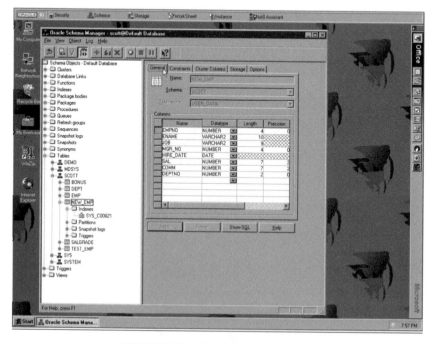

FIGURE 5.7 The Schema Manager

We must keep in mind that this is the maximum size of the record. In reality the space held by the record may be less. This is due to the following:

❑ The data type varchar2 stands for variable length character. This means that if the number of bytes for the column data being inserted is less then the defined column length then the remaining bytes are not used. For example if the last name of the person is "Jones" then only five bytes are used to store the five characters.

❑ For number fields the same is true. The internal representation for the number may require less than the maximum number of bytes.

CREATING A VIEW

A view is a tailored presentation of data stored in one or more tables. A view can be used to hide various details of the underlining table from the person(s) that are accessing the table data.

Example of creating view (refer to Display 5.2):

```
SQLPLUS> create view empvu
SQLPLUS> as select empno,ename,job
SQLPLUS> from emp;
```

DISPLAY 5.2

In this example we have created a view called "empvu" from the table "emp." The view "empvu" consists of three columns: empno, ename, and job. The end user that needs access to employee names and their jobs would access the view rather than the underlying table.

Now we can access the data using the view as shown in Display 5.3.

```
SQLPLUS> select *
SQLPLUS> from empvu;
```

DISPLAY 5.3

The SCHEMA MANAGER utility can also be used to create the view as shown in Figure 5.8.

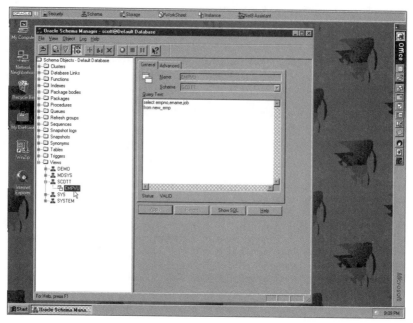

FIGURE 5.8 The Schema Manager utility

CREATING A SYNONYM

A synonym is an alias for a table or view. When a user wants to access a schema object such as a table or view that belongs to another user (the object is in another person's schema) they need to prefix the schema object with the name of the schema where the object is stored. A synonym can be created as either private or public. If the synonym is created as a public synonym then all the users of the database would have access to it because all of the users are in the Oracle role called public. If the synonym is created as private then only the owner/creator of the synonym would have access to it.

Example of Create Synonym

In this example we are accessing the emp table that belongs to Wally Jones (userid wjones). To select from the table owned by wjones we would type (refer to Display 5.4):

```
SQLPLUS> select * from
SQLPLUS> wjones.emp;
```

DISPLAY 5.4

To create a public synonym the owner (W.Jones) would issue the CREATE SYNONYM statement:

> SQLPLUS> create public synonym
> SQLPLUS> emp for wjones.emp;

DISPLAY 5.5

If we want to access the emp table we can refer to the synonym rather then the actual table, thus eliminating the need to prefix the schema name onto the object being selected.

> SQLPLUS> select * from .emp;

DISPLAY 5.6

The creation of the synonym can also be accomplished using SCHEMA MANAGER as shown in Figure 5.9.

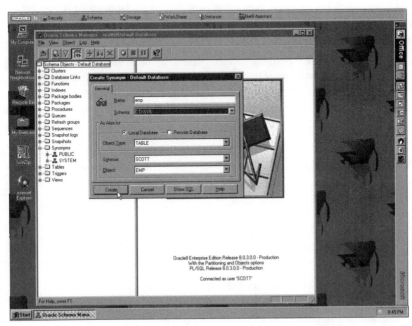

FIGURE 5.9   The creation of the synonym

DATABASE ACCESS/SECURITY

One of the activities of a DBA is to create user accounts. The DBA must also be able to give users access to the various database objects, and grant users the privileges to perform different operations.

CREATING A USER

To create a user the DBA issues the CREATE USER command as shown in Display 5.7.

```
SVRMGR80> create user scott
SVRMGR80> identified by tiger
SVRMGR80> default tablespace user_data
SVRMGR80> temporary tablespace
SVRMGR80> temporary_data
SVRMGR80> profile user
SVRMGR80> quota 15M on user;
```

DISPLAY 5.7

In the example we are creating the user "SCOTT" and assigning them the password "tiger." We are also assigning the user to a DEFAULT TABLESPACE. This means that whenever the user SCOTT creates a schema object, the object will be created in the tablespace called USER_DATA.

The user SCOTT is assigned to a default tablespace. When the user SCOTT sorts their data (issues a SQL select command with the SORT keyword) the data will be sorted in the tablespace called **TEMPORARY_DATA** (Oracle performs all sorting of data in the tablespace designated as the user's temporary tablespace as shown in Figure 5.10.

The user SCOTT is also assigned a quota on the default tablespace. This means that the user SCOTT can create as many database objects as they want as long as they do not exceed the 15M quota.

❑ Session idle time.

❑ Session connect time.

❑ Number of sessions that the user can have.

❑ Amount of CPU resources the end user can use.

To keep any one user from using all the resources in a given tablespace the DBA can assign a quota to each user (see Figure 5.11).

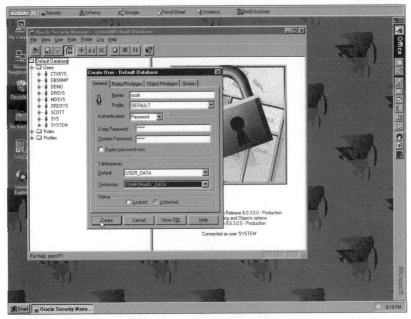

FIGURE 5.10 TEMPORARY_DATA

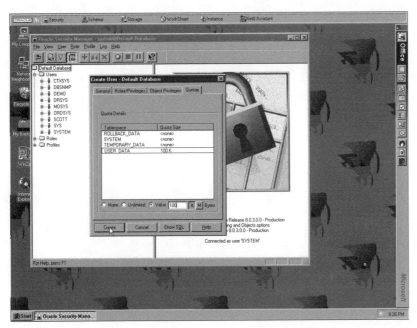

FIGURE 5.11 The DBA can assign a quota to each user

In the example SCOTT is also given a profile. The profile allows for the following control of the end-users session. The profile *user* can be created by issuing the command (refer to Display 5.8):

```
SQLPLUS> create profile user
SQLPLUS> sessions_per_user 1
SQLPLUS> idle_time 20
SQLPLUS> connect_time 600;
```

DISPLAY 5.8

A profile can be <u>ALTER</u>'ed or <u>DROP</u>p'ed.

❑ drop profile user;

❑ alter profile user idle_time 100;

The user SCOTT can change their password by issuing the command (refer to Display 5.9):

```
SVRMGR80 > alter user scott
SVRMGR80 >  identified by
SVRMGR80 > new_password;
```

DISPLAY 5.9

OBJECT AND SYSTEM PRIVILEGES

For users to be able to access the database the users must be granted access privileges. The SQL*PLUS "GRANT" is used to issue (grant) various privileges.

Granting the privilege to connect to the database and create a table in the schema owned by Scott (refer to Display 5.10):

```
grant <privilege> to <user/role/public> (general format)
```

```
SVRMGR80 > grant create session,
SVRMGR80 > create table to scott;
```

DISPLAY 5.10

In this example the user SCOTT is given the privilege to create a session and tables. With the Oracle RDBMS, users must first be created and then given the privilege to connect to the database or create schema objects.

Privileges like create table, create view, etc. can also be revoked. To revoke a privilege, issue the SQL REVOKE command (refer to Display 5.11):

```
SVRMGR80 > revoke create table
SVRMGR80 > from scott;
```

DISPLAY 5.11

A user can be granted the privilege to alter another user's tables/schema object. To do this the user is granted the ALTER TABLE <table_name> privilege. A user can also be granted the privilege to alter any table in the database as shown in Display 5.12.

```
SVRMGR80 > grant alter
SVRMGR80 > any table to scott;
```

DISPLAY 5.12

A user can also be granted privileges which that user can then grant to another user. This is done by using the "WITH ADMIN OPTION" as shown in Display 5.13.

```
SVRMGR80 > grant create user,
SVRMGR80 > alter user, drop user
SVRMGR80 > to scott with admin option;
```

DISPLAY 5.13

The DBA will often be called on to review the privileges that the users have been granted. To view the privileges the various users have, use the data dictionary view TABLE_PRIVILEGES.

The following query will list the privileges for the user specified by <oracle_uid>, where <oracle_uid> equals the users Oracle userid.

```
SVRMGR80 > select grantee,
SVRMGR80 > privilege, admin_option
SVRMGR80 > from sys.dba_sys_privs
SVRMGR80 > where grantee = '<oracle_uid>;
```

DISPLAY 5.14

The DBA will often be called on to remove a user from the system. This is accomplished with the DROP USER command.

The following statement will drop the person with userid "scott" (refer to Display 5.15).

```
SVRMGR80 > drop user scott;
```

DISPLAY 5.15

To monitor a user's session the system view "v$session" is used. The view v$session can be used to see what command a user is currently executing and other information such as the users session id, schema name, etc. (use the SQL*PLUS command DESCRIBE or refer to the Oracle7 Server Administrators for a list of the columns in the view).

In the following example the query being issued will return the userids of all persons that have a session established and the SQL command that they are executing (refer to Display 5.16):

SVRMGR80 > select username,
SVRMGR80> command from v$session;

DISPLAY 5.16

Access privileges can also be created using the SECURITY MANAGER utility as shown in Figure 5.12.

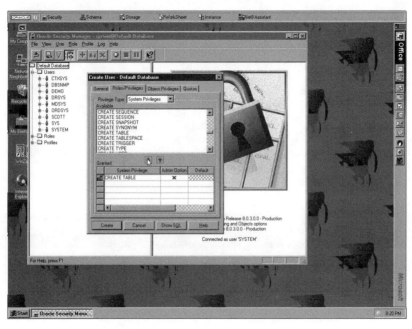

FIGURE 5.12 The Security Mnanger utility

The user SCOTT is also assigned various system privileges. Privileges such as create table, create index, create synonym, and create view are needed by most application developers and database administrators.

The end user also needs to be assigned privileges to objects that are not owned by them. These objects are not in their schema. Assigning additional object privileges is shown in Figure 5.13.

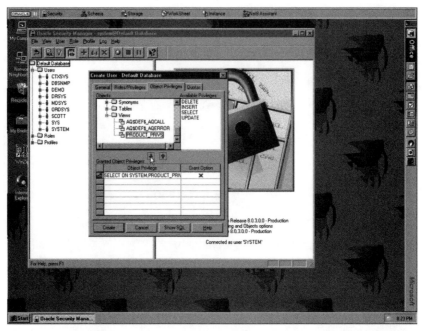

FIGURE 5.13 Assigning additional object privileges

ROLES

Roles are used to reduce the number of privileges that the DBA has to grant to individual users. Rather then granting privileges to individual users the DBA can create a role and grant a set of privileges to the role. As new users join the organization they can be placed into a predefined role.

In the following example we'll assume that we're the DBA for the XYZ Company. In the XYZ Company, all managers have the ability to create tables and synonyms for those tables. Rather than granting privileges to each manager the DBA can choose to create a role called MANAGER and place those persons that are managers into that role (refer to Display 5.17).

```
SVRMGR80 > create role manager;
SVRMGR80 > grant create synonym,
SVRMGR80 > create tableto manager;
SVRMGR80 > grant manager to scott;
```

DISPLAY 5.17

In Figure 5.14 SECURITY MANAGER is used to create the role "MANAGER" and assign privileges to it. After the role is created and privileges assigned the DBA can "GRANT" the role to the various end users.

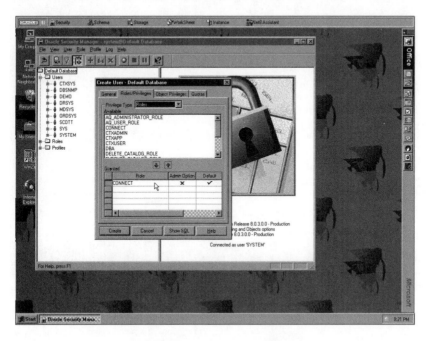

FIGURE 5.14 The role Manager

HELPFUL DATA DICTIONARY VIEWS

The tables and views in the Oracle data dictionary provide the DBA with the information that is needed to manage end-user accounts. The Oracle data dictionary is also the central repository for information concerning database performance. A complete description of all of the tables is in the book *Oracle8 Server Administrators Guide*. The objects in the Oracle data dictionary include:

❑ Tables and views that are owned by the Oracle user SYS or SYSTEM.

❑ Data dictionary objects that start with USERS are data dictionary objects that the individual user has created (see Table 5.2).

TABLE 5.2 Examples of User-Created Objects

View Name	Description
USER_CATALOG	Tables, views, synonyms, sequences owned by the user
USER_CONSTRAINTS	Description of the user's own constraints
USER_INDEXES	Description of the user's own indexes
USER_SEQUENCES	Description of the user's own sequences
USER_SYNONYMS	Description of the user's own synonyms
USER_TABLES	Description of the user's own tables
USER_USERS	Information about the current user
USER_VIEWS	Description of views owned by the user

Data dictionary objects that start with ALL are objects to which the user has been granted access, as in Table 5.3.

TABLE 5.3 Examples of Accesible Objects Granted to User by DBA

View Name	Description
ALL_CATALOG	Tables, views, synonyms, sequences accessible by the user.
ALL_CONSTRAINTS	Constraints on all accessible objects.
ALL_INDEXES	Description indexes accessible by the user.
ALL_SEQUENCES	Description of sequences accessible by the user.
ALL_SYNONYMS	Description synonyms accessible by the user.
ALL_TABLES	Description tables accessible by the user.
ALL_USERS	Information about all users of the database.
ALL_VIEWS	Description of views accessible by the user.

Data dictionary objects that start with DBA can only be accessed by the users SYS and SYSTEM. All other users must be granted access to the objects that are owned by the user SYS (Table 5.4).

TABLE 5.4 SYSTEM-Owned Objects

View Name	Description
DBA_CATALOG	Tables, views, synonyms, sequences owned by the SYS user.
DBA_CONSTRAINTS	Description of all database constraints
DBA_INDEXES	Description of all indexes in the database
DBA_SEQUENCES	Description of all sequences in the database
DBA_SYNONYMS	Description of all synonyms in the database
DBA_TABLES	Description of all tables in the database
DBA_USERS	Information about all users of the database
DBA_VIEWS	Description of all views in the database
DBA_DATA_FILES	Listing of the location and size of the RDBMS data files
DBA_FREESPACE	Listing of free space in the various tablespaces
DBA_EXTENTS	List the number of extents for a segment
DBA_TABLESPACES	Description of the various tablespaces that make up the database

The objects in the data dictionary should never be deleted or modified.

CONSTRAINTS

An integrity constraint is a mechanism used by the RDBMS to prevent invalid data entry into a table. One very important use of an integrity constraint is to enforce various business rules. Integrity constraints prevent DML statements from modifying a table if a business has been violated.

Types of Integrity Constraints

There are four basic types of integrity constraints.

1. NOT NULL: All row/column entries must have a value. A NOT NULL constraint enforces the rule that a value must be entered. An example would be to enforce the constraint that every employee in a company's employee table have a last name and a first name.
2. UNIQUE: A unique constraint enforces the rule that no two columns can have the same value for a specified column. An example of a UNIQUE constraint would be that all employees in the company must have a unique employee number (now we see a sequence generator should be set when adding new employees).

3. PRIMARY KEY: A table can have only one primary key. The properties of a PRIMARY KEY constraint are that the row/column data have no null values and no duplicate values.

   We see that a PRIMARY KEY CONSTRAINT is a combination of the NOT NULL and the UNIQUE key constraints. An example would be the companies department table. In the department table the department number can be defined as a PRIMARY KEY (this would enforce the rule that every department in the company must have a number and the number must be unique).

4. FOREIGN KEY—Referential integrity is enforced through the use of FOREIGN KEY constraints. Referential integrity means that a column in one table (called the dependent or child table) must have a corresponding value in another table (called the parent table). An example would be that every employee name that is added to the company's employee table be placed in a department that already exists. In this case the child table is the employee table, and the parent table is the department table. The link is that both the employee table and the department table have a column for department number.

The following will show how constraints are created (refer to Display 5.18).

```
SQLPLUS> create table emp
SQLPLUS> (empno     NUMBER(10) PRIMARY KEY,
SQLPLUS> ename      VARCHAR2(20) NOT NULL,
SQLPLUS> job        VARCHAR2(10),
SQLPLUS> hiredate   DATE,
SQLPLUS> sal        NUMBER(9,2),
SQLPLUS> deptno     NUMBER(4) NOT NULL
SQLPLUS> CONSTRAINT fkey_dept REFERENCES
SQLPLUS> dept);
```

DISPLAY 5.18

Constraints can also be created when the table is created using SCHEMA MANAGER rather then using a command-line tool like SQL*PLUS or SERVER MANAGER (see Figure 5.15).

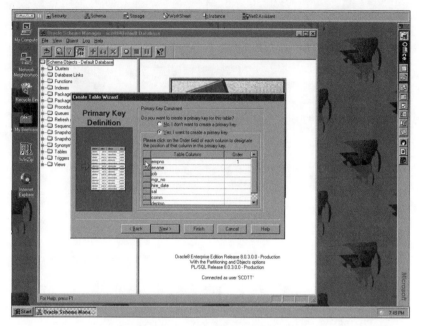

FIGURE 5.15 The Schema Manager

In this example the column *empno* is defined as a PRIMARY KEY. According to our definition of a PRIMARY KEY it is both NOT NULL and UNIQUE. The columns *ename* and *deptno* are defined as NOT NULL. The end user must enter a value for empno, ename and deptno because of the constraints that exist.

In Figure 5.16 the column *empno* cannot have any duplicate values in it. The RDBMS will create a unique index that is associated with the column *empno*. The index is automatically created when the constraint is enabled and dropped when the constraint is disabled.

Constraints can also be added after the table is created. This is accomplished by using the "ALTER TABLE" instruction:

```
alter table emp
add PRIMARY KEY (empno) DISABLE;
```

The DISABLE clause will keep the creation of the constraint from failing if some of the rows violate the constraint. This is because the rule is not enforced. To enable the constraint issue (refer to Display 5.19):

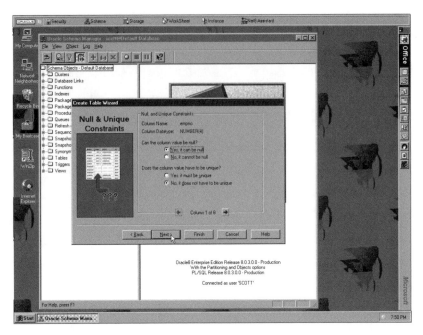

FIGURE 5.16   The column empno is defined as a Primary Key

```
SQLPLUS> alter table emp
SQLPLUS> ENABLE PRIMARY KEY;
```

DISPLAY 5.19

The enabled constraint can be disabled by issuing the command (refer to Display 5.20):

```
SQLPLUS> alter table emp
SQLPLUS> DISABLE PRIMARY KEY;
```

DISPLAY 5.20

Constraints can also be dropped as shown in Display 5.21.

```
SQLPLUS> alter table emp
SQLPLUS> DROP PRIMARY KEY,
SQLPLUS> DROP CONSTRAINT fkey_dept;
```

DISPLAY 5.21

Referential Integrity and Foreign Key Constraints

Referential integrity states that a foreign key value must match an existing primary key value. In the above example the column *deptno* in the table *emp* is defined as a foreign key. This means that in order to insert a record into the emp table there must be a matching value in the *dept* table's *deptno* column. The referential integrity between the dept table and the emp table is created using SCHEMA MANAGER as shown in figure 5.17.

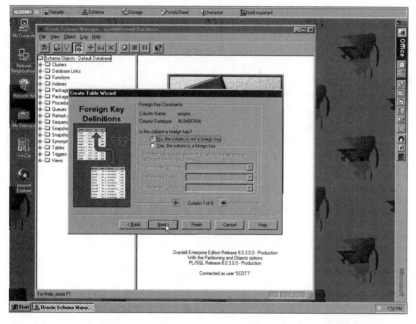

FIGURE 5.17 The referential integrity between the dept table and the emp table is created using Schema Manager

The following insert (refer to Table 5.5 and Table 5.6) into the table *emp* will fail because there is no corresponding value in the table *dept*:

insert into emp(333333,g.brown,CEO,96-03-03,5000.00,60)

TABLE 5.5   Emp Table

EMPNO	ENAME	JOB	HIREDATE	SAL	DEPTNO
111111	r.jones	mgr	96-05-05	1000.00	10
222222	v.smith	VP	92-01-02	3000.00	30

TABLE 5.6   Dept Table

DEPTNO	DEPT_NAME	DEPT_LOC
10	Finance	NY
20	IS	NJ
30	Manufacturing	SF

In summary, integrity constraints allow us to enforce business rules on the data that is being placed into the database.

LOADING DATA

DBAs and application developers must sometimes be able to load large amounts of data into the Oracle database at one time. Often this data comes from non-Oracle sources such as an ASCII file. When large amounts of non-Oracle data must be loaded into the Oracle database the utility SQL*LOADER (SQLLDR) should be used. The alternative to using SQL*LOADER is to use several SQL INSERT commands to load the data into a table.

The utility SQL*LOADER has several keywords that must be passed to it. In the example below we see that the user must pass their userid and password. We also see that the name of a control file is also passed. It is the contents of the control file that tells SQL*LOADER how to load the data into the database. The last parameter that is being passed tells SQL*LOADER where to write all output messages to.

```
Syntax:sqlldr userid=uid/pw control=file.ctl log=file.log

Sample SQL*LOADER control file  = file.ctl:
    LOAD DATA
    INFILE 'loadme.dat' <--- Name of file containing the data
    to be loaded.
    INTO TABLE emp

    (empno          POSITION(01:04),
    ename           POSITION(06:15),
```

```
job                     POSITION(17:25),
mgr                     POSITION(27:30),
sal                     POSITION(32:39),
Comm                    POSITION(41:48),
deptno                  POSITION(50:51))
```

Sample ASCII file = "loadme.dat"

```
7782 CLARK   MANAGER    7839  2572.50   10
7839 KING    PRESIDENT  7542  5500.00   10
7934 MILLER  CLERK      7782  920.00    10
7566 JONES   MANAGER    7839  3123.75   20
7499 ALLEN   SALESMAN   7698  300.00    30
7654 MARTIN  SALESMAN   7810  1400.00   30
7658 CHAN    ANALYST    7566  3450.00   20
```

In the next example a TAB delimited file will be loaded into a table. The DESCRIBE instruction is used to show the structure of the table that the data will be loaded into (refer to Display 5.22).

```
SVRMGR80> describe hawb

Table or View hawb
Name           Null?              Type
-----------------------------      --------
HAWB_NO                           VARCHAR2(l0)
HAWB_ORIG                         VARCHAR2(l0)
HAWB_ DEST                        VARCHAR2(10)
HAWB_SHIPPER_NAME                 VARCHAR2(80)
```

DISPLAY 5.22

The data consists of two records that will be loaded into the table:

```
7457820812,,'BAH',"PACIFIC PROPELLER INC"
989714666,"LAX","BRU","AIRMOTIVE SERVICE"
```

The control file that will be used is:

```
LOAD DATA
INFILE '4198.dat'
BADFILE 'hawb.bad'
DISCARDFILE 'hawb.dsc'
```

```
APPEND
INTO TABLE oracle.hawb
FIELDS TERMINATED BY','OPTIONALLY ENCLOSED BY ""
TRAILING NULLCOLS
(HAWB_NO,
HAWB_ORIG,
HAWB_DEST,
HAWB_SHIPPER_NAME)
```

To load the data, issue the instruction shown in Display 5.23.

```
DOS> sqlldr80 userid=oracle/user control=hawb.ctl log=4198hawb.log
```

DISPLAY 5.23

Fast Data Loading

When loading large amounts of data it is often desirable to bypass the normal RDBMS processing. This can be accomplished by using the *direct path load* feature of SQL*LOADER. The direct path load method will bypass writing the data to the SGA. Instead the data blocks will be written directly to the data files on the disk. The syntax for using the direct path load feature is:

```
Syntax: sqlldr userid=uid/pw control=file.ctl log=file.log
        direct=true
```

Using direct path loading can greatly reduce the time to load large amounts of data. Because the normal RDBMS processing is being bypassed, there can be no active transactions against the table. In the event of a media failure during a direct path load (refer to Chapter 6, "Database Backup and Recovery") if redo log file archiving is enabled (the database is running in ARCHIVELOG mode) recovery is possible. If redo archiving is not enabled then media recovery is not possible.

LOADING DATA USING ENTERPRISE MANAGER

Loading data into the Oracle database can be done using Oracle's command line SQL*LOADER (SQLLDR), EXPORT or IMPORT. Data can also be loaded using *ENTERPRISE MANAGER*. ENTERPRISE MANAGER provides the user with a GUI for using SQL*LOADER, IMPORT and EXPORT. It is also used to schedule batch jobs for execution. In the following examples we see how to load data using *ENTERPRISE MANAGER*.

The first time that the user logs into *ENTERPRISE MANAGER* the utility will create a profile for that user (this occurs automatically as soon as the user logs in). This is only done the first time that the user tries to access *ENTERPRISE MANAGER* (see Figure 5.18).

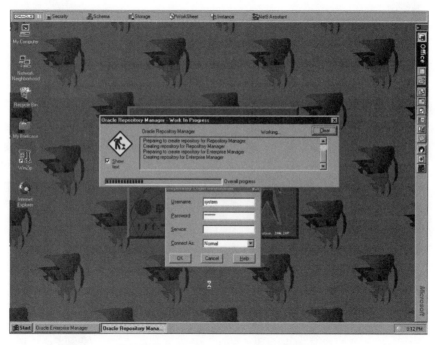

FIGURE 5.18 The Enterprise Manager

After the end-user's repository has been created the user can create a "JOB" as shown in Figure 5.19.

Next we create a name for our batch job (see Figure 5.20). The name and description indicate that we plan on using SQL*LOADER to batch load data into a database table.

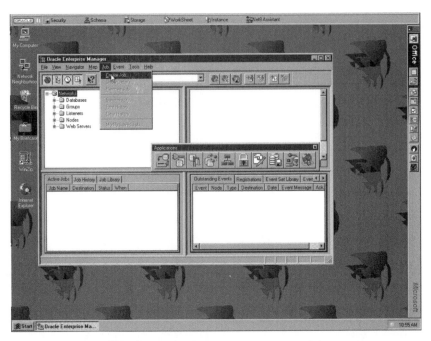

FIGURE 5.19   The user can create a Job

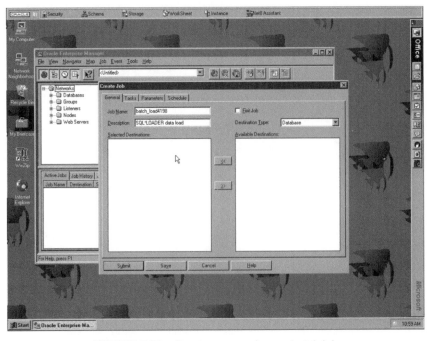

FIGURE 5.20   Create a name for our batch job

The ENTERPRISE MANAGER utility can perform several different types of batch operations. These operations include SQL*LOADER, IMPORT, and EXPORT. In Figure 5.21 we see that we must choose which task we want to perform.

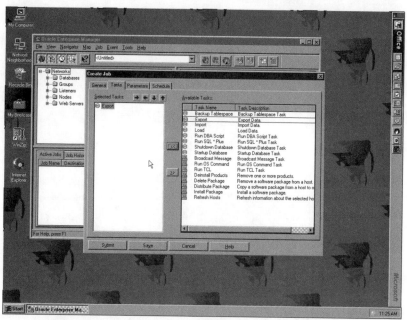

FIGURE 5.21   We must choose which task we want to perform

Next we specify the location of the loader's control file (this file is not the same as the database's control file (refer to Figure 5.22).

We can also specify which files should be used for logging the progress of the loader utility (refer to Figure 5.23).

The last step is the scheduling of the batch job(refer to Figure 5.24).

Once the job is submitted it will be executed based on the schedule that was specified.

IMPORT/EXPORT

SQL*LOADER is the right utility to use when large amounts of non-Oracle data must be loaded into the system at one time. But what if we want to transfer data from one Oracle database into another. To be more specific what if we need to populate an empty database from an existing database. First we would have to decide if we need all of the objects in the existing database of just a few of the tables. Regardless of the amount of data we would use the Oracle IMPORT and EXPORT utilities.

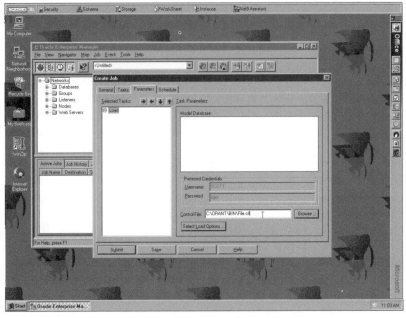

FIGURE 5.22   Specify location of loader's control file

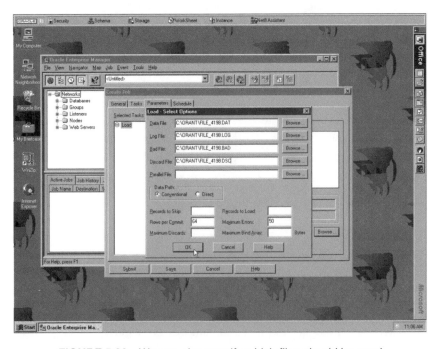

FIGURE 5.23   We can also specify which files should be used

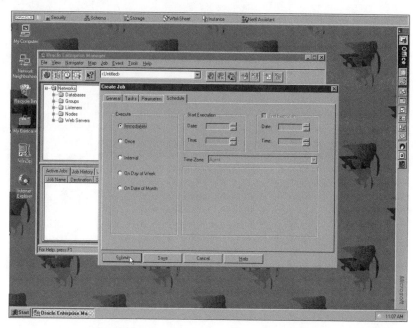

FIGURE 5.24   The scheduling of the batch job

To export the entire database a full export is performed as shown in Display 5.24:

DOS> exp80 userid=scott/tiger full=y grants=y file=exp.dat

DISPLAY 5.24

We can also use the export feature of ENTERPRISE MANAGER. This is done by selecting the EXPORT task from the CREATE JOB window as shown in Figure 5.25.

In the example shown in Figure 5.25, the user "scott" is performing a full export. The exported data will be placed into the file called today.exp.

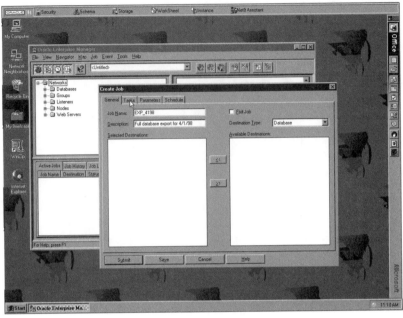

FIGURE 5.25   The Export task from the Create Job window

If the user "scott" only wanted to export the emp and the dept tables they would have used this syntax below:

```
exp userid=scott/tiger tables=(emp,dept) grants=y file=exp.dat
```

DISPLAY 5.25

To import the full database into the new system the user "scott" would code the following (refer to Display 5.26):

```
imp userid=scott/tiger full=y file=exp.dat
```

DISPLAY 5.26

If only the dept and emp tables had to be imported, the import statement would have been coded as shown in Display 5.27.

```
imp userid=scott/tiger tables=(emp,dept), grants=y
```

DISPLAY 5.27

Importing large amounts of data often causes the RDBMS to run out of space in the rollback segments. This occurs because the inserting of large amounts of data causes the RDBMS to store the previous state of the tables. This data must be stored in the rollback segments. To get around the problem the DBA can cause the IMPORT utility to execute a commit after each record is loaded. Issuing the commit releases the space in the rollback segments. This technique will allow you to manage the size of the rollback segments and help ensure that your import does not fail. To use this technique the DBA would issue the instruction (shown in Display 5.28).

```
imp userid=scott/tiger full=y file=today.exp commit=y
```

DISPLAY 5.28

This will prevent the RDBMS from running out of space in the rollback segments (issuing the error message ORA-1547: failed to allocate extent of size *nnn* in segment *'name'*).

We can choose to use the command-line version of IMPORT for our loading job. If we want to schedule the job for import and we want the import to take place at some future time, then ENTERPRISE MANAGER provides the job-scheduling capability that is required for unattended data loading (refer to Figure 5.26).

MANUAL DATABASE CREATION

In Chapter 3 we used the utility ORAINST to install the Oracle RDBMS. This option installed the necessary software that was required and also created the database. In this section we investigate how to create a database manually (without using the installer ORAINST).

1. Copy the init<SID>.ora and config<SID>.ora files into the ORACLE_HOME\database directory. As discussed earlier, the init<SID>.ora and config<SID>.ora files contain the database initialization parameters.
2. Start the server manager utility (refer to Display 5.29)

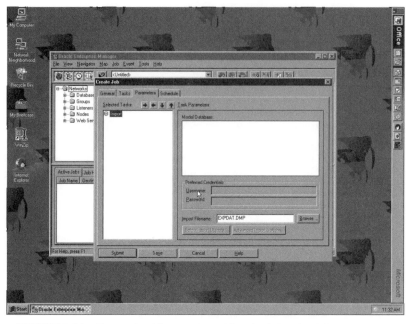

FIGURE 5.26 Enterprise Manager provides the job-scheduling capability

DOS> SVRMGR80

DISPLAY 5.29

3. Log in as the internal user as shown in Display 5.30.

SVRMGR80 > connect internal

DISPLAY 5.30

4. Start the Oracle instance, but DO NOT mount and open the database. This step will start the Oracle background processes PMON, SMON, LGWR DBWR and the server processes (refer to Display 5.31).

SVRMGR80 > startup nomount

DISPLAY 5.31

5. Next we will execute the create database script shown below. The first thing that the script does is creates a log file to capture any possible errors. Next the "CREATE DATABASE" command is executed. Some of the parameters that should be set when creating a database are the location and size of the redo log files, the size of the SYSTEM tablespace, and the NLS character set that will be used (refer to Display 5.32).

SVRMGR80 > @create_mydb

DISPLAY 5.32

6. After the create database statement has been processed we create a rollback segment in the SYSTEM tablespace for recoverability purposes.

7. Next we must run the Oracle supplied scripts that create objects in the Oracle data dictionary. The script CATALOG.SQL creates the DBA_, USER_, ALL, and V$_, data dictionary objects. The script CATAUDIT.SQL creates the Oracle tables used for auditing the database. CATPROC.SQL is used to create the database objects that are required for the support of the procedural option (PL/SQL). The script UTLXPLAN.SQL creates the data dictionary objects that are required for the utilities that are used for SQL statement tuning such as TKPROF. The script CATDBSYN.SQL is run by the user SYSTEM. The script creates the private synonyms that the user SYSTEM will use to reference the objects in the data dictionary without having prefixed the database objects name with the schema name "SYS" (the user SYS owns the objects in the Oracle data dictionary).

8. The next step is to create the additional tablespaces. The tablespaces that should be created are TEMP for sorting, RBS for additional rollback segments and USERS for storing the tables associated with the applications that the database will support.

9. After the tablespaces have been created, additional rollback segments should be created and brought on line.

10. The last step is to bring the rollback segment that was created earlier (in the SYSTEM tablespace) off line and then drop it.

```
##############################################
# Database Creation Script: CREATE_MYDB.SQL #
##############################################
spool create_mydb.log
create database MYDB
logfile group 1 ('C:\ORANT\database\log_1.dbf',
                'C:\ORANT\database\log_2.dbf') size 2M,
        group 2 ('C:\ORANT\database\log_3.dbf',
                  'C:\ORANT\database\log_4.dbf') size 2M
maxlogfiles 9
datafile 'C:\ORANT\database\system01.dbf' size 25M
maxdatafiles 255
maxinstances 1
noarchivelog
character set WE8ISO8859P9
/

create public rollback segment system_pub
storage (initial 50k next 50k minextents 1 maxextents 50)
    tablespace system;
alter rollback segment system_pub online;

@@C:\ORANT\rdbms\admin\catalog.sql
@@C:\ORANT\rdbms\admin\cataudit.sql
@@C:\ORANT\rdbms\admin\catproc.sql
@@C:\ORANT\rdbms\admin\utlxplan.sql

connect system/manager

@@C:\ORANT\rdbms\admin\catdbsyn.sql

create tablespace TEMP
    datafile 'C:\ORANT\database\temp01.dbf' size 20M reuse
    default storage (initial 1M next 1M
          minextents 1 maxextents 120)
/
create tablespace ROLLBACK
    datafile 'C:\ORANT\database\rol101.dbf' size 20M reuse
    default storage (initial 1M next 1M
          minextents 2 maxextents 120)
```

```
/
create tablespace USERS
     datafile ' C:\ORANT\database\user01.dbf' size 50M reuse
     default storage (initial 200K next 200K
          minextents 1 maxextents 120)
/

create rollback segment PRS_1 storage (initial 1M next 1M min-
     extents 2 maxextents 120) tablespace ROLLBACK
/
create rollback segment PRS_2 storage (initial 1M next 1M min-
     extents 2 maxextents 120) tablespace ROLLBACK
/
create rollback segment PRS_3 storage (initial 1M next 1M min-
     extents 2 maxextents 120) tablespace ROLLBACK
/
create rollback segment PRS_4 storage (initial 1M next 1M min-
     extents 2 maxextents 120) tablespace ROLLBACK
/
alter rollback segment PRS_1 online
/
alter rollback segment PRS_2 online
/
alter rollback segment PRS_3 online
/
alter rollback segment PRS_4 online
/
alter rollback segment SYSTEM_PUB offline
/
drop public rollback segment SYSTEM_PUB
/
spool off
exit
```

The DBA should also run the script PUPBLD.SQL. The script will create the product user profile tables. The product user profile is used to disable the end-user's ability to issue operating system commands from SQL*PLUS. It is also used to disable the user's ability to connect to the database as another user. The routine is located in the $ORACLE_HOME\sqlplus\admin directory and must be run by the user SYSTEM. Running this script will also prevent the message "product user profile does not exist" each time an end user logs into SQL*PLUS. The product user profile table has the following columns:

```
Column Name Description
PRODUCT      Set to SQL*PLUS.

USERID       Names of the users whose commands are being
             disabled.

ATTRIBUTE    Command that is being disabled.

CHAR_VALUE   Set to "DISABLEED"
```

DATABASE AUDITING

Auditing is the process of examining database access. Implementing auditing of the database is often useful to:

1. Keep track of who is accessing the database.
2. Keep track of who is modifying the database.

As part of implementing an auditing scheme we must understand what are the database operations that can be audited. The following is a list of the types of database activities that can be audited.

1. End-user sessions.

```
SVRMGR80 > audit session scott, irma;
```

DISPLAY 5.33

In Display 5.33 the sessions for the user "SCOTT" and "IRMA" are audited. The database DML/DDL operations that are executed (such as INSERT, DELETE UPDATE, SELECT, etc.) by the two users will be stored in the audit table.

To obtain information about when the users "SCOTT" and "IRMA" logged off of the system, the DBA would issue the following query (refer to Display 5.34):

```
SQPLUS > select username,logoff_time from
SQPLUS > sys.dba_audit_session;
```

DISPLAY 5.34

2. Auditing use of privileges (refer to Display 5.35).

SVRMGR80 > audit create table;

DISPLAY 5.35

In this example the privilege "CREATE TABLE" is audited. The userid of the database users that issue the "CREATE TABLE" command will be stored in the audit table.

3. Modifications made to database objects (refer to Display 5.36).

SVRMGR80 > audit insert on emp;

DISPLAY 5.36

In this example we are auditing changes made to the table emp. This is often helpful for tracking who is making changes to the various tables that support the database's various applications.

The DBA or any database user with the proper privileges can audit the database. Auditing must be enabled before it can be used to track database access. When auditing is enabled and the SQL auditing statements arte executed, the RDBMS will store the audit records in the table SYUS.AUD$. To enable auditing the init<SID>.ora parameter "AUDIT_TRAIL" is set to "DB" (the default is "NONE" for no auditing). The DBA must run the script CATAUDIT.SQL. This script will create the main audit table SYS.AUD$ and various audit views. A brief summary of the function of the various auditing views is listed in Table 5.7.

TABLE 5.7 Functions of Various Auditing Views

AUDIT TABLE	AUDIT TABLE DESCRIPTION
DBA_AUDIT_EXISTS	Audit trail records created by the AUDIT EXIST command.
DBA_AUDI_OBJECT	Audit records for database object auditing.
DBA_AUDIT_SESSION	Audit records for session auditing.
DBA_AUDIT_STATEMENT	Audit records for statement auditing.
DBA_AUDIT_TRAIL	Collection of all the system audit records.

Protecting the Audit Trail

The DBA should protect the audit trail. The term "protect the audit trail" means keep track of who is modifying the auditing table SYS.AUD$. To protect the audit trail the DBA should enter the following (refer to Display 5.37):

```
SVRMGR80 > audit insert, update, delete on
SVRMGR80 > SYS.AUD$ by access;
```

DISPLAY 5.37

The above command will cause the RDBMS to audit access to the audit table SYS.AUD$.

The auditing process creates records in the table SYS.AUD$. It is the responsibility of the DBA to monitor and control the size of the table. The SQL command TRUNCATE can be used to drop records from the audit table.

ORACLE TABLE/DATABASE REPLICATION TECHNIQUES

BACKGROUND

Many IS organizations support 24 x 7 operations for their Oracle database/application installations. To support this type of activity it is often advantageous to duplicate various tables on a machine other then the database server. This situation can arise if we have an OLTP application such as an order entry system that accesses the same tables that the ad hoc management reporting system accesses. In this case the ad hoc tool will interfere with the response time of the OLTP application. To resolve this problem we can duplicate the tables that the order entry system accesses onto a different machine. The other machine can be used by the management reporting system, therefore improving the overall response time of the order entry application. In this situation one server is called the database server and the other is called the replicated server (replication server).

There are three different techniques used to replicate Oracle RDBMS tables. The three database-replication techniques are:

1. SNAPSHOT
2. Database COPY
3. Remote Procedure Call (RPC)

DATABASE REPLICATION USING ORACLE SNAPSHOT

A snapshot is a copy of one or more tables. The machine where the original tables are located is called the master (and contains the master tables). The machine that contains the replicated tables is called the snapshot and contains the copied or "snapshot tables." In order to use Oracle's SNAPSHOT feature the DBA should do the following:

❏ Both the master server and the replication server must use the Oracle Distributed Option. This is supported on all Oracle databases provided that it was purchased and installed.

❏ Run the utility CATSNAP.SQL. The utility will create the Oracle data dictionary objects that the RDBMS needs to support the snapshot feature.

❏ Set up a database link from the replication server to the master server using SQL*NET (v1 or v2) as shown in Display 5.38.

```
SVRMGR80> CREATE DATABASE LINK dblink
SVRMGR80> connect to scott identified by tiger
SVRMGR80> USING '<SQLNET ALIAS>';
```

DISPLAY 5.38

❏ Issue the statement "CREATE SNAPSHOT" on the replication server using the database link. This will create a base table on the snapshot machine called SNAP$_<snapshot_name> (the base table should never be modified) and a view of the base table which is the snapshot. Another view will be created on the master machine. The view is called MVIEW$__<snapshot_name> and is used by the master to refresh the snapshot. The statement should be issued with the "REFRESH" option to control the refresh rate of the replicated tables. In the following example the table my_table is being replicated on another machine. The refresh rate for the snapshot is every 7 days (refer to Display 5.39).

❏ Creation of a SNAPSHOT log on the server. This log is used by the Oracle RDBMS. It ensures that only the records that have been changed since the last SNAPSHOT are updated on the replication server (this will also reduce the amount of network traffic that database replication can produce).

❏ Create an index on the snapshot base table to improve queries on the replication server.

```
SVRMGR80>  CREATE SNAPSHHOT s_my_table
SVRMGR80>  TABLESPACE users
SVRMGR80>  STORAGE (initial 50K NEXT 50K)
SVRMGR80>  REFRESH FAST
SVRMGR80>  START WITH sysdate
SVRMGR80>  NEXT sysdate+7
SVRMGR80>  AS SELECT * FROM my_table@dblink;
```

DISPLAY 5.39

The drawbacks to using SNAPSHOT are:

1. The replicated tables are read only. Therefore snapshots can only be queried.
2. Database integrity constraints are not supported on the replicated server. Snapshots cannot be joined. The tables can be joined if a complex snapshot is used (SNAPSHOT with a join clause) but the refresh feature is not supported for complex SNAPSHOTs as that would generate more network traffic because the entire table is replicated.
3. A SNAPSHOT statement must be written for all tables that are to be replicated.

DATABASE REPLICATION USING COPY

The second technique uses the SQL*PLUS command "COPY" to replicate the database. The DBA would do the following:

❏ Create a database link from the replication server to the server as shown in Display 5.40.

```
SVRMGR80> CREATE DATABASE LINK dblink
SVRMGR80> connect to scott identified by tiger
SVRMGR80> USING '<SQLNET ALIAS>';
```

DISPLAY 5.40

❏ Issue the "COPY" command on the replication server using the database link. The command "COPY" should be issued with the REFRESH option. This will ensure that only the updates are copied from the server to the replication server.

DATABASE BACKUP/ RECOVERY

It is important that the DBA define a database backup and recovery strategy. The investment in the time it takes to define and implement a database backup and recovery strategy will pay off the first time that your important data needs to be recovered after a system hardware failure. The different types of software and hardware failures include:

1. Media failure: The physical media is damaged (disk). A power outage or failure of the disk read/write mechanical system could have caused this.
2. User thread failure: The user session was abnormally terminated. This could occur if a personal computer (PC) client does not end its session correctly (such as powering off the PC instead of first exiting from the application). The PMON thread monitors user threads. If a user thread terminates abnormally, the PMON thread will roll back the uncommitted statements and release all resource locks.
3. Instance failure: One of the Oracle threads (SMON, PMON, LGWR, DBWR) terminated abnormally. Instance recovery is the job of the SMON thread.

Before we address database recovery we first discuss database backup. The reason why we cover database backup first is because it influences the options that we have for database recovery. There are two methods used to backup a database. The two methods are physical backup and a logical backup.

PHYSICAL BACKUP

This is an operating system backup. It saves the database data files onto tape or some other storage media. This type of backup is often used to recover the database to the point of failure.

LOGICAL BACKUP

The logical backup technique uses the IMPORT/EXPORT utilities to create the backup copy of the database. A logical backup will backup the contents of the database. In Figure 6.1 a logical backup is created using the utility ENTERPRISE MANAGER. A logical backup can be used to recover the database to the last backup.

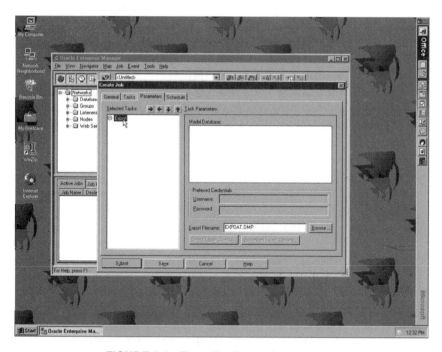

FIGURE 6.1   The utility Enterprise Manager

Both methods can be used to restore a database. But what happens if the disk that holds one of the tablespace data files is damaged. Restoring the data from an IMPORT/EXPORT does not allow you to correct the damaged data file problem. To recover the database we must first restore the tablespace's data files. For these types of situations the backup strategy to use is the physical backup.

TYPES OF PHYSICAL BACKUPS AND DATABASE MODES

For a physical backup (often referred to as an operating system backup) the data files, redo log files and control files are saved on a backup media such as a tape storage system. The backup is accomplished by using both Windows NT operating system utilities and Oracle database utilities.

There are two different types of physical backups. One type is called a "COLD" backup and the other type is called a "HOT" backup. When choosing the type of backup strategy to use the following should be considered:

- ❏ Can the database be shutdown so that a database backup can be taken. If the answer is no, then a hot database backup is the backup strategy to use. A hot backup is often used in IS shops that support 24 x 7 access.

- ❏ A hot backup can be used to recover the database to the point in time of failure. Database recovery from a cold backup will only restore the database to the time when the last backup was taken. The data that was entered between the time the last backup was taken and the time that the system failure occurred are lost. Recovery from a hot backup can help minimize data lost.

- ❏ A hot database backup requires more disk space then a cold database backup (the reason for this will be covered later in this chapter).

COLD BACKUP

The first step in creating a cold backup s to determine the locations of the log files, control files and the database files. The following commands can be issued to find the locations of these files:

1. Obtain a full list of data files as shown in Display 6.1.

SVRMGR30 > select * from dba_data_files;

DISPLAY 6.1

2. Obtain a full list of the redo log files as shown in Display 6.2.

SVRMGR > select member from v$logfile;

DISPLAY 6.2

3. Obtain a full list of the control files as shown in Display 6.3.

SVRMGR > select * from v$controlfile;;

DISPLAY 6.3

After determining the locations of the log files, data files and control files the database must be shutdown as shown in Display 6.4.

SVRMGR > connect internal
SVRMGR > shutdown

DISPLAY 6.4

Once the database is shutdown the DBA can exit the SVRMGR utility and copy the log files, data files and control files onto the backup media (refer to Figure 6.2).

FIGURE 6.2 The SVRMGR utility

Usually the backup media is a tape device. The Windows NT operating provides a utility for backing up disk files to tape as shown in Figure 6.3.

The DBA should proceed to copy the control files, log files and data files to the backup media. Once the backup has been completed the DBA can restart the database.

We can also use Oracle's backup utility to create our cold backup as shown in Figure 6.4.

The utility can be used to create a cold backup of the database without writing any SQL (refer to Figure 6.5).

The backed up database files can be saved into any directory or into the default directory C:\ORANT\BACKUP (refer to Figures 6.6 and 6.7).

When the backup utility has completed a message is written to the screen (see Figure 6.7)

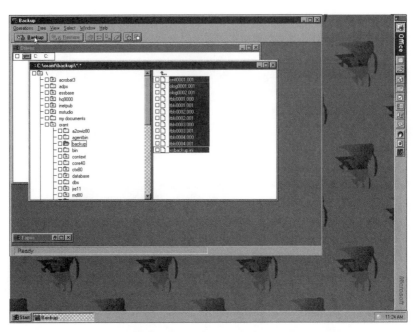

FIGURE 6.3   Windows NT backup

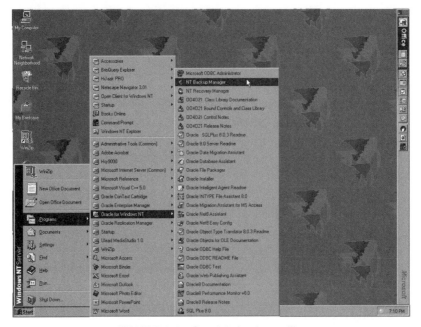

FIGURE 6.4   Oracle's backup utility

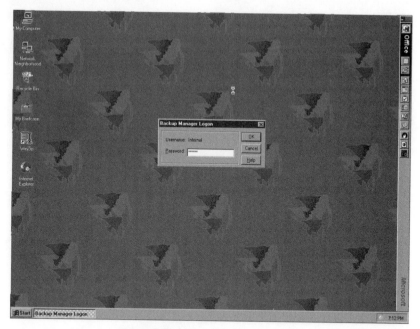

FIGURE 6.5 Create a cold backup

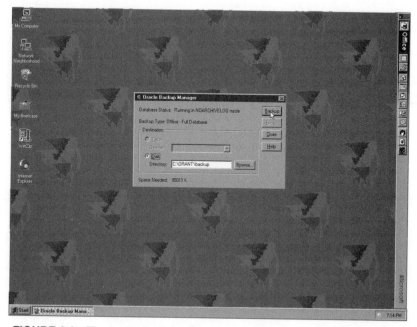

FIGURE 6.6 The backed up database files can be saved into any directory

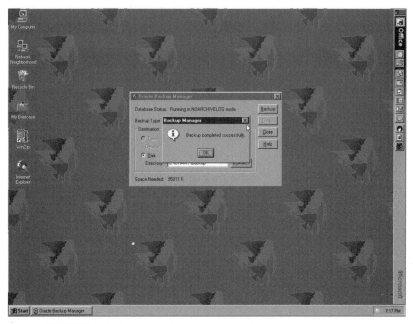

FIGURE 6.7   The completed message is written to the screen

At this point the DBA should backup the saved files. The files should be backed up to tape using the Windows NT backup utility (as shown earlier) or some other backup utility.

HOT BACKUP

Many IS shops are supporting 24 x 7 operations where the database cannot be brought down without inconveniencing the end users. In these situations it is best to take a hot database backup.

Before we introduce the technique for creating a hot backup we must first cover the different modes that the database can be running in. One mode is called ARCHIEVELOG mode and the other mode is called NOARCHIVELOG mode.

The ARCH Thread—When the database is started or switched to ARCHIVE-LOG mode another Oracle thread called "ARCH" is started. The ARCH thread functions by writing the data from the on-line redo log files to off line storage. When the RDBMS is created it has at least two redo log files.   While the LGWR thread is writing the redo log buffers to one of the redo log files the ARCH thread will write the contents of the other redo log file to off line storage (another disk device). When the redo log file that the LGWR thread is writing to is full, a log switch will occur. The LGWR thread will then begin writing the redo log buffers to the other redo log file (refer to Figure 6.8).

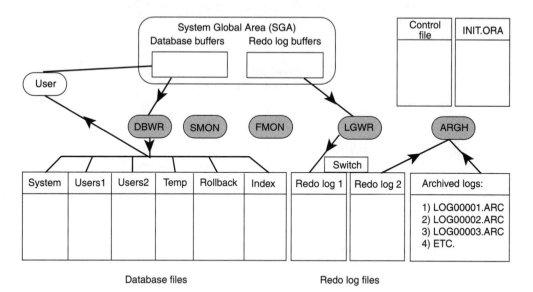

FIGURE 6.8 The LGWR thread

Before creating the database the DBA should make the following additions to the init<sid>.ora file:

```
LOG_ARCHIVE_START = TRUE

LOG_ARCHIVE_DEST = %ORACLE_HOME%\database\archive

LOG_ARCHIVE_FORMAT = "%%ORACLE_SID%%T%TS%S.ARC"
```

If all the on-line redo log files are filled before they can be archived all database operations will be suspended until archiving has been completed. It is also VERY important that the directory containing the archived log files not become full. If the archive directory becomes full the ARCH thread will not be able to archive the redo log files. The DBA should always monitor the percentage of space used in the archive directory.

The database can be placed into ARCHIVELOG mode at database creation time or after the database has been created. To create the database in ARCHIVELOG mode the DBA should issue the following command (refer to Display 6.5).

```
SVRMGR30 > create database test
SVRMGR30 > datafile 'system0l.dbf' size 23M
SVRMGR30 > logfile group1 'file1.log' size 50K group2 'file2.log' size
SVRMGR30 > 50K  archivelog;
```

DISPLAY 6.5

To change from ARCHIVELOG mode to NOARCHIVELOG mode (or vice versa) the database must be mounted but not open as shown in Display 6.6.

```
SVRMGR > connect internal
SVRMGR > startup mount
SVRMGR > alter database noarchivelog;
SVRMGR > alter database open;
```

DISPLAY 6.6

To restart archiving the database must be mounted but not open (see Display 6.7):

```
SVRMGR > connect internal
SVRMGR > startup mount
SVRMGR > alter database archivelog;
SVRMGR > alter database open;
```

DISPLAY 6.7

The reader should note that in each case listed here the database was shutdown prior to connecting to it as the user INTERNAL.

This technique can also be used to place the database in ARCHIVELOG mode if it was originally created in NOARCHIVELOG mode. To see if the database is running in ARCHIVELOG mode issue the following command (shown in Display 6.8).

SVRMGR30 > select log_mode from v$database;

DISPLAY 6.8

Creating a hot backup requires that the archived redo log files be copied to a backup media (usually tape) before the data files are backed up. The following script is an example of what the archive script would look like. Note that before the archive log files are copied the instruction ALTER SYSTEM SWITCH LOGFILE is issued.

Next the individual tablespaces and control files must be backed up. The Oracle RDBMS must be told when a hot backup of the tablespace data files and control files has begun and when it has finished. The following script illustrates how to create a hot backup. The script can be executed from the command-line utility SERVER MANAGER:

```
################################
# Script: CREATE_ONLINEB.SQL #
################################
spool online_backup.log
connect internal

alter tablespace USERS begin backup;
copy C:\ORANT\DATABASE\USR1ORCL.ORA C:\ORANT\back-
    up\tbls0001.000
alter tablespace USER end backup;

alter tablespace TEMP begin backup;
copy C:\ORANT\DATABASE\TMP1ORCL.ORA C:\ORANT\back-
    up\tbls0003.000
alter tablespace TEMP end backup;

alter tablespace ROLLBACK begin backup;
copy C:\ORANT\DATABASE\RBS1ORCL.ORA C:\ORANT\back-
    up\tbls0002.000
alter tablespace ROLLBACK end backup;

alter tablespace SYSTEM begin backup;
copy C:\ORANT\DATABASE\SYS1ORCL.ORA C:\ORANT\back-
    up\tbls0004.000
alter tablespace SYSTEM end backup;
```

```
alter database backup controlfile to 'C:\ORANT\back-
    up\cntrl.dbf';

spool off
exit
```

The script uses the commands "ALTER DATABASE BEGIN BACKUP" and "ALTER DATABASE END BACKUP" to signal the start and end of the backup of a tablespace.

The DBA can also use the Oracle backup utility to create a hot backup of the database. In the Figure 6.9 the utility ENTERPRISE MANAGER is used to access the Oracle backup utility.

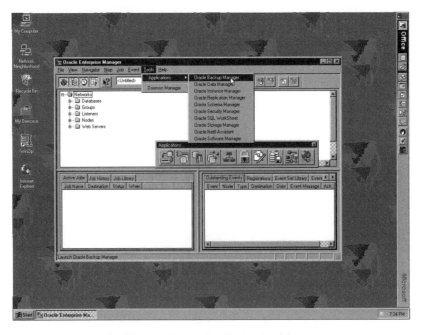

FIGURE 6.9   The utility Enterprise Manager

The utility allows us to choose which tablespaces we want to include in the backup. It is a good practice to backup all data files at the same time (refer to Figure 6.10).

The utility will issue the SQL ALTER TABLESPACE BEGIN/END commands that must be issued when creating a hot backup of the database (refer to Figure 6.11).

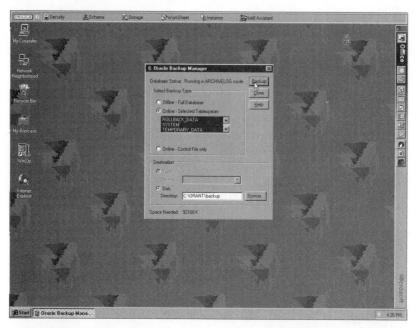

FIGURE 6.10 It is a good practice to backup all data files at the same time

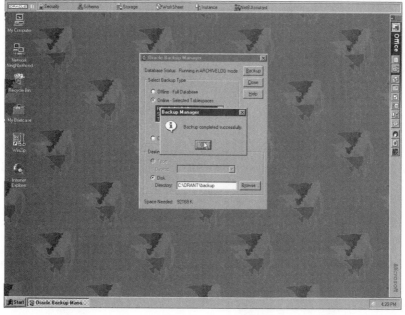

FIGURE 6.11 The utility will issue the SQL ALTER TABLESPACE BEGIN/END commands

All database files should be saved to a backup media. The files that are saved should include backups of the control files, log files, data files and archived log files (refer to Figure 6.12).

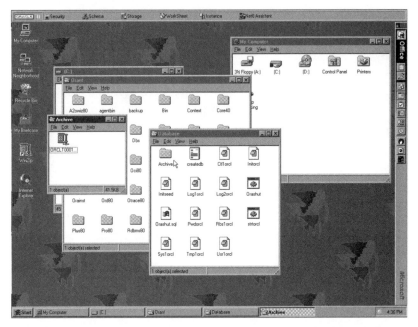

FIGURE 6.12   All database files should be saved to a backup media

To ensure that there is always a recent backup of your database a backup should be taken on a daily basis. The backup should have the date written on it and then stored in a safe location.

DATABASE RECOVERY

In the previous section we covered the different techniques that are used to create a backup of an Oracle database. The three techniques include:

1. Logical backup using the EXPORT utility.
2. Cold physical backup. This technique included shutting down the database and using one of the operating system commands to save the data files onto the backup media.

3. Hot physical backup. This technique allows us to create a backup of the database while the database is still on line. The technique is implemented using the "ALTER TABLESPACE BEGIN/END BACKUP" commands and one of the operating system commands to save the data files onto the backup media.

Earlier in the chapter it was stated that there are several failures that can occur. Errors that are caused by a damaged disk (containing one or more of the Oracle data files) will usually require that the disk be changed and the data files on the old disk restored to the new disk. In this section we will cover restoring the database from the various types of backups.

RECOVERY USING A COLD BACKUP

To recover the Oracle RDBMS from a cold backup the DBA would do the following:

1. Restore backup files from the backup media. The control files, log files and data files must be restored into the exact locations from where they were originally copied.
2. Start the utility SVRMGR and connect as the internal user (see Display 6.9).

```
DOS% SVRMGR30
SVRMGR30 > connect internal
```

DISPLAY 6.9

3. Start the database (Display 6.10). When the database instance is started the SMON thread will apply the contents of the redo log entries to the data files. This thread is called roll forward. After applying the contents of the redo log files to the data files the SMON thread will apply the data in the rollback segments to undo uncommitted changes in the data blocks. This is called the roll back thread.

```
SVRMGR30 > startup
```

DISPLAY 6.10

At this point the database has been restored/recovered from the cold backup. Notice that the database has been recovered to the point in time when the last cold backup was taken. The data that was entered between the time of the last database backup and the time when the database was restored is lost.

DATABASE RECOVERY FROM A HOT BACKUP

The hot backup technique lets the DBA restore the database to the point in time of failure. The technique gives the DBA the greatest possibility of recovering all committed data after a disk failure. Database recovery from a hot backup involves the restoring of the tablespaces from the data files that are stored on the backup media.

It is possible that one of the disk drives that contains a data file will malfunction. In this situation the damaged disk drive must be repaired. If the disk drive can be repaired without rebooting the server it is also possible to recover the database without taking the entire database off line. End users can continue to access tables that are stored in the tablespaces/data files that are not stored on the damaged disk drive.

Database recovery from a hot backup uses the following commands:

❏ RECOVER TABLESPACE: Used to recover all the data files that make up the tablespace. The database must be on line if this command is used.

❏ RECOVER data file: Used to recover an individual data file.

❏ RECOVER DATABASE: Used to recover all tablespaces. For systemwide recovery the database cannot be open.

Open Database Recovery

It is often desirable to recover the database when users are still logged on. In this situation one or more of the data files need to be recovered. If a data file requires recovery the Oracle RDBMS will issue the message: *"Media Recovery Required for datafile <Datafile_Name.DBF>."* It is possible to recover the damaged data file without shutting down the database. This is desirable because there may be other applications that are accessing data files/tablespaces that are not damaged (why should we bring down the manufacturing application when it is the human resources application that is not working because the data file containing the human resources table is damaged?).

The following technique can be used to repair a damaged data file while the database is still up, and end-user applications that access other tables/data files are running with no problems.

1. Take the affected tablespace off line as shown in Display 6.11.

```
SVRMGR30 > ALTER TABLESPACE USERS OFFLINE;
```

DISPLAY 6.11

2. If the disk that contains the data files is damaged then it must first be repaired. After the disk has been repaired, restore the tablespace's data file from the backup media. The data file must be restored into the same directory that is was taken from.
3. Restore the archive log files back into the archive log directory.
4. Start database recovery. This will start the recovery process. The Oracle RDBMS will prompt the user for the locations of the archived log files (that is why it is important to restore the archived files back into their original location). To start automatic media recovery enter the RECOVER DATABASE OR DATAFILE command.

To recover the data file associated with a tablespace issue the command as shown in Display 6.12.

```
SVRMGR30 > RECOVER DATAFILE
SVRMGR30 > C:\<directory_location>/users01.dbf ;
```

DISPLAY 6.12

To recover all data files that make up the tablespace, issue the command (refer to Display 6.13):

```
SVRMGR30 > RECOVER
SVRMGR30 > TABLESPACE users;
```

DISPLAY 6.13

At this point Oracle starts media recovery on the data file that represents the tablespace called USERS. The SMON thread will apply the contents of the on-line and off-line log files to the data file. The SMON thread will analyze the log sequence numbers written into the database's control file and apply the appropriate log files as specified by the log sequence numbers to the data file. This is the roll forward process. Next the rollback process is performed. The data in the log files will also be used to reconstruct the rollback segments. Once the rollback segments have been reconstructed they are applied to the data file to undo the uncommitted changes.

Next the restored tablespace is brought back on line. After the last log file has been applied the RDBMS will issue a message saying "Media recovery complete." At this point the DBA can alter the tablespace on line (see Display 6.14).

```
SVRMGR30 > ALTER TABLESPACE
SVRMGR30 > USERS ONLINE;
```

DISPLAY 6.14

At this point the damaged tablespace has been repaired and all the tablespaces for the database are on line.

Closed Database Recovery

The technique just outlined showed how to recover the database if only one or a few tablespaces are damaged. In the situation where the database has been shut-down and the DBA has to perform media recovery before end-user applications can be started, the DBA should use closed database recovery. The following technique can be used to recover the database after the damaged disk(s) has been:

1. If the disk that contains the data files is damaged then it must first be repaired. After the disk has been repaired, restore the tablespace's data file from the backup media. The data file and archived log/log files should be restored as shown earlier using the UNIX TAR or CPIO utilities.

2. Start the Oracle instance and mount the database but do not open it (refer to Display 6.15).

```
SVRMGR > STARTUP MOUNT;
```

DISPLAY 6.15

3. Start database recovery. This will start the recovery process. The Oracle RDBMS will prompt the user for the locations of the archived log files (that is why it is important to restore the archived files back into their original location). First start by bringing the restored data file on line and then start automatic media recovery (see Display 6.16).

```
SVRMGR30 > ALTER DATAFILE
SVRMGR30 > <directory_location>\users01.dbf
SVRMGR30 > OFFLINE;
SVRMGR30 > RECOVER DATAFILE
SVRMGR30 ><directory_location>\users01.dbf ;
```

DISPLAY 6.16

Will recover the data file associated with a tablespace or issue the instruction (refer to Display 6.17):

```
SVRMGR30 > ALTER DATAFILE
SVRMGR30 > C:\<directory_location>\
SVRMGR30 > users01.dbf ONLINE;
SVRMGR30 > RECOVER TABLESPACE
SVRMGR30 > users;
```

DISPLAY 6.17

This will recover all data files that make up the tablespace.

At this point Oracle starts media recovery on the data file that represents the tablespace called USERS. The SMON process will apply the contents of the on-line and off-line log files to the data file. The SMON process will analyze the log sequence numbers written into the database's control file and apply the appropriate log files as specified by the log sequence numbers to the data file. This is the roll forward process. Next, the rollback process is performed. The data in the log files will also be used to reconstruct the rollback segments. Once the rollback segments have been reconstructed they are applied to the data file to undo the uncommitted changes.

During the recovery phase the RDBMS prompts for the locations of the various redo log files. If all the log files are applied to the database then the recovery is called "complete recovery." Incomplete recovery is performed if:

❑ All archive log files are not available.

❑ Point-in-time recovery is desired. This type of recovery uses the command:

```
RECOVER DATABASE UNTIL CANCEL
```

or

```
RECOVER DATABASE UNTIL TIME '1997-11-14:18:45:01';
```

4. Bring the restored tablespace back on line. After the last log file has been applied the RDBMS will issue a message saying "Media recovery complete." At this point the DBA can alter the tablespace on-line (as shown in Display 6.18).

```
SVRMGR30 > ALTER DATABASE OPEN;
```

DISPLAY 6.18

Special Database Open Instructions

If all the required on/archived log files are not present (some of the log files may have been damaged) or if the control file had to be restored from a backup, then the redo log information needs to be reset in the control file before the database can be opened. This is done by issuing the following command after media recovery has been completed (refer to Display 6.19).

```
SVRMGR30 > ALTER DATABASE OPEN;
```

DISPLAY 6.19

Database recovery can also be done using the utility RECOVERY MANAGER. This utility will issue all of the SQL commands associated with recovering the database using either a hot or a cold backup (see Figure 6.13).

The DBA will be presented with a GUI that will prompt them for the type of database recovery that they want to perform. In Figure 6.14 the database is being recovered from a cold backup of the database.

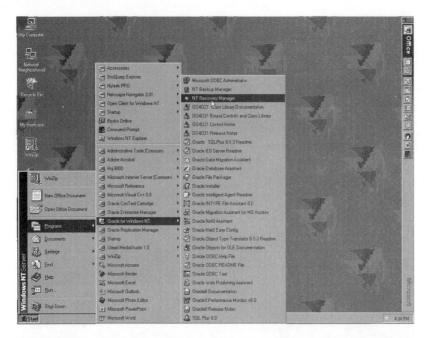

FIGURE 6.13 The SQL commands associated with recovering the database

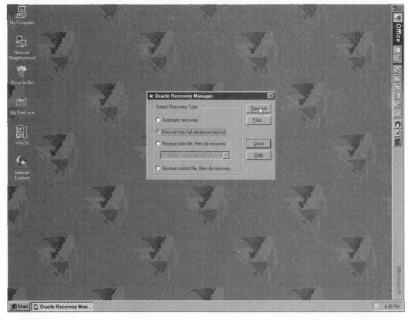

FIGURE 6.14 The database is being recovered from a cold backup

In this case the data files, log files and control files were used to restore the database. This was a database restoration from a cold backup. To restore the database using a hot backup the DBA can choose to restore all tablespaces associated with the database. To do this the Automatic Recovery option is chosen (refer to Figure 6.15).

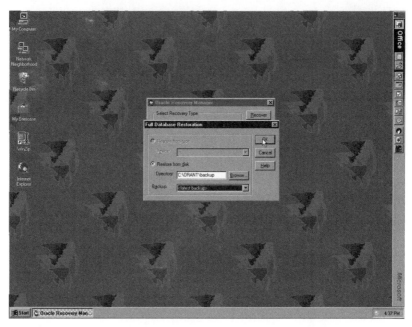

FIGURE 6.15   The Automatic Recovery option

The DBA can also use RECOVERY MANAGER to recover only certain tablespaces (tablespaces that are damaged) as shown in Figure 6.16.

SUMMARY

There are several techniques that can be used to backup an Oracle database. When choosing which database backup technique to use the DBA should consider:

❑ Does the RDBMS support a 24 x 7 operational environment?
❑ In the event of a disk failure can a loss of data be tolerated?

In most cases if the answer to the first question is "yes," and the answer to the second question is "no" then the hot database backup technique is the right choice. If the recovery technique dictates that a hot backup of the database should be used

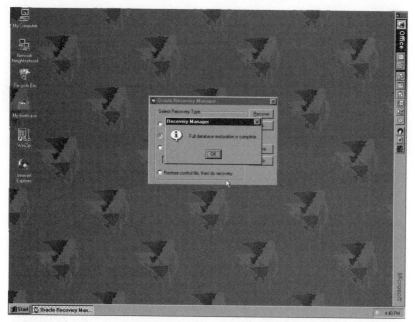

FIGURE 6.16 The Recovery Manager

for recovery then the database must be run in ARCHIVELOG mode. Running the database in ARCHIVELOG mode also gives the DBA greater flexibility when recovering the database.

DATABASE PERFORMANCE ANALYSIS AND TUNING

The architectural view of a database server is shown in Figure 7.1. The system consists of several different parts. The CPU is responsible for executing the machine instructions. The memory and cache hold data in RAM that is needed by the CPU. The disk system holds data that will or may be used by the CPU (when the CPU needs the data that is on the disk it will be brought into the machine's RAM).

The Oracle RDBMS relies on the underlying machine hardware and operating system. Therefore it is important to monitor and optimize how the machine uses RAM, the CPU, and the disk or storage subsystem.

The first step in analyzing system performance is to gather information related to the system. The data that is gathered is compared to the database manufacturers guidelines. If the performance statistics are not within the guidelines then the DBA should tune the system. To tune the system the DBA must be able to manage the various resources that are used by the RDBMS. The various resource management areas include:

❏ Memory management

Since memory access is much faster than disk access, it is desirable for data request to be satisfied by memory access rather than disk access. Therefore it is important that we distribute memory in such a way that we optimize Oracle's use of it.

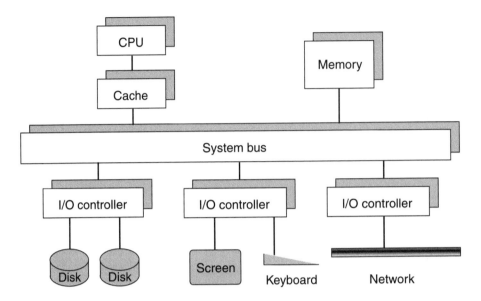

FIGURE 7.1   The architectural view of a database server

❏ CPU management

How to obtain the best system/job throughput. In theory, maximum throughput occurs when the system CPU is operating at 100 percent capacity. But application load spikes are dynamic making it impossible to maintain 100 percent utilization.

❏ Disk I/O management.

I/O bottlenecks are often the easiest performance problems to identify. In a system that uses multiple disk drives it is important that the data be distributed so that I/O contention is minimized.

❏ SQL statement tuning

Database performance is directly related to how fast the RDBMS can process SQL statements. SQL statement tuning involves analyzing how the SQL statement is processed by the RDBMS, and what can be done to make the statement run faster.

MEMORY MANAGEMENT TUNING

In Chapter 2, the architecture of the Oracle RDBMS was described. The description of the RDBMS showed that it consists of a memory structure called the SGA and several background and shadow threads. A shadow thread is a separate dedicated server thread that acts on behalf of a particular user. One thread is created for each user who connects to the database. Any request a user has for the database is performed through the shadow thread for that user. When a shadow thread must read from the database, it checks to see if the data exists in the SGA. If the data exists in the SGA, the shadow thread reads it from the memory. If the shadow thread doesn't find the data in memory, it goes directly to the data files and reads the data into the SGA. When a shadow thread must write to the database, it writes into the SGA only. At a later time, the DBWR writes this data out to disk.

The function of the LGWR thread was also described in Chapter 2. We saw that the main function of the LGWR thread was to manage the storage in the portion of the SGA called the redo log buffers. The LGWR thread manages the redo log buffer space by writing it buffers to the redo log files on the disk. The redo log files contain a history of all transactions to enable the database to perform an instance recovery. A minimum of two redo logs is required, and it's possible to use more. When a redo log fills, a log switch occurs. At log-switch time, all new redo information goes to the next redo log file in line. If the system is running in ARCHIVELOG mode, the previous log file is copied out to an archive log file. With a recent backup, the redo log files, and the redo log archive files, complete database recovery is possible should there be a storage subsystem failure.

When tuning memory management, one of the things we are trying to find is the optimum sizes for the database buffer cache, redo log buffers, and the shared pool (the shared pool consists of the data dictionary cache plus the library cache).

The following steps should be followed when analyzing and tuning memory management:

1. Make sure the SGA fits into one shared memory segment. The size of the SGA can be SVRMGR manager as shown in Display 7.1.

```
SVRMGR30 > SHOW SGA

NAME                  VALUE
--------------------- ----------
Fixed Size              47936
Variable Size          9962624
Database Buffers       40960000
Redo Buffers            102400
```

DISPLAY 7.1

The kernel parameter SHMMAX should be at least equal to the size of the SGA. The Oracle installation and configuration guide will suggest a starting value for SHMMAX. The size of the SGA can be controlled by adjusting the INIT<sid>.ORA parameters DB_BLOCK_BUFFERS, DB_BLOCK_SIZE, and LOG_BUFFER.

2. Optimize the database buffer cache. User data is stored in the part of the SGA called the database buffer cache. In order to determine if the database buffer cache is sized correctly the user must calculate the database buffer cache hit ratio. The database buffer cache is defined as:

```
HitRatio = 1 - (physical reads / (db block gets + consistent
          gets))
```

The values for physical reads, db block gets and consistent gets, can be determined by querying the Oracle performance table V$SYSSTAT as shown in Display 7.2.

```
SQLPLUS> select name,value
SQLPLUS> from v$sysstat
SQLPLUS> where name in ('db block gets','consistent gets','physical
SQLPLUS> reads');

NAME                                                      VALUE
---------------------------------------------------- ----------
db block gets                                             37804
consistent gets                                          143915
physical reads                                              338
```

DISPLAY 7.2

The database buffer cache hit ratio is 99.81

The size of the database buffer cache is equal to DB_BLOCK_BUFFER x DB_BLOCK_SIZE. The database block size cannot be changed after the database has been created. The parameter DB_BLOCK_BUFFER is used to increase the amount of memory available for the database buffer cache.

3. Optimize the redo log buffer. Oracle stores data that is being changed by various transactions in the redo log buffers. The following query can be used to determine if the redo log buffer is sized correctly (refer to Display 7.3):

The redo space request should be close to zero. A nonzero value means that the buffer may be too small. In that case we need to increase the size of the buffer so that threads are not waiting to access the redo log buffer (such as the LGWR thread or a server thread). The INIT<sid>.ORA parameter LOG_BUFFER controls the size of the redo log buffer.

```
SQLPLUS> select name, value
SQLPLUS> from v$sysstat
SQLPLUS> where name = 'redo log space requests';

NAME                                                    VALUE
-------------------------------------------------- ----------
redo log space requests                                    0
```

DISPLAY 7.3

4. Optimize the data dictionary cache. Various database operations cause the RDBMS to access its system tables. These system tables are stored in the Oracle data dictionary. The objects in the data dictionary are stored in the system tablespace. When the RDBMS needs access to its system tables the tables are read into the data dictionary cache (which resides in the section of RAM that is reserved for the SGA). To tune the data dictionary cache we need to obtain the data dictionary GET MISSES/GETS ratio. This can be found by querying the table V$ROWCACHE as shown in Display 7.4:

```
SQLPLUS> select sum(getmisses)
SQLPLUS> "MISSES",sum(gets)
SQLPLUS> "GETS",sum(getmisses)/sum(gets) "RATIO"
SQLPLUS> from v$rowcache;

MISSES    GETS     RATIO
---------- ---------- ----------
916       88598    .010338834
```

DISPLAY 7.4

The ratio should be less then 10%. The data dictionary cache is part of the shared pool. The size of the shared pool is controlled by the INIT<sid>.ORA parameter SHARED_POOL_SIZE.

5. Optimize the library cache. The parsed representation of SQL statements that Oracle is executing is stored in the library cache. Prior to executing an SQL statement Oracle has to parse the statement if there is no parsed representation of the statement in the library cache. The library cache ratio can be obtained by querying the table (refer to Display 7.5):

```
SQLPLUS> select sum(pins)
SQLPLUS> "executions",sum(reloads)
SQLPLUS> "misses",(100*(sum(reloads)/sum(pins)))
SQLPLUS> "LIBCACHE%" from v$librarycache;

executions   misses  LIBCACHE%
---------- ----------   ----------
    14320      15     .104748603
```

DISPLAY 7.5

The library cache ratio should be between one and three percent. The library cache is part of the shared pool. The size of the shared pool is controlled by the INIT<sid>.ORA parameter SHARED_POOL_SIZE.

6. Minimize the amount of disk I/O used for sorting. This can be achieved by monitoring the sort area while the application is running. The query shown in Display 7.6 will gather information on the number of sort runs that occur on disk "sorts(disk)" and the sorts that are using memory "sorts(memory)."

```
SQLPLUS> select name, value
SQLPLUS> from v$sysstat
SQLPLUS> where name IN ('sorts(memory)', 'sorts(disk)');

NAME                                          VALUE
---------------------------------------------   -------------
sorts(memory)                                  1001
sorts(disk)                                       6
```

DISPLAY 7.6

The number of sort runs to disk should be around ten percent. The INIT<sid>.ORA parameter SORT_AREA_SIZE is used to control the amount of RAM used for the sort area.

Increasing the size of the sort reduces the amount of memory that can be allocated to the rest of the system. The DBA should check if additional memory is available for sorting before increasing the sort parameter.

CPU MANAGEMENT

Managing the CPU for the RDBMS will often involve changing the init<ORACLE_SID>.ora parameter called PROCESSES. This parameter specifies the number of threads Oracle8 can create for your CPU. This number must also include the Oracle8 service and background threads. The number of Oracle8 service threads is two, and the number of background threads is typically six. Therefore, the parameter value must be at least the maximum concurrent connections expected (concurrent connections cannot exceed 500) plus two service threads and six background threads.

System activity can be observed using the Windows NT Performance Monitor (refer to Figure 7.2).

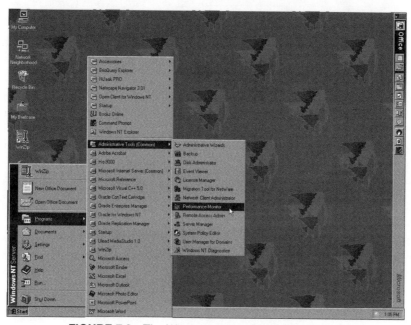

FIGURE 7.2   The Windows NT Performance Monitor

System statistics such as the percentage of processor time spent in the states user and privileged can be monitored by adding them to the Performance Monitor graph as shown in Figure 7.3.

In most Windows NT systems the majority of the system processor utilization is in user mode. The DBA should verify the system processor utilization by running Performance Monitor and looking at the percentage of processor time spent in privileged and in user time for the Oracle process (Process: percentage of User Time divided by percentage of Privileged Time). Privileged time should be considered as operating system overhead, such as time spent in the I/O subsystem or in system calls. The higher the ratio of user to privileged time, the better (refer to Figure 7.4).

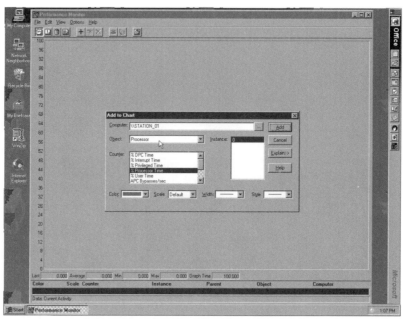

FIGURE 7.3   Adding to the Performance Monitor

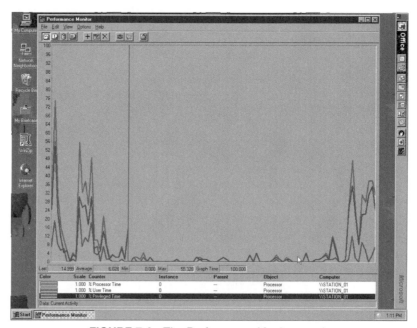

FIGURE 7.4   The Performance Monitor graph

DISK I/O MANAGEMENT

In a well-tuned system there is little or no waiting on I/O. This indicates that the system processors always have some work to do while there is outstanding I/O. You can verify this by running the Windows NT Performance Monitor and observing the processor utilization (Processor: percentage of Processor Time), the disk utilization (LogicalDisk divided by PhysicalDisk Transfers/sec), the length of the processor queue (System: Processor Queue Length), and the threads performing I/O operations (Thread: percentage of Processor Time).

There are several things that the DBA should do to ensure that the disk I/O is being used in an efficient manner. The following is a list of things that should be considered:

1. Place redo log files on their own disk device. Redo log files are written to disk in a circular manner. Disk response time is dependent on how long it takes the disk subsystem to find the data to the disk. This time is called seek time (time to move the disk heads in and out) and latency (delay time due to disk rotational delay). By placing the redo log files on their own disk device we can control disk access time by minimizing disk seek and latency times. This is very important for applications that make heavy use of the LGWR thread. Applications that have a lot of INSERT and UPDATE activity will utilize the LGWR thread more than applications that have less INSERT and UPDATE activity.

2. Use asynchronous I/O. In a disk system that uses synchronous I/O the DBWR thread must wait for a disk I/O request to complete before it can work on another request. In a system that uses asynchronous I/O the DBWR thread does not have to wait for the disk I/O to complete before it can start to satisfy another disk request.

3. For systems that do not have asynchronous I/O the number of DBWR writer threads should be set equal to the number of disks containing database files.

4. Reduce tablespace fragmentation. In an ideal situation, a segment's data is stored in a single extent. When a segment has multiple extents, there is no guarantee that the extents will be stored next to each other. These pockets of discontinuous storage are called fragments. Fragmentation increases the amount of I/O that must be performed to access the data. To solve the problem the technique to use is to export the tablespace's data (tables, views, etc.), then drop and recreate tablespace.

To check for tablespace fragmentation the table SYS.DBA_EXTENTS is used (refer to Display 7.7):

```
SVRMGR > select tablespace_name,
SVRMGR> file,block_id,size,segment
SVRMGR> from sys.dba_extents;
```

DISPLAY 7.7

This will produce the output shown in Figure 7.5.

Tablespace	File	Block Id	Size		Segment
SYSTEM	1	2	25		SYS.SYSTEM
	1	27	25		SYS.SYSTEM
	1	52	60		SYS.C_OBJ#
		1	112	5	SYS.I_OBJ#
			.		
			.		
			.		
		1	8,232	12	SYS.SAVE_ROLL
	1	8,244	3		<free>
	1	8,247	512		TP1.IACCOUNT
	1	8,759	512		TP1.IACCOUNT
	1	9,271	5		SYS.SAVE_STATS
	1	9,276	5		SYS.SAVE_KQR
		1	9,286	100	TP1.HISTORY
	1	9,386	93		SYS.SAVE_STATS
	1	9,479	5		SYS.I_OBJ1
	1	9,484	41		SYS.C_OBJ#
	1	9,525	8		SYS.I_OBJ2
	1	9,533	12		SYS.I_XREF1
	1	9,545	5		<free>
	1	9,550	5		<free>
	1	9,555	5		<free>
	1	9,560	5		<free>
	1	9,565	5		<free>
	1	9,570	5		<free>

FIGURE 7.5   The output

5. Only one DBWR thread is activated in the init.ora file. Oracle8 for Windows NT uses the asynchronous I/O capabilities of Windows NT. Asynchronous I/O allows the Database Writer (DBWR) and/or the Log Writer (LGWR) thread to avoid blocking on I/O. With the asynchronous I/O capabilities of the operating system and Oracle8, only one DBWR thread is necessary in the system. This cuts down on system idle time that might occur when the DBWR is blocked on I/O.

6. To achieve maximum performance on data files being accessed sequentially, the disk(s) must be dedicated to this purpose. Of primary importance are the Oracle transaction log files, which are accessed in a sequential, write-only fashion. Other partitions with little I/O activity, such as the operating-system partition, can share the disk(s) with the redo logs

7. Random I/Os are balanced across all drives allocated to data and indexes. In a typical multiuser database system, file access is random. You should spread these files out over as many physical disks as necessary to achieve random I/O rates that do not exceed recommendations. You can best achieve this by using disk striping (available with the Compaq SMART Array Controller or similar controllers from other vendors).

8. Physical disk I/O rate capacities are not exceeded. Avoid overloading an individual disk with random I/O. Based on Compaq testing, random I/O should not exceed 60 tranactions per second per drive for 4-gigabyte drives, 50 per second per drive for 2-gigabyte drives, or 40 per second per drive for 1-gigabyte and 500-megabyte drives

Most questions concerning CPU and disk I/O performance can be observed using the Windows NT utility PerfMon. The counters to focus on are:

❏ Processor: percentage of ProcessorTime. When you suspect a processor upgrade may be necessary, measure this counter. If the processor counter measures 80 percent or more for an extended period of time, this could be a good indication that the processor is in need of an upgrade.

❏ System: Processor Queue Length. This can also be measured to figure out if a processor upgrade is necessary. If the number of threads waiting to be processed is greater than two, the processor may be a bottleneck for the system.

❏ Processor: Interrupts/sec. When you suspect a hardware device is malfunctioning in the system, measure this counter. If the Processor-Interrupts/sec increases and the processor time does not, a hardware device could be sending bogus interrupts to the processor. Locate the hardware device and replace it.

❏ Memory: Cache Faults, Page Faults and Pages/sec. When you suspect that there is not enough system memory, these counters should be measured. They indicate the frequency your system needs to swap pages to the hard disk swap file. If this counter is high, chances are the need for memory is also high.

❏ PhysicalDisk/LogicalDisk:%Disk Time. When you suspect the hard disk is a system bottleneck, measure this counter. This counter shows you how much processor time is being spent servicing disk requests. Measure this counter against Processor:% Processor Time to see if the disk requests are using up a notable amount of processor time.

❏ PhysicalDisk/LogicalDisk: Disk Bytes/Transfer. When you are trying to find out how fast your hard disks are transferring data, measure this counter.

❏ PhysicalDisklLogicalDlsk: Current Disk Queue Length: When you are thinking about upgrading your hard disk, measure this counter. This counter shows you how much data is waiting to be transferred to the disk. If the queue is long, processes are being delayed by disk speed.

The Windows NT server performance is optimized using the control panel. The Windows NT menu Select Control Panel > Network > Services > Server > Properties (shown in Figure 7.6) sequence is used to access the display.

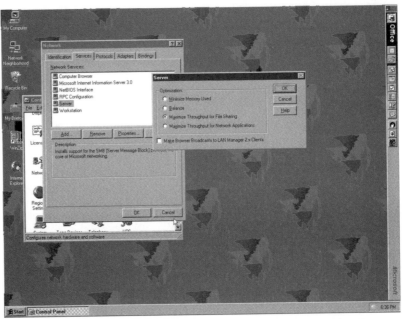

FIGURE 7.6 The Windows NT menu Select Control Panel > Network > Services > Server > Properties

Minimize Memory Used: This setting provides the best performance for less than ten users.

Balance: This setting provides the best performance for 10 through 64 users.

Maximize Throughput For File Sharing: This setting provides the best performance for more than 64 users, by maximizing the memory available for file sharing. This is the default setting.

Maximize Throughput For Network Applications: This setting is used for supporting distributed applications.

ADDITIONAL TUNING TIPS

There are additional things that the DBA can do to ensure that the RDBMS environment is optimally configured. The following "TIPS" will help when considering the optimal environmental setting of the server.

TIP 1

To configure your Microsoft server, use Control Panel/Network to choose Server from the Installed Network Software list, and then choose Configure. Change the relationship of memory allocated to the network connections and memory allocated to applications running on the server by choosing Maximize Throughput for Network Applications (the default is Maximize Throughput for File Sharing). This optimizes the server memory for Oracle8 Server, because it performs its own memory management for caching files and network

TIP 2

If Oracle8 is dedicated to being a database server only, you can reduce overhead on the processor(s) by stopping various services. The minimum services needed are Server and OracleServiceSSSS (Windows NT represents the Oracle8 server process as OracleServiceSSSS, where SSSS is the system ID), but I recommend Event-Log and Workstation as well. You also need one or more services, depending on the versions of SQL*Net and protocols supported, to support user connections through SQL*Net (for example, OracleTCPListener). Turn off services by using the Control Panel/Services dialog.

TIP 3

Most of the system processor utilization is allocated to the shadow threads and not the background threads. Use Performance Monitor to verify the system processor utilization at the Oracle thread level (Thread: % Processor Time). Make sure that the users' shadow threads are getting the majority of the system processor time.

TIP 4

To reduce excess I/O, tune the Oracle8 Server data cache to provide maximum use of available resources. Oracle8 Server buffers are tuned with the parameter DB_BLOCK_BUFFERS. Because Oracle8 Server is a single process, multithreaded application, all the threads share the memory from the single process. To find out how much memory is available for buffers, use Performance Monitor (Memory: Available Bytes) to observe the amount of available memory left in the system. Do not use all the available memory for buffers, because this may cause swapping to occur. System performance degradation caused by swapping more than undoes the advantages acquired by tuning the Oracle8 Server buffers

TIP 5

The default DB_BLOCK_SIZE is 2,048. The value to which DB_BLOCK_SIZE is set depends on the type of transaction load you have when performance is the most critical. If performance is most crucial during applications that primarily access the database in a random fashion (small threads or updates scattered throughout the database), you should use a block size of 2,048. On the other extreme, if most of the applications are sequentially accessing the database when performance is most crucial, you need a block size of 8,192. If you are uncertain of the transaction load or have an even split of random and sequential access during this critical time, use a block size of 4,096

TIP 6

You'll find a minimal performance difference when using FAT (file allocation table), NTFS (NT file system), or RAW file partition in Windows NT.

ROW CHAINING AND MIGRATION

When an UPDATE statement increases the amount of data in a row so that the row no longer fits in its data block, the ORACLE RDBMS will try to find another block with enough free space to hold the entire row. If such a block is available, ORACLE moves the entire row to the new block. This is called migrating a row. If the row is too large to fit into any available block, ORACLE splits the row into multiple pieces and stores each piece in a separate block. This is called chaining a row. Rows can also be chained when they are inserted.

Migration and chaining, are detrimental to performance because:

❑ UPDATE statements that cause migration and chaining perform more disk I/O.
❑ Queries that select migrated or chained rows perform more disk I/O.
❑ Leads to database fragmentation.

The DBA can identify migrated and chained rows in a table by using the SQL command ANALYZE with the LIST CHAINED ROWS option. This command collects information about each migrated or chained row and places this information into a specified output table. The definition of a sample output table named CHAINED_ROWS appears in a SQL script available in the ORACLE_HOME/ rdbms/admin directory. The name of the script is UTLCHAIN.SQL.

CORRECTING MIGRATION AND CHAINING

To reduce migrated and chained rows in an existing table, follow the steps below:

1. Use the ANALYZE command to collect information about migrated and chained rows (refer to Display 7.8):

```
SQLPLUS> ANALYZE TABLE emp LIST
SQLPLUS> CHAINED ROWS;
```

DISPLAY 7.8

2. Query the table containing the collected migration/row chaining statistics as shown in Display 7.9.

```
SQLPLUS> SELECT * FROM chained_rows WHERE table_name = 'emp';

OWNER_NAME  TABLE_NAME  CLUSTER_NAME  HEAD_ROWID      TIMESTAMP

----------  ----------  ------------  ----------      ---------
   SCOTT    EMP                       0000236C.0003.0001    08-SEP-95
   SCOTT    EMP                       0000236C.0002.0001    08-SEP-95
   SCOTT    EMP                       0000236C.0001.0001    08-SEP-95
```

DISPLAY 7.9

3. The results from the query shown in the last step have three migrated or chained rows. To eliminate the migrated rows:

   a.   Create an intermediate table with the same columns as the original table to hold the migrated and chained rows (refer to Display 7.10):

```
SQLPLUS> CREATE TABLE int_emp
SQLPLUS> AS SELECT * FROM emp
SQLPLUS> WHERE ROWID IN
SQLPLUS> (SELECT head_rowid FROM chained_rows
SQLPLUS> WHERE table-name = 'emp');
```

DISPLAY 7.10

b. Delete the migrated and chained rows from the existing table as shown in Display 7.11.

```
SQLPLUS> DELETE FROM emp
SQLPLUS> WHERE ROWID IN
SQLPLUS> (SELECT head_rowid
SQLPLUS> FROM chained_rows
SQLPLUS> WHERE table_name = 'emp');
```

DISPLAY 7.11

c. Insert the rows of the intermediate table into the original table as shown in Display 7.12.

```
SQLPLUS> INSERT INTO emp
SQLPLUS> SELECT *
SQLPLUS> FROM int_emp;
```

DISPLAY 7.12

d. Drop the intermediate table as shown in Display 7.13:.

```
SQLPLUS> DROP TABLE int_emp;
```

DISPLAY 7.13

4. Delete the information collected in Step 1 from the output table as shown in Display 7.14.

```
SQLPLUS> DELETE FROM
SQLPLUS> chained_rows
SQLPLUS> WHERE table_name = 'emp';
```

DISPLAY 7.14

5. Use the ANALYZE command again and query the output table.
6. Any rows that appear in the output table are chained rows. Increasing the block size of the database will help to reduce chained rows. It may not be possible to avoid chaining in all situations. If a table contains a LONG or long CHAR or VARCHAR2 columns chaining is often unavoidable.

MINIMIZING MIGRATION AND ROW CHAINING

In the previous sections we covered the identification of migrated and chained rows in a table. In order to minimize migration and row chaining the block size for the database can be increased. Another thing that will help minimize migration and row chaining for tables that have LONG or long VARCHAR2 fields is to set the value of the percent free (PCTFREE) to a value between 30 and 50 percent.

The percent free for a table can be increased/altered by issuing the command shown in Display 7.15.

```
SQLPLUS> ALTER TABLE emp
SQLPLUS> PCTFREE 30
 SQLPLUS> PCTUSED 60;
```

DISPLAY 7.15

The block size for the database is set at database creation time and can only be altered by recreating the database. The block size parameter DB_BLOCK_SIZE can be set in either the INIT<sid>.ORA or the CONFIG<sid>.ORA files. The block size should be set to either 4096 bytes or preferably 8192 bytes to minimize row chaining.

INDEXES AND SQL STATEMENT TUNING

BACKGROUND

In the previous sections we focused on tuning the various parts of the Oracle RDBMS. In this section we'll focus on tuning the SQL statements that are processed by the RDBMS.

The statement below is an SQL query. The query retrieves the name, salary and department number for all employees in the "emp" table named Jones (refer to Display 7.16).

```
SQLPLUS> select ename,sal,deptno
SQLPLUS> from emp
SQLPLUS> where ename = 'RJones';
```

DISPLAY 7.16

In this example the query will result in a full scan of the table "emp" if the field "ename" has not been indexed. An analogy would be trying to find RJones in the phone book by starting on the first page of the book. In the phone book example we could speed our search by using the books index to find the page number where people named Jones are listed (of course we could rely on luck and just open the book hoping that we would get the right page).

In general, indexing of the data in a table allows for faster queries. This is done by replacing the full-table scan with an index scan.

WHAT SHOULD BE INDEXED?

The first thing that we should ask ourselves is: "What should be indexed?" When choosing what columns to index in a table the DBA should consider the following:

❑ Index the columns that appear frequently in the "WHERE" clause of the queries. In the above example the column "ename" appears in the "WHERE" clause and is therefore a candidate for indexing.

In the example in the previous section we created an index on the emp table by issuing the statement shown in Display 7.17.

```
SQLPLUS> create index ind_name
SQLPLUS> on emp(ename);
```

DISPLAY 7.17

❑ Index columns that are used for table joins are shown in Display 7.18.

```
SQLPLUS>select ename, salary, loc
SQLPLUS>from emp, dept
SQLPLUS where emp.deptno = SQLPLUS>
dept.deptno;
```

DISPLAY 7.18

In this example the fields "deptno" in the tables "emp" and "dept" should be indexed.

❑ Columns that have few distinct values (low cardinality) should not be indexed. Therefore the column that indicates a person's gender is not a good candidate for indexing.

❑ Statements that are frequently modified are not good candidates for indexing. This is because the data and the index must be modified when an UPDATE, INSERT or DELETE is executed on a row which has columns that are indexed. The DBA must always weigh query speed against UPDATE/DELETE/INSERT speed.

❑ LONG and LONG RAW columns cannot be indexed.

❑ Do not index small tables. For small tables (tables with less then 200 data blocks) a full-table scan is often faster then an index scan.

❑ If a query returns more than 20 percent of the rows in the table, a full-table scan is often faster than an index scan.

❑ Oracle's rule-based optimizer looks at the order of table names in the FROM clause to determine the driving order for the query. Ensure that the last table in the FROM clause is the table that will return the smallest number of rows. Table joins should be driven from tables returning fewer rows rather than tables returning more rows. In other words, the table that returns the fewest rows should be listed last. This usually means that the table with the most rows is listed first.

Composite Indexes

It is possible to create one index that is used to cover multiple columns. This type of an index is called a composite index. An example of a query that could benefit from using a composite index would be (refer to Display 7.19):

```
SQLPLUS> select first_name, last_name
SQLPLUS> from emp
SQLPLUS> where first_name = "Amy" and
SQLPLUS> last _name = "Jones";
```

DISPLAY 7.19

In this example we could create two separate indexes, one to cover the column first_name and the other to cover the column last_name. But if we are always going to issue the same query (meaning that we will always query for both first and last name), then creating a single index (composite) is desirable.

To create a composite index we would issue the statement shown in Display 7.20.

```
SQLPLUS> create index first_last
SQLPLUS> on emp (first_name,
SQLPLUS> last_name)
SQLPLUS> in tablespace indexes;
```

DISPLAY 7.20

This statement will create a composite index called first_last. The composite index will cover the columns first_name and last_name from the table "emp." The index will be created in the tablespace called indexes.

When choosing composite indexes the DBA should consider the following:

❏ If we created a composite index on both first and last name but submitted our query as (refer to Display 7.21):

In this example the composite index will not be used because the leading portion of the first column is not included in our query. In general, if a composite index is created using columns ABC the index will be used to search for the combinations A, AB, ABC but not for the column combinations AC, BC and C. When creating the index the column specification should be from most selective to least selective.

```
SQLPLU> select first_name,last_name
SQLPLUS> from emp
SQLPLUS> where last_name = "Jones";
```

DISPLAY 7.21

SQL STATEMENT ANALYSIS TOOLS

It is often desirable to analyze how your SQL statement was executed. The analysis will show whether a full-table scan is being performed or if the data had to be merged/joined or sorted in order for the query statement to be processed. For this type of analysis the utility TKPROF with the EXPLAIN plan is used. TKPROF with the EXPLAIN plan output also shows the amount of time that it takes the RDBMS to fetch, parse and execute the SQL statement.

Setting Up TKPROF (Turning on Tracing)

To use TKPROF the DBA should do the following:

1. Modify the INIT<ORACLE_SID>.ORA to include the following parameters:

```
TIMED_STATISTICS = TRUE: This will allow for the reporting of
    CPU execution time.
MAX_DUMP_FILE_SIZE = 100: This is the maximum size of the
    trace file in operating system blocks.
USER_DUMP_DEST = \your_dir: This is the location of the direc-
    tory that will contain the trace file.
```

2. Enable tracing for your session by issuing the statement shown in Display 7.22.

```
SVRMGR30> ALTER
SVRMGR30> SESSION SET
SVRMGR30> SQL_TRACE =
SVRMGR30> TRUE;
```

DISPLAY 7.22

3. Execute the SQL statement.
4. Observe the output using TKPROF (see also Table 7.1). To get the utility TKPROF to output a SQL trace/Explain Plan issue the following statement:

```
TKPROF my_statements_file.trc sql_exp.sav
     SORT=((EXECPU,FCHCPU) explain=my_uid/pw.
```

Where my_statements_file.trc is the trace file and sql_exp.sav will contain the output data. One of the data entries in the file sql_exp.sav would look like:

```
select objno, site_no, site_name, site_type, address, city,
     state, country_code, status
from table_site
where objno IN (268437028)
```

call	count	cpu	elapsed	disk	query	current	rows
Parse	1	0.04	0.03	0	0	0	0
Execute	1	0.00	0.01	0	0	0	0
Fetch	1	0.00	0.00	1	1	0	0
total	3	0.04	0.04	1	1	0	0

```
Misses in library cache during parse: 1
Optimizer goal: CHOOSE
Parsing user id: 8 (SA)
```

Rows	Execution Plan
0	SELECT STATEMENT GOAL: CHOOSE
0	NESTED LOOPS
0	NESTED LOOPS
0	TABLE ACCESS GOAL: ANALYZED (BY ROWID) OF 'TABLE_SITE'
0	INDEX GOAL: ANALYZED (RANGE SCAN) OF 'OBJINDEX' (NON-UNIQUE)

TABLE 7.1 SQL Trace/Explain Plan Explanation

Variable	Description
count	Number of times the statement was parsed, fetched or executed.
cpu	Total CPU time in seconds.
elapsed	Total system elapsed time in seconds.
disk	Total number of data blocks read from the data files on disk.
query	Total number of buffers retrieved for queries.
current	Total number of buffers retrieved for INSERT, UPDATE, and DELETE statements.
rows	Total number of rows processed by the SQL statement.

For SELECT statements the number of rows returned appears in the fetch step. For UPDATE, DELETE, and INSERT statements the number of rows returned appears in the execute step.

TYPES OF INDEXES

In the this example we saw that the table access is via an index scan. This means that the value was retrieved by first accessing the index OBJINDEX. The index contains the rowid of the desired records. Rather than performing a full-table scan to access the data the RDBMS can use the rowid to access the data directly.

As stated earlier, an index is used to speed access to table data. Oracle supports both the B*-tree and the bit-mapped index. The B*-tree index structure (shown in Figure 7.6) consists of branch blocks and leaf blocks. The upper levels of the index are the branch blocks. The lowest level of the index contains the leaf blocks. Leaf blocks contain every indexed data value and the rowid that is used to locate the record.

Oracle also supports bit-mapped indexes. Bit-mapped indexes work by:

1. Assigning a bit pattern for each distinct column value (key).
2. This results in a bit-map key pair.
3. The pairs are stored in a B*-tree ordered by the key.
4. RDBMS converts bit-map to rowid for fast data retrieval.

Depending on the application/query, bit-mapped indexes can speed access to data. Bit-mapped indexes should be used when:

❑ There are columns that have low cardinality. In general between 100 and 1000 distinct values is considered high cardinality (depending on the size of the database).

❑ There are queries that have multiple "AND/OR" clauses.

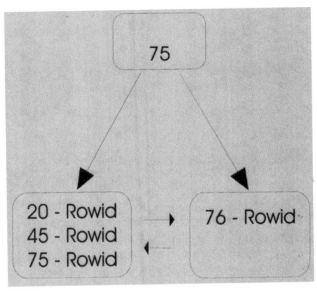

FIGURE 7.7   B*-tree Index Structure

SUMMARY

Database performance analysis involves finding where bottlenecks exist in the system. Tuning involves the reduction or elimination of the bottleneck. Database performance will vary as the goals of the business change. To keep up with these changes the DBA should collect and analyze the various database performance statistics. It is important to look for trends in the collected data. This will give the DBA an indication of how the database performance is changing as the business changes, such as additional end users are added or more applications are added to the system.

When database performance is not acceptable the DBA should investigate to see if performance can be improved. The areas that the DBA investigates should include:

❑ Memory management

❑ CPU management

❑ Disk I/O management

❑ SQL statement tuning

DATABASE CAPACITY PLANNING

The DBA is responsible for ensuring that there is enough disk space available to support the various end-user applications that access the database. To do this the DBA must have some knowledge of the applications that will use the RDBMS. This chapter focuses on estimating the amount of disk space that is required for application support. This includes estimating the amount of disk space required by the table data and its indexes. We will also estimate the amount of disk space that is required for the tablespaces TEMP and ROLLBACK.

SIZING TABLE SEGMENTS AND TABLESPACES

The starting point for sizing a database should be to determine the amount of space required for the various tables and then the space required for the tablespace that will hold the tables.

Lets review the table sizing calculation that was performed in Chapter 5, "Database Objects, Access and Security." In Chapter 5 we created the table "emp" to hold the employee information. The query shown in Display 8.1 was issued to create the "emp" table.

```
SQLPLUS> create table emp
SQLPLUS> (empno number (4),
SQLPLUS> ename varchar2(I 0),
SQLPLUS> job varchar2 (9),
SQLPLUS> mgr_number number(4),
SQLPLUS> hiredate_date,
SQLPLUS> sal number (7,2),
SQLPLUS> comm number (7,2),
SQLPLUS> deptno number (2));
```

DISPLAY 8.1

The records that will make up the table have eight columns as shown in Table 8.1.

TABLE 8.1 Emp Table Record Format

empno	ename	job	mgr_number	hire_date	sal	comm	deptno

To compute the size of a record we would use the following technique:

❏ Number fields are computed using the formula: *number of bytes = precession/ 2 + 1*. In our example we would compute the number of bytes used by the fields empno, mgr_number, sal, comm and deptno. This would result in the following computation: number of bytes = $(4/2+1) + (4/2+1) + (7/2+1) + (7/2+1) + (2/2+1) = 17$ bytes.

❏ One character requires one byte. Therefore the fields denoted by varchar2 will result in the following computation: number of bytes = $10 + 9 = 19$ bytes.

❏ Date fields require 7 bytes.

By adding another three bytes to our calculation (for the row header) we get:

```
Row Size = 3 + 17 + 19 + 7 = 46 Bytes
```

If we were to add ten people per month to the table the table will require 920 bytes:

```
Amount of table storage = 10 * Row Size * Number of Months =
    10 * 46 * 2 = 920 Bytes
```

The above calculation should be done for all tables that the DBA plans to contain in a single tablespace. By adding the number of bytes required for each table and multiplying by a specified time period the DBA can estimate the amount of storage required for the tablespace over a given period of time. The values for the extent sizes should be chosen as follows:

❏ The initial/next extent size parameters for the tablespace should be set to the same value as the initial/next extent parameters for the table with the largest initial/next extent size. When a table is created it will inherit the storage parameters of the tablespace if the table storage parameters are not explicitly specified when the table is created.

❏ The DBA should try to minimize extent fragmentation. To do this the DBA should try to minimize the number of extents that a table requires by trying to contain all data in a single extent. In practice this is often very difficult. In our example the DBA would choose an initial/next extent size of 1 KB to hold two months worth of data in a single extent.

SIZING INDEX SEGMENTS AND TABLESPACES

To compute the size of the tablespace required for storing indexes we must first determine how much space is required to store the index. To compute the space required to store an index, and therefore the values for the storage parameters initial and next, the following method can be used:

1. Compute the amount of space required for the dataspace

    Dataspace Size = Block Size minus Block Header Size (this assumes the PCTFREE for indexes is approximately zero). Using a blocksize of 4096 (4KB) and a block header size of 159 bytes we can compute the dataspace size:

    ```
    Dataspace Size = 4096 - 159 = 3937 bytes
    ```

2. Next we must compute the average entry size by using the formula:

    ```
    Average Entry Size = Entry Header + ROWID + Average
    Row Size
    ```

    The size of the ROWID is 6 bytes and the Entry Header requires 2 bytes. The Average Row Size from our table sizing calculation was 46 bytes. Therefore the Average Entry Size is:

    ```
    Average Entry Size = 2 +6 + 46 = 54
    ```

3. Next the number of blocks required for the index is computed using the formula:

    ```
    Number Of Blocks = 1.05 (Number Of NULL Rows) * (Average
    Entry Size)/Dataspace
    ```

4. The number of bytes required for an index is computed by converting blocks to bytes (using the value of the init<SID>.ora parameter DB_BLOCK_SIZE).

The size of the indexes tablespace can be computed by using the formula:

```
Tablespace size = Index Size * Number Of Indexes * MAXEXTENTS
```

SIZING ROLLBACK SEGMENTS AND TABLESPACES

One of the tablespaces that should be sized and routinely monitored is the rollback segment tablespace. Rollback segments are used to store undo information. A rollback segment consists of contiguous multiblock pieces called extents. The segment uses these extents in an ordered circular fashion, moving from one to the next after the current extent is full. A transaction writes a record to the current location in the rollback segment and advances the current pointer by the size of the record (refer to Figure 8.1).

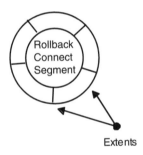

Extents

FIGURE 8.1   A transaction writes a record to the current location

What undo information is and why it is required can be shown by using the following example:

❑ I start a query and print against the emp table at 9:00.

❑ At 9:10 Amy issues an update and commit against all rows in the emp table.

❑ At 9:30 my program completes its query and prints.

In this situation we need to record the way that the emp table looked when my query began. If there was no recording of how the table looked before my query began, then my query would produce incorrect information. My query would produce a report where one part of the report represents how the data looked before Amy's update and the other part how the table looked after Amy's update.

But before we can determine the size of the rollback segment tablespace we must first determine:

❑ How many rollback segments do we need.

❑ How large should each rollback be.

The first question can be answered by using the rule:

❑ One rollback segment per every four concurrent users.

Therefore if we have a system where the number of concurrent users is eight then we need at least two rollback segments.

The second question can be answered by using the following technique:

Determine the size of the initial and next extent storage definition parameters. The initial and next extent parameters should be used to determine the initial = next use the formula:

```
Extent Size = 1.25 (M/n)
```

Where n equals the maximum number of extents for a rollback segment and M equals the amount of undo data that each segment will hold. The value for n should be less then the MAXEXTENTS clause in the create rollback segment statement. For example if MAXEXTENTS = 120 set n = 100. To determine the value of M we need to estimate how much undo information we need to store. If we choose to store 2 MB of undo data then the initial = next extent size should be 1.25 * (2000000/100) = 25 KB. (See Figure 8.2.)

Now that we know the size of the rollback segments we can determine the size of the rollback segment tablespace. The size of the tablespace can be determined by:

```
Tablespace size = MAXEXTENTS * Extent Size * Number Of
    Segments
```

In our example we would have:

```
Tablespace size = 100 * 25000 * 4 = 10 MB.
```

In the Figure 8.3 we see that we can also create our rollback segments using the *STORAGE MANAGER* utility.

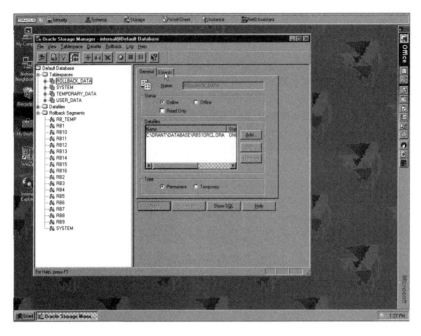

FIGURE 8.2 The Storage Manager

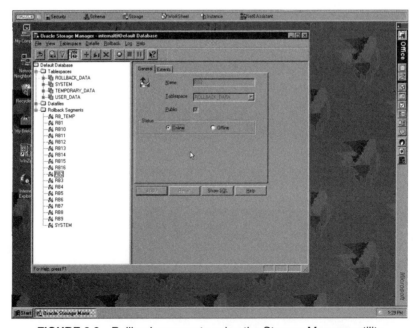

FIGURE 8.3 Rollback segments using the Storage Manager utility

We have developed one technique for estimating the amount of storage required for rollback segments and its tablespace. There are some basic principles that apply to rollback segment space management for both ORACLE version 7 and 8. Some of the most important principles are:

- ❏ A transaction can only use one rollback segment to store all of its rollback (undo) records.
- ❏ Multiple transactions can write to the same extent.
- ❏ The head of the rollback segment never moves into a rollback extent currently occupied by the tail.
- ❏ Extents in the ring are never skipped over and used out of order as the head tries to advance.
- ❏ If the head cannot use the next extent, it allocates another extent and inserts it into the ring.

It is evident that transaction time as well as transaction size is important. Therefore it is worthwhile for us to develop a better technique for estimating the storage required for rollback segments.

There are two issues that need to be considered when deciding if your segment is large enough. First, you want to make sure that transactions will not cause the head to wrap around too fast and catch the tail. This causes the segment to extend in size, per the principles mentioned above. Second, if you have long running queries that access data that frequently changes, you want to make sure that the rollback segment doesn't wrap around and prevent the construction of a read-consistent view.

The number of rollback segments needed to prevent contention between processes can also be determined with the help of the storage manager utility and with the use of the V$WAITSTAT table. The rollback monitor column "header waits/ sec" gives an indication of the current rollback segment contention. Waits are a definite indication of contention. The following V$WAITSTAT query will display number of waits since instance startup (refer to Display 8.2).

```
SQLPLUS> SELECT *
SQLPLUS> FROM V$WAITSTAT
SQLPLUS> WHERE OPERATION = 'buffer busy waits'
SQLPLUS> AND CLASS = 'undo segment header';
```

DISPLAY 8.2

To find out the size and number of rollback segments needed to handle normal processing on the database the DBA will have to do some testing. One test is to start with small rollback segments and allow your application to force them to extend. Here are the steps to run such a test.

❑ Create a rollback segment tablespace.

❑ Select a number of rollback segments to test (use the estimate one rollback segment per every four concurrent users) and create them in the rollback segment tablespace.

❑ Create the rollback segments so that all extents are the same size. Choose an extent size that you suspect will need between 10 to 30 extents when the segments grow to full size.

❑ Each rollback segment should start with two extents before the test is run. This is the minimum number of extents any rollback segment can have.

❑ Activate only the rollback segments that you are testing by making the status "in use." The only other segment that should be "in use" is the system rollback segment.

The maximum size any one of the rollback segments reaches during the test is the size you want to use when configuring. This size we will call the "minimum coverage size". If there is contention, adjust the number of segments and rerun the test. Also, if the largest size requires fewer than ten extents, or more than 30, it is a good idea to lower or raise the extent size, respectively, and rerun the test. Otherwise you may be wasting space.

For sizing rollback segment extents, each extent should be of the same size. In fact, for all strategies listed below we assume that all rollback segments have extents of the same size and that the size of the rollback tablespace is some multiple of the common extent size. The number of extents for an individual segment should be around 20.

We now have some good base estimates for the size and number of your rollback segments needed during normal processing.

ORACLE8 also provides features to simplify the management of rollback segments. These additions assist in the managing of segment size, managing segment availability, and monitoring rollback activity.

In the rollback segment storage clause, the PCTINCREASE parameter was replaced by a parameter called OPTIMAL (back in ORACLE7). This specified the optimal size of a rollback segment in bytes. It can also be specified in kilobytes or megabytes. The RDBMS tries to keep the segment at its specified optimal size. The size is rounded up to the extent boundary, which means that the RDBMS tries to have the fewest number of extents such that the total size is greater than or equal to the size specified as OPTIMAL. If additional space is needed beyond the optimal size, it will eventually deallocate extents to shrink back to this size. The process of deallocating extents is performed when the head moves from one extent to the next. At this time, the segment size is checked and the RDBMS determines if the next extent should be deallocated. The extent can only be deallocated if there are no active transactions in it. If necessary, the RDBMS will deallocate multiple extents at one time until the segment has shrunk back to its optimal size. The RDBMS always deallocates the oldest inactive extents as they are the least likely to be used for read consistency.

SETTING UP ROLLBACK SEGMENTS

After calculating the size and the number of rollback segments required, we can see how the rollback segment tablespace should be configured. There are three different transaction environments.

- ❏ Steady average transaction rate
- ❏ Frequent large transactions
- ❏ Infrequent large transactions

Our first goal is to estimate the size of the rollback information (undo) generated by a transaction. This can be done with the help of the following script.

```
define undo_overhead=54
DROP TABLE undo$begin;
DROP TABLE undo$end;
CREATE TABLE undo$begin ( writes number );
CREATE TABLE undo$end ( writes number );
CREATE TABLE test1 (col1 number, col2 varchar2(1);
INSERT INTO test1 values (1, 'N');
INSERT INTO test1 values (1,'Y');
INSERT INTO test1 values (2,'Y');
commit;
INSERT INTO undo$begin
     SELECT sum(writes) FROM v$rollstat;
set termout on
set feedback on
UPDATE test1 SET col1=99 WHERE col3 ='Y';
REM Note : The test transaction can be executed from a SQL
REM script file.
set termout off
set feedback off
INSERT INTO undo$send
     SELECT sum(writes) FROM v$rollstat;
set termout on
set  feedback on
```

```
SELECT  ( ( e.writes - b.writes) - &undo_overhead)
" number of bytes generates"
      FROM undo$begin b, undo$end e;
set termout off
set feedback off
DROP TABLE undo$begin;
DROP TABLE undo$end;
DROP TABLE test1;
```

This script will determine the amount of undo generated during the transaction. The result of the test is accurate if it is performed while nothing else is occurring on the database. The UNDO_OVERHEAD defined in the script is a constant which compensates for the unavoidable overhead of the "INSERT INTO undo$begin..." statement.

The use of the OPTIMAL clause is a very handy tool. However the DBA should be aware of its limitations. One potential problem is that extent allocation and deallocation is expensive in regards to performance. This means that an OPTIMAL setting may decrease performance if it is too low. Another potential problem is that you are never guaranteed when a rollback segment will shrink down to its optimal size. Remember from the previous discussion that a rollback segment only shrinks when it attempts to move into another extent and sees that the extent meets the requirements for deallocation.

For databases where the transaction rate has no fluctuation (has a steady average transaction rate), there is a simple technique that can be used to configure the tablespace. Create a tablespace that will fit your calculated number of rollback segments with the minimum coverage size you have determined. Make all extents the same size. For a safety net, you may allocate some additional space in the tablespace to allow segments to grow if they need to. If you elect to do this, use the OPTIMAL feature to force all rollback segments to free up any additional space they allocate beyond their determined size requirement. You do not want to make OPTIMAL smaller than the minimum coverage size. Otherwise performance will suffer due to excessive segment resizing.

Databases with frequent large transactions are the hardest case to deal with. We will define frequent as the time between large transactions being less than the time needed to allow all rollback segments to shrink back to optimal size. A large transaction is one in which we don't have enough space to create all rollback segments of the size necessary to handle its rollback information. Because we cannot depend on the segment shrinking in time to allow repeated large transactions, OPTIMAL is not really an option for this environment. There are basically two options that you can choose from for your rollback segment tablespace. One is to reduce the number of segments so that all are large enough to hold the largest transactions. This option will introduce contention and will cause some degradation in performance. It is a reasonable choice if performance is not extremely critical.

The second option is to build one or more larger rollback segments and make sure that large transactions use these segments. The SET TRANSACTION USE ROLLBACK SEGMENT command is necessary to control the placement of these large transactions. This option is difficult to implement if large transactions are being run with ad hoc queries and there is no systematic control of large transactions.

For cases where large transactions are rare, the DBA can use the OPTIMAL feature to set up a flexible rollback segment scheme, one where you are not concerned about which rollback segment a large transaction falls upon. The key is to leave enough free space in the rollback tablespace that the largest transaction's rollback information can fit entirely into it. To do this, create the rollback tablespace with the space needed for your calculated number of segments and their minimum coverage size plus this additional space. Then set the OPTIMAL for each segment equal to the minimum coverage size. Using this technique, transactions will randomly make one of the segments grow and eat up the free space, but the segment will release the space before the next large transaction comes along. Note that you are sacrificing some performance for this flexibility.

SIZING TEMPORARY SEGMENTS AND TABLESPACES

The size of the temporary tablespace can be determined by using a technique similar to the one used for sizing rollback segments. We start by determining the size of the initial/next extent values. This can be done by using the formula.

```
Extent Size = 1.25 (M/n)
```

Where n = the maximum number of extents for the segment and M = the largest sort to disk. As in the case of sizing rollback segments we'll let n = 100. We will estimate the largest disk sort to be three times the size of the init<SID>.ora parameter SORT_AREA_SIZE. For our case we make the following computation:

```
Extent Size = 1.25 (306000/100) =  380 KB
```

The size of the tablespace can be determined by performing the following computation:

```
Tablespace size = MAXEXTENTS * Extent Size
```

In our example we would make the following computation:

```
Tablespace size = 100 * 380000 = 38 MB
```

We stated earlier that the temporary tablespace is used for sorting data. One technique for determining the efficiency of sorting is to determine how much sorting is getting accomplished in memory, therefore reducing disk I/O. To determine how much sorting is being performed in memory and how much requires disk IO we issue the query shown in Display 8.3.

```
SQLPLUS> SELECT name, value
SQLPLUS> from v$sysstat
SQLPLUS> where name IN ('sorts(memory)', 'sorts(disk)');

NAME                                                VALUE
-------------------------------------------         ----------
sorts(memory)                                       1001
sorts(disk)                                             6
```

DISPLAY 8.3

The DBA can reduce the number of sorts that require disk I/O by increasing the memory sort area. This is done by increasing the init<SID>.ora parameter SORT_AREA_SIZE. By increasing the sort area the DBA can realize the following benefits:

1. Reducing the number of sort runs decreases the number of merge operations that the RDBMS must perform.
2. Reducing the number of sort runs decreases the number of I/O.

In Figure 8.4 we see that we can create the TEMPORARY tablespace using STORAGE MANAGER. We see that we can also increase the amount of storage for a given tablespace. This can be done automatically by using the auto data file extend enhancement to extend the size of the data file. This new feature eliminates the need to add a data file when increasing the amount of space in a given tablespace. This feature can be used to automatically extend the data file for any of our tablespaces.

SUMMARY

The calculations allow you to estimate the amount of disk space required for the various Oracle tablespaces/data files. The DBA should always monitor the amount of space remaining in a particular tablespace to ensure that there is enough storage remaining in the table to accommodate table growth.

The following PL/SQL procedure calculates the amount of space remaining in the USERS tablespace (the procedure can be modified for any tablespace).

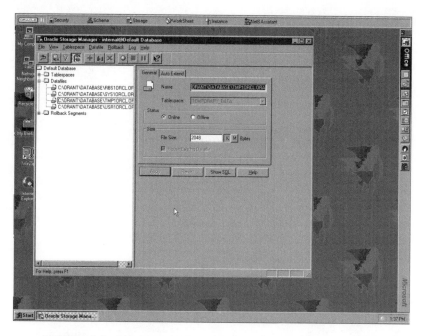

FIGURE 8.4 The Temporary tablespace using Storage Manager

```
CREATE OR REPLACE procedure pct_users   IS
     free_bytes     number;
     total_free     number := 0;
     total_bytes    number := 0;
     tot_bytes      number;
     pct_used       number(10,4) := 0;
     CURSOR freesp IS
     select bytes from sys.dba_free_space where
     tablespace_name = 'USERS';
     CURSOR totalsp IS
     select bytes from sys.dba_data_files where
     tablespace_name = 'USERS';
BEGIN
     open freesp;
     open totalsp;
   loop
     fetch freesp into free_bytes;
     exit when freesp%notfound;
     total_free := total_free + free_bytes;
   end loop;
```

```
loop
  fetch totalsp into tot_bytes;
  exit when totalsp%notfound;
  total_bytes := total_bytes + tot_bytes;
end loop;
  close freesp;
  close totalsp;
  pct_used := ((1-(total_free/total_bytes))*100);
  dbms_output.put_line ('USERS TABLESPACE total free space
  in BYTES = ' || total_free);
  dbms_output.put_line ('USERS TABLESPACE total size in
  BYTES = ' || total_bytes);
  dbms_output.put_line ('percentage of USERS TABLESPACE
  storage used = '|| pct_used);
END pct_users;
/
```

The output would yield the following output.

```
USERS TABLESPACE total free space in BYTES = 42827776
USERS TABLESPACE total size in BYTES = 52428800
percentage of USERS TABLESPACE storage used = 18.3125
PL/SQL procedure successfully completed.
```

The DBA should also monitor the number of extents that a segment has. This should be done to ensure that the MAXEXTENTS for the segment is not exceeded. The following script can be used to monitor the number of extents for indexes and tables:

```
spool ext_num.log
set pagesize 120
col tablespace_name heading 'TSPACE_NAME' format a11
col segment_name heading 'TABLE NAME' format a10
col extents heading '# OF EXTENTS' format 99,990
col next_extent heading 'NEXT EXTENT' format 99,990,000
col max_extents heading 'MAX. EXTENT' format 99,990
col pct_increase heading 'PCT_INCR' format 99,990

select s.tablespace_name, s.segment_name,
    s.extents,s.next_extent,s.max_extents,s.pct_increase
            from   user_segments s, user_tables t
            where  s.segment_type = 'TABLE'
            and    s.extents > 2
            and    s.segment_name = t.table_name
            order  by s.segment_name;
```

```
col segment_name heading 'INDEX NAME' format a15

select s.tablespace_name, s.segment_name,
    s.extents,s.next_extent,s.max_extents,s.pct_increase
        from    user_segments s, user_indexes t
        where   s.segment_type = 'INDEX'
        and     s.extents > 1
        and     s.segment_name = t.index_name
        order   by s.segment_name;

spool off
```

The resulting output from executing the script will be:

TSPACE_NAME TABLE NAME		# OF EXTENTS	NEXT EXTENT MAX.	EXTENT PCT_INCR	
USERS	EMP_SCH_IN	4	114,688	121	20
USERS	EMP_TABL	3	90,112	121	20
USERS	EMP_CONT	7	212,992	121	20

TSPACE_NAME TABLE NAME		# OF EXTENTS	NEXT EXTENT MAX.	EXTENT PCT_INCR	
INDEXES	IND_F_NAME	2	163,840	120	50
INDEXES	IND_L_NAME	2	163,840	120	50

APPLICATION DEVELOPMENT FOR DBAs

INTRODUCTION

In Chapter 1, we saw that a database is often used as an information repository for end-user applications. It was also stated that end-user applications can be written using various programming tools. An order-entry system will have an end-user interface that the sales representative uses to record the customer's order. The resulting order information is stored in the database tables that are allocated to the order-entry application. In a client/server environment the data entry screen communicates with the database through SQL*NET and the underlying software/hardware.

Because the database is the information repository for end-user applications the DBA is often called on to work with or in some cases be the application developer. The application development role will often include such activities as modeling business functions, determining which application development tools to use, writing and testing the application. The role of the DBA does not end with system installation. The DBA is also responsible for system performance and capacity planning. The performance of the system and the growth of the system is influenced by the design of the system. Therefore it is very important that the DBA be part of the application-development cycle.

ENTITY-RELATIONSHIP MODELING

End-user applications are used to satisfy or automate a business requirement. Therefore it is important to understand the business requirements that the application is written to satisfy. The entity-relationship model shows how the business requirements will be satisfied by the application. The ER model also provides the framework for understanding how the application should be written. Some of the other reasons for using an ER model include:

❑ Models can be changed quickly.

❑ Models show the alternatives to satisfying a business requirement.

❑ Models can be used to estimate system capacity requirements.

ENTITY-RELATIONSHIP MODEL COMPONENTS

The ER model is a graphical technique for capturing business information and the relationships between the data. The ER model consists of the following components.

1. Entities—The things of significance about the information that is held. Entities often become the tables or views that an application will use.
2. Relationships—Describes how the entities are related. The different types of relationships include one to one (1:1), one to many (1:M), many to one (M:1), many to many (M:M) and optional relationships.
3. Attributes—The specific information that describes the entity. Attributes often become the columns in the tables. An attribute can be mandatory (must always have a value), optional (can be NULL) or unique. The symbol '*' is used for an attribute that is mandatory, o is used for attributes that are optional and # is used to show that the attribute is unique.

The graphical components of the ER model are shown in Figure 9-1.

The ER model is used to convey business information. For example, a computer manufacturer might construct the following ER model to show the relationship between the computer and the motherboard (shown in Figure 9-2).

This is an example of a one to one relationship (1:1) where the relationship is mandatory in one direction and optional in the other.

The sales organization of a company might develop the following ER model to show the relationship between a sales representative and a customer (shown in Figure 9-3).

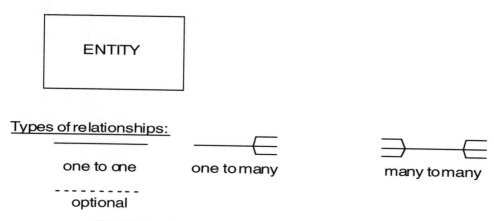

FIGURE 9.1 The graphical components of the ER model

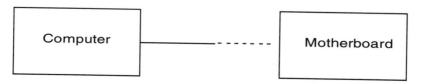

FIGURE 9.2 One to one relationship

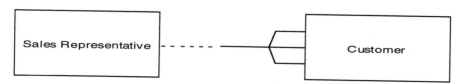

FIGURE 9.3 One to many relationship

This is an example of a one to many relationship. We see that the relationship is optional between sales representative and customer. In this case optional means that the sales representative *may* be assigned one or more customers rather then the mandatory relationship that the sales representative *will* be assigned one of more customers.

An entity may have many attributes. For example, the entity customer may have the attributes customer number, customer name, customer phone number and item purchased. The graphical representation of the customer entity may look like the one shown in Figure 9-4.

```
Customer Number
Customer Name
Phone number
Item Purchased
Date purchased
```

FIGURE 9.4   The graphical representation of the customer entity

We can enforce the applications business rules by assigning constraints to the various attributes. The graphical representation of assigning constraints to the entities attributes is shown in Figure 9-5.

```
#*  Customer number
*   Customer name
o   Phone number
*   Item Purchased
*   Date purchased
```

FIGURE 9.5   Attributes with assigned constraints

Each customer is assigned a unique customer number (UID). The customer number is also mandatory. This makes the customer number a primary key (refer to Chapter 5 for a complete explanation of key constraints). The other mandatory fields are customer name, item purchased and the date when it was purchased. The customer's phone number is optional in this example.

Applications are written to satisfy a business requirement. The ER modeling technique is best shown by example. The business requirements that will be the basis for an ER model could be summarized using the following narrative.

My name is K.E. Nell. I am the owner and operator of KEN's Kennel. At KEN's Kennel we board pets while their owners are out of town. When the owner brings in their pet we obtain the name of the owner, the name of each pet, the age of each pet and the pet's weight, species, gender, color and breed.

We also need information about the customer. We need their name, address, home phone, their veterinarian's name and phone number, and when they will be returning for the pet.

I house each pet in a very spacious kennel suite during their stay. The larger pets reside in a 30 x 20 foot kennel and the smaller pets get a nice cozy 10 x 5 foot kennel suite. For the pet's safety and comfort only one pet is housed in a kennel suite.

In the narrative we must first find the entities or *"things of significance."* The characteristics of an entity include:

❑ An entity is an object of interest/significance to the business.

❑ An entity is a noun.

❑ An entity is a category or class.

One possible ER model for the scenario is shown in Figure 9-6.

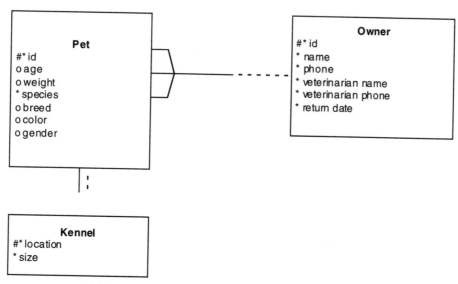

FIGURE 9.6   One possible ER model for the scenario

We see that the things that are of interest are pet, owner, and kennel. Once the entities are known the attributes can be assigned to the entities. The relationship between the entities can also be determined. In this example an owner can have more then one pet but a pet can only have one owner (M:1). We also see that there is a 1:1 relationship between pet and kennel (only one pet in a room at a time). Based on the ER model the DBA can write the SQL "CREATE TABLE" statements that will create the tables PET, OWNER, and KENNEL.

NORMALIZATION

Database normalization is used to eliminate data redundancy in the database design. There are three rules that are used to normalize the data. These rules are summarized below.

First normal form (1NF): All attributes must be single valued. A repeated attribute indicates a missing entity.

The example below shows a simple ER model for seating arrangement at a concert. The entity CONCERT not only contains the person's name and registration number but also the seat numbers that are in the concert hall (refer to Figure 9-7).

```
CONCERT
Ticket number
Name
seat1
seat2
seat3
seat4
...
seat 100
```

FIGURE 9.7   A Simple ER model for seating arrangement at a concert

By applying the 1NF rule the ER model resembles the one shown in Figure 9-8.

FIGURE 9.8   The 1NF rule ER model

Second normal form (2NF): An attribute must depend upon its entity's entire unique identifier. The following example is of a bank that has several accounts. The ER model is defined to have the entities ACCOUNT and BANK. By applying the 2NF rule we see that the attribute *bank location* is not dependent on the UID *account number* (refer to Figure 9-9).

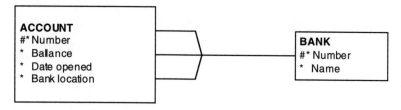

FIGURE 9.9   The attribute bank location is not dependent on the UID account number

The attribute bank location is dependent on the entity bank. This results in the following change to the ER model (refer to Figure 9-10).

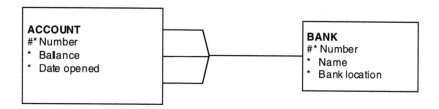

FIGURE 9.10   The attribute bank location is dependent on the entity bank

Third normal form (3NF): A non-UID attribute cannot be dependent upon another non-UID attribute.

This example represents the ER model for an order-entry system. The attributes customer name and customer address are dependent on the customer ID (refer to Figure 9-11).

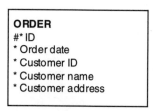

FIGURE 9.11   The ER model for an order-entry system

To place the model in 3NF we create a new entity called *customer*. The attributes *customer name* and *customer address* are moved to the entity *customer* because they are dependent on *customer ID* (refer to Figure 9-12).

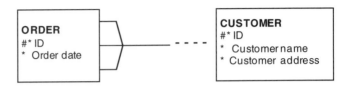

FIGURE 9.12   The attributes customer name and customer address
are moved to the entity customer

HOW IT ALL FITS TOGETHER

A complete end-user application consists of the database that is used to store table data and a user input screen. The client application (user input screen) connects to the database through SQL*NET. Client applications can be written using Developer 2000 (Oracle*Forms, Oracle*Reports and Oracle*Graphics), Visual C++/Basic or HTML are some of the more popular application development tools.

Because of the growth of the Internet, the language HTML has become very popular. HTML-based applications can be distributed to many users via the Internet. These applications usually consist of data input forms. The information that is entered into the form can be transferred to the database via a Common Gateway Interface (CGI). A CGI is a software routine that is usually used to link an HTML web page to a database. There are several languages that can be used to develop a CGI. The languages that a CGI can be written in include in the precompiler PRO*C/C++ (C/C++ with imbedded SQL) and the scripting language PERL.

A web-based application may consist of a series of forms and informational screens. The forms can be used to gather information that will be used to create a customer profile. After the end user enters the data into the form the CGI routine is executed. The data is passed from the form to the CGI routine. The CGI will parse the data and INSERT it into the appropriate database table.

The following HTML code will create the web page that is shown in Figure 9-13.

```
<html>
<head>
<title> On Line Registration System</title>
</head>
<body>
<h2> World Wide Web Registration Form </h2>
<form method="POST" action=      >
<p> First Name :  <input name="fname"></p>
<p> Last Name :  <input name="lname"></p>
```

```
<p> Address : <input name="address"></p>
<p> Phone Number : <input name="phone"></p>
<p><input type="submit" value="Register Me"></p>
</form>
</body>
</html>
```

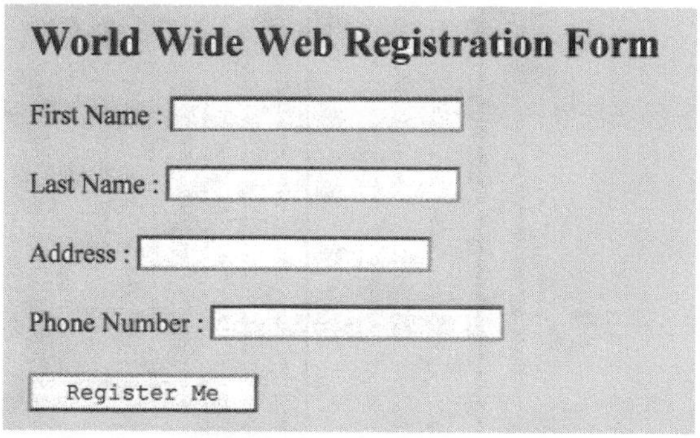

FIGURE 9.13 HTML web page

The following code fragment is an example of a PERL CGI script that could be used to insert the end-user data into the table called *CUSTOMER_TABLE*.

```
#Build SQL file
  open (tmpSQLfile, ">$InsertUserSQLFile") || print "Error:
    couldn't open the file: $InsertUserSQLFile.<BR>\n";

    print tmpSQLfile "spool $InsertUserResultsFile\;\n";

    print tmpSQLfile "
    insert into customer_table values(
                '$firstname',
                '$lastname',
                '$address',
                '$phone',
                        SYSDATE)\; \n";

    print tmpSQLfile "commit\;\n\n";
}


    print tmpSQLfile "spool off\;\n";
    print tmpSQLfile "exit\;\n";
```

```
close tmpSQLfile;

# Run the sqlplus command to put the data into the database
table customer_table.

system ("sqlplus -s admin/admin@SERVR @$InsertUserSQLFile
>log_file");
```

ORACLE WEB ASSISTANT

Oracle8 provides database administrators and application developers with a new utility (see Figure 9-14) for generating HTML called *"WEB ASSISTANT."*

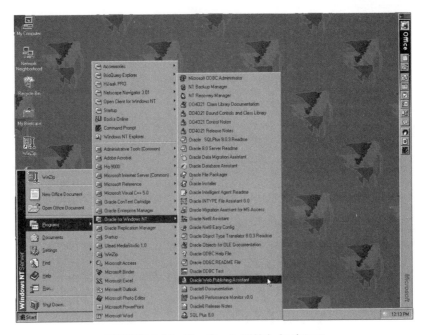

FIGURE 9.14 The Oracle8 Web Assistant

The Oracle8 *WEB ASSISTANT* can be used to generate both static and dynamic HTML (see Figure 9.15).

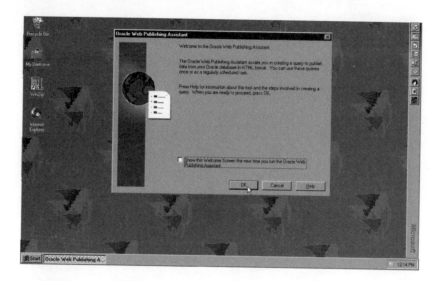

FIGURE 9.15 Static and dynamic HTML

By pressing the option *"NEW"* (refer to Figure 9-16) the DBA can create static or dynamic HTML

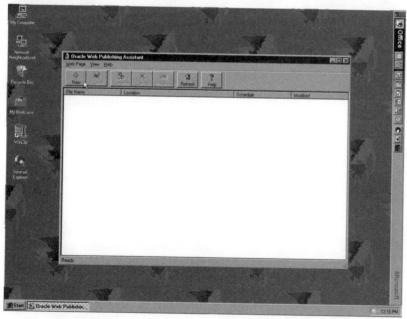

FIGURE 9.16 The DBA can create static or dynamic HTML

The DBA can also choose the frequency with which the HTML file will be regenerated (dynamic HTML) or will the HTML be generated only once (for static HTML) as shown in Figure 9-17.

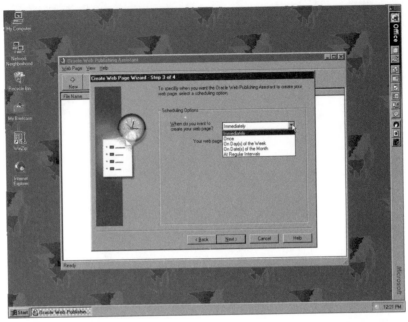

FIGURE 9.17 Frequency of generation.

DBAs can choose to create a query and let the *WEB ASSISTANT* generate the HTML template, or choose to supply their own HTML template as shown in Figure 9-18.

The completed HTML can be viewed using any standard web browser as shown in Figure 9-19.

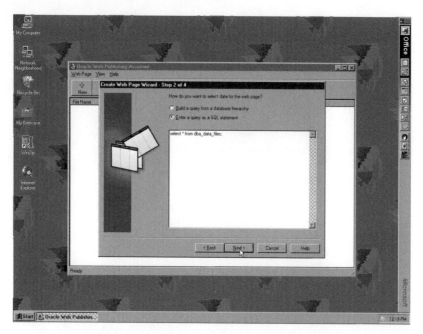

FIGURE 9.18 DBAs can supply their own template

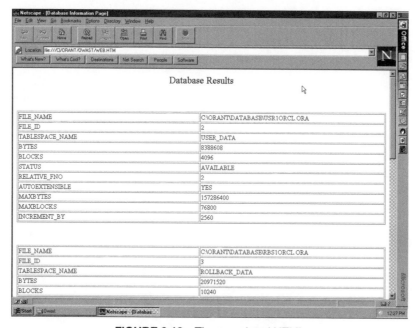

FIGURE 9.19 The completed HTML

VLDB

Scalability of an RDBMS is very important in the current business environment. Oracle8 provides several scalability features for its RDBMS. These features include:

❑ Supports hundreds of terabytes of data. The theoretical upper limit is 512 petabytes.

❑ Supports as many as 30,000 users

❑ Supports more files, more columns per table, and larger columns.

One important addition to Oracle8 is the use of partitioning technology to improve the database's availability and manageability. Partitioning lets database administrators carry out storage management and maintenance chores on segments of a database without bringing down the entire database.

Separating table data into manageable units by splitting the table data according to design considerations is called table partitioning. While logically it remains one large table, it is being split into ten separately manageable units, each with the same logical attributes, but possibly different physical characteristics, such as storage allocation.

How do you manage a large table of 10GB or more? Can you still back it up in the time that is allotted at night for backups? What about reorganizing, reloading or purging the data? As the tables grow so does the time required to perform these operations. Soon it will no longer be possible to do the maintenance at night. Partitioning is designed to solve these kinds of problems. By physically partitioning one table into smaller chunks while still treating it as one database entity we gain a much higher level of flexibility. Especially when it comes to managing and maintaining large tables.

By using table partitioning we can take advantage of Oracle's "divide and conquer" paradigm. Data is now manipulated at the partition and not at the table level. So, I can back up the first six months of table data, while the most current data is available for use. Or I can design table partitions where read-only data will be separated from read-and-write data and build my backup strategy around that. In most cases partition-level operations can be performed in parallel as well, thus speeding up the DML operations on large tables.

In May 1997 the magazine *Client Server Computing* interviewed one of its customers that uses an Oracle database. AT&T Corporation's Consumer Markets Division is very interested in the scalability and partitioning capacities of Oracle8. In the article, the AT&T lead system developer for order status at the division stated, "Our database is currently 130 gigabytes, and we'll be over 200 gigabytes by the end of the year. The organization is currently producing tables that can be as large as 30 gigabytes and indexes that can be up to 12 gigabytes in size."

Creating a partitioned table is simple. We can partition our table based on different requirements. For example we can partition a large table that is used for order entry based on a date range. The SQL to create the table is shown in Display 10.1.

```
SQLPLUS> CREATE TABLE orders98
SQLPLUS> (cust_no  NUMBER(6)
SQLPLUS> product_no NUMBER(15)
SQLPLUS> amount  NUMBER(4)
SQLPLUS> order_date DATE
SQLPLUS> )
SQLPLUS> PARTITION BY RANGE
SQLPLUS> (
SQLPLUS> PARTITION ts1 VALUES LESS THAN ('01-APR-98') TABLESPACE ts1,
SQLPLUS> PARTITION ts2 VALUES LESS THAN ('01-JUL-98') TABLESPACE ts2,
SQLPLUS> PARTITION ts3 VALUES LESS THAN ('01-OCT-98') TABLESPACE ts3,
SQLPLUS> PARTITION ts4 VALUES LESS THAN ('01-JAN-98') TABLESPACE ts4);
```

DISPLAY 10.1

Partitioned Views were introduced in the Oracle7.3 release. Partitioned View uses UNION ALL operation on underlying multiple tables. In other words, you have to create multiple tables and combine them using the CREATE VIEW UNION ALL syntax.

Our large table is still a single database entity that happens to be stored in separate physical chunks. What has changed between Oracle7 and Oracle8 releases is that the unit of data management in Oracle7 was at the table level. In Oracle8 the unit of data management is at the partition level. Essentially, this unit of data management does not need to grow, just the number of those units.

In addition, even though reasons for Partitioned Views in Oracle7 are the same as Partitioned Tables in Oracle8, one of the limiting factors for Partitioned Views is the length of SQL statement itself. The SQL statement sets a limit on number of tables that can be used in Partitioned View. Because Oracle8 partitions are on a single table, no restrictions of this kind exist.

TABLE STRIPING

Table Striping is a technique of separating portions of a table and splitting them between several devices. Performance gains from striping tables can be significant. However, the major difference between Striped Table in Oracle7 and Partitioned Table in Oracle8 is that no administrative operations are allowed on separate stripes of the table. Backup, reload and purging of the table must be done at the table level. In Oracle8 partitions are separate units of data. As a result different operations can be performed on different partitions of the same table. I can back up the various individual partitions of a table while end users are accessing other partitions of the same table. In addition, it is very cumbersome to logically define the boundaries of stripes in Oracle7. In Oracle8 it can be done using the keyword VALUES LESS THAN.

PARTITIONING GUIDELINES

Each Table Partition should be stored in a separate tablespace. Controlling the allocation of specific data files allows a degree of control not available before. The DBA can control which operating system file will have specific ranges of table data. The advantages include:

❏ Improved availability

❏ Better administration

❏ Enhanced performance

How many partitions to define is an important question. Many considerations exist. Often they conflict with one another. Most important ones need to be chosen. Where do we need to improve the most, is it availability or ease of maintenance?

Or is it performance? One of the easiest considerations is the size of the table. Partitions should be small enough so you can easily manage them, do backups or possibly rebuild when needed. If your backup strategy includes export and your operating system file size limit is 2Gb, you would benefit from sizing the partitions to fit into a single file system.

Every table usually has only a certain amount of data that changes. The majority of the data will remain unchanged once entered. In Oracle7.3, backup of the table required the entire table be backed up, even though up to 80 percent of data never changed. By implementing the partitioning strategy where read-only data is separated from read-update data, we can reduce the backup time significantly. By placing a read-only data into a separate partition and into its own tablespace, we need only to back it up once, while the read-update data is being backed up regularly.

When deciding how to partition a table consider the parallel analyze capability in Oracle8. Since partitions can be analyzed independently of one another, we can break up data based on analysis needs. In a data warehouse it might be beneficial to create a new partition for each nightly load and analyze in parallel. Balancing partition size is very important. If data for November, December and January is significantly larger, partitioning by month will not take data skew into account and result in a few very large partitions and many small ones. Consider breaking up these monthly partitions into weekly partitions and balance partition sizes across the table.

If a partition has to be dropped and a global index exists on the table, the entire global index will be invalidated. At that point the index cannot be used and must be rebuilt. All the data access would have to be done without using the global index. The main issue here is trading performance for availability. Data access via global index is much faster, but the impact on availability when using global indexes should also be considered. Global indexes are usually much faster that local indexes. It might be necessary to avoid local indexes and use global indexing strategy instead.

SQL SUPPORT FOR TABLE PARTITIONING

SQL commands to manage partitions are available through the Oracle Enterprise Manager (OEM) as well as in SQL*PLUS. Some of the standard SQL partition operations include:

- ❏ Alter table... add partition...
- ❏ Alter table... drop partition...
- ❏ Alter table... truncate partition...
- ❏ Alter table... move partition...
- ❏ Alter table... split partition...
- ❏ Alter table... exchange partition...
- ❏ Alter index... rebuild partition...

DATA DICTIONARY AND TABLE PARTITIONS

Several new views have been added to the Data Dictionary in Oracle8. Some of them are:

- ❏ USER_PART_TABLES
- ❏ USER_PART_KEY_COLUMNS
- ❏ USER_PART_INDEXES
- ❏ USER_PART_HISTOGRAMS
- ❏ USER_PART_COL_STATISTICS
- ❏ USR_IND_PARTITIONS
- ❏ DBA_IND_PARTITIONS
- ❏ DBA_ANALYZE_OBJECTS
- ❏ ALL_TAB_PARTITIONS
- ❏ ALL IND_PARTITIONS

MIGRATING FROM PARTITIONED VIEWS TO PARTITIONED TABLES

There are only two steps in this migration. First, create a Partitioned Table matching the existing partitioned view. Second, use the command "ALTER TABLE EXCHANGE PARTITION" on each of the tables in the partitioned view with empty partitions in the Oraele8 partitioned table. Rebuild the indexes after the data has been exchanged.

CONCLUSION

Serious considerations need to be given when designing partitions. What may work very well for availability and manageability of the data may be different if the design is for optimal performance. Each factor needs to be weighed separately with the most important one being the main design consideration. Partitioning improves performance of queries and allows some new parallel operations not possible prior to Oracle8.

ADDITIONS TO THE ORACLE DATA DICTIONARY

The following is a descriptive list of the various views that have been added to the Oracle8 Data Dictionary.

1. ALL_ALL_ TABLES and DBA_ALL_TABLES and USER_TABLES—This view will show all relational information as well as all object tables accessible to the user.
2. ALL_ARGUMENTS—This view lists all arguments in the object which are accessible to the user.
3. ALL_CLUSTERS and DBA_CLUSTERS and USER_CLUSTERS—This view lists all clusters accessible to the user.
4. ALL_COL_PRIVS and DBA_COL_PRIVS and USER_COL_PRIVS—This view lists grants on columns for which the user or PUBLIC is the grantee.
5. ALL_COLL_TYPES and DBA_COL_TYPES and USER_COL_TYPES—This view lists the named collection types accessible to the user.
6. ALL_DIRECTORIES and DBA_DIRECTORIES and USER_DIRECTORIES— This view contains information about directories accessible to the user.

7. ALL_IND_PARTITIONS and DBA_IND_PARTITIONS and USER_IND_PARTITION—This view gives information on each index partition.

8. ALL_LIBRARIES and DBA_LIBRARIES and USER_LIBRARIES—This view lists all the libraries that a user can access.

9. ALL_LOBS and DBA_LOBS and USER_LOBS—This view displays the LOBs contained in tables accessible to user.

10. ALL_METHOD_PARAMS and DBA_METHOD_PARAMS and USER_METHOD_PARAMS—This is a description view of all method parameters of types accessible to the user.

11. ALL_METHOD_RESULTS and DBA_METHOD_RESULTS and USER_METHOD_RESULTS—This is a view for method results of types accessible to the user.

12. ALL_NESTED_TABLES and DBA_NESTED_TABLES and USER_NESTED_TABLES—This view describes the nested tables in tables accessible to the user.

13. ALL_OBJECT_TABLES and DBA_OBJECT_TABLES and USER_OBJECT_TABLES—Lists description of all the object tables.

14. ALL_PART_COL_STATISTICS and DBA_PART_COL_STATISTICS and USER_PART_COL_STATISTICS—List of column statistics and histogram information.

15. ALL_PART_HISTOGRAM and DBA_PART_HISTOGRAM and USER_PART_HISTOGRAM—List of histogram data for histograms on table partitions.

16. ALL_PART_INDEXES and DBA_PART_INDEXES and USER_PART_INDEXES—Lists object-level partitioning information for all partitions.

17. ALL_PART_KEY_COLUMNS and DBA_PART_KEY_COLUMN and USER_PART_KEY_COLUMN—Describes partitioning key columns for partitioned objects that the current user can access.

18. ALL_PART_TABLES and DBA_PART_TABLES and USER_PART_TABLES—This view lists object-level partitioning information for partitioned tables the current user can access.

19. ALL_REF and DBA_REF and USER_REF—This view describes the REF columns and REF attributes in the object-type column.

20. ALL_REGISTERED_SNAPSHOTS and DBA_REGISTERED_SNAPSHOTS—This view lists all registered snapshots.

21. ALL_REPCOLUMN and DBA_REPCOLUMN and USER_REPCOLUMN—This view is used with Advanced Replication.

22. ALL_REPGENOBJECTS and DBA_REPGENOBJECTS and USER_REPGENOBJECTS—This view is for Advanced Replication Option.

23. ALL_SNAPSHOT_REFRESH_TIMES and DBA_SNAPSHOT_REFRESH_TIMES and USER_SNAPSHOT_REFRESH_TIMES—Used by the advanced replication option. The view shows the last time the snapshot was refreshed.

24. ALL_TAB_COL_STATISTICS and DBA_TAB_COL_STATISTICS and USER_TAB_COL_STATISTICS—This view contains column statistics and histogram information.

25. ALL_TAB_HISTOGRAMS and DBA_TAB_HISTOGRAMS and USER_TAB_HISTOGRAMS—This view lists histograms on tables and views accessible to users.

26. ALL_TYPES and DBA_TYPES and USER_TYPES—This view displays all types accessible to the user.

27. ALL_TAB_PARTITIONS and DBA_TAB_PARTITIONS and USER_TAB_PARTITIONS—Lists each table partition and its information.

28. ALL_TYPE_ATTRS and DBA_TYPE_ATTRS and USER_TYPE_ATTRS—This view displays the attributes of types accessible to the user.

29. ALL_TYPE_METHOD and DBA_TYPE_METHOD and USER_TYPE_METHOD—This lists the types accessible to the user.

30. DBA_PENDING_TRANSACTIONS—This view describes pending transactions

31. DBA_REGISTERED_SNAPSHOT_GROUPS—This view lists all the snapshot groups at the site.

32. DBA_QUEUE_TABLES—Describes names and types of the queue in all of the queue tables created in the database.

33. DBA_QUEUES and USER_QUEUES—This view describes the operational characteristics for every queue.

The following lists the new additions to the Oracle DYNAMIC PERFORMANCE VIEWS:

1. V$ARCHIVE_DEST —This view describes all archive log destinations.

2. V$ARCHIVED_LOG—This view displays the archive log information from the control file.

3. V$BACKUP_CORRUPTION—This view describes information about corruptions in the data file backups. This information is read from the control file.

4. V$BACKUP_DATAFILE—Displays backup data file and backup control file information from the control file.

5. V$BACKUP_DEVICE—Displays information on supported backup devices.

6. V$BACKUP_PIECE—Displays information on the backup pieces from control file.

7. V$BACKUP_REDOLOG—Displays information about archived logs in backup sets from the control file.

8. V$BACKUP_SET—This view displays backup set information from the Oracle control file.
9. V$BUFFERPOOL—This view lists all the buffer pools available for that instance.
10. V$CLASS_PING—Displays the number of blocks pinged per block class.
11. V$CONTROLFILE_RECORD_SECTION—This view displays information about control file record sections.
12. V$COPY_CORRUPTION—Displays information about data file copy corruptions. The information is obtained from the control file.
13. V$DATAFILE_COPY—This view displays data file copy information from the control file.
14. V$DATAFILE_HEADER—Displays information from the data file headers.
15. V$DELETED_OBJECT—This view displays information on deleted archived logs, data file copies and backup pieces from the control file.
16. V$DISPATCHER_RATE—Provides statistics for the dispatcher process.
17. V$EXECUTION_LOCATION—Displays information on the parallel query execution tree location.
18. V$LOADPSTAT—SQL-loader statistics compiled during execution of a direct load.
19. V$OFFLINE_RANGE—This view contains information on off line data files.
20. V$SESSION_LONGOPS—This view displays the status of certain long-running operations.
21. V$SESSION_OBJECT_CACHE—Contains object cache statistics for the current user session.
22. V$SESSION view New column PDML_ENABLED—This will allow to see if a parallel DML has been enabled.
23. V$SUBCACHE—Displays subordinate cache information, currently loaded into library cache memory.
24. V$TABLESPACE—Displays tablespace information from the control file.
25. V$TRANSACTION_ENQUEUE—This view displays locks owned by transaction state object.

WHAT IS SQL?

The programming language called Structured Query Language (SQL) is used to define, access, and manipulate information that is stored in a relational database. Some of the attributes and features of the SQL language are:

1. SQL
    - ❏ Developed by IBM for System R.
    - ❏ Oracle introduced the first commercial SQL product in 1979.
    - ❏ IBM introduced SQL/DS (VM) in 1982 and DB2 (MVS) in 1984.
    - ❏ First official ANSI standard established in 1986, and revised in 1989.

2. SQL is a nonprocedural language used to process a set of records.
3. Simple and intuitive syntax.
    - ❏ CREATE/DROP/ALTER all database objects including tables and indexes.
    - ❏ INSERT/SELECT/UPDATE/DELETE rows.
    - ❏ GRANT/REVOKE privileges.

INTRODUCTION TO SQL*PLUS

QUERYING THE DATABASE

The purpose of this section is to introduce the reader to Oracle's version of SQL called SQL*PLUS. This section is centered on querying the database (getting the desired information from the tables that make up the database). We will work with the tables called "emp" and "dept." Running the script DEMOBLD.SQL creates the tables. The script is located in the directory C:\ORANT\DBS. The script can be run using the utility SQL*PLUS.

As stated earlier we will be working with the two tables called "emp" and "dept" for the employees' table and the department table. The "emp" table contains information about the people that work for a fictitious company and the "dept" table contains information about the departments that the company is divided into. The structure of the "emp" table is shown in Figure B.1.

EMPNO	ENAME	JOB	MGR	HIREDATE	SAL	COMM	DEPTNO

FIGURE B.1   The emp table

The structure of the "dept" table is shown in Figure B.2.

DEPTNO	DNAME	LOC

FIGURE B.2   The dept table

Please execute the following instructions and observe the output.

1)   describe dept
     desc emp;

These commands will display the structure of the emp and the dept tables.

```
2)    select dname,deptno
      from dept;
```

This will list all of the departments and the corresponding department numbers as stored in the "dept" table.

```
3)    select distinct job
      from emp;
```

Displays only distinct job entries. If a job description is stored in the database multiple times only one occurrence is displayed.

```
4)    select distinct job "JOB LIST"
      from emp;
```

Same as the previous query except the column heading will be "JOB LIST"

```
5)    select ename, job, sal
      from emp
      where deptno = 30;
```

Displays all employees that are in department 30.

```
6)    select ename, job,sal
      from emp
      where job <> 'MANAGER';
```

Lists the name, job description, and salary for all persons that are not managers.

```
7)    select ename,job,deptno,hiredate
      from emp
      where ename like 'Mo%';
```

This displays all employees whose names start with "Mo." Note the use of the wild card character %.

```
8)    select ename, sal, job
      from emp
      where deptno = 10
      order by sal desc;
```

This will display the salary, jobs and employee names with the data sorted in descending order based on the salaries.

```
9)   select ename, sal, job
     from emp
     where deptno = 10
     order by 2;
```

Same as the previous example except that we told it to order the data with respect to the second column (sal).

```
10)  select ename, loc, emp.deptno
     from emp, dept
     where emp.deptno = dept.deptno;
```

This will join the two tables to produce a listing showing the person's name, location and department provided that there is a match between the deptno column in the emp table and the deptno column in the dept table.

LOADING/UPDATING THE DATABASE

The purpose of this lab is to continue to introduce you to SQL*PLUS. Log into SQL*PLUS just as in the previous section. Execute the following commands and review the output.

```
11)  insert into dept
     values(50, 'finance', 'los angeles');
```

This will insert the department number, department name and department location into the dept table.

```
12)  insert into emp (empno, ename, hiredate, sal, deptno)
     values (s_ emp_empno.nextval,'lerner','01-jan-
     92',2000,30);
```

This will insert a new record for the new employee's name, Lerner (note that only certain columns are loaded).

```
13)  insert into dept
     values (&deptno, '&dname', '&loc');
```

This will prompt you for the department number, department name and the location. Then the record is inserted into the dept table.

14)
```
update emp
set job = 'salesman', deptno = 30
where empno = 7566;
```

This will change the job title and department number for the employee who has employee number 7566.

15)
```
update emp
set job = 'sales'
where job = 'salesman';
```

This will change the job title salesman to sales. Now try changing it back.

16)
```
select ename, sal, comm, sal+comm from emp
where job = 'salesman'
and comm > .25*sal
order by 4
```

This will display the compensation for salespeople whose commission is greater then 25 percent of their salary (note that the sal and comm columns were added together).

USING SQL*PLUS FUNCTIONS

In the next exercise we want to convert a null value to a non-null value for the purpose of evaluating and expressing the use of the null value function (NVL).

17)
```
select ename, job, sal, comm, nvl (sal, 0) + nvl (comm, 0)
from emp where deptno = 30;
```

Note that if the value of either the sal column or the comm column is null the number zero is returned rather then a null value.

18)
```
select avg(sal), max(sal), sum(sal)
from emp
where job = 'salesman';
```

This will display the average salary, the maximum salary and the sum of the annual salaries for all sales people.

INTRODUCTION TO PL/SQL

Standard ANSI SQL is a nonprocedural language. By nonprocedural we mean that there is no mechanism for creating the decision clauses such as if-then-else and do-while loops for repetitive calculations. PL/SQL is an extension to regular SQL that addresses the nonprocedural nature of SQL. PL/SQL also allows us to execute a program based upon an event occurring.

Programs written in PL/SQL are called subprograms. The three different types of subprograms are:

1. Procedure: A procedure is a program that performs a specific function.
2. Function: A function is similar to a procedure but a function has a return clause.
3. Trigger: A trigger is a stored program that is associated with a specific table and is invoked when a specific event occurs.

PL/SQL PROGRAM/BLOCK LAYOUT

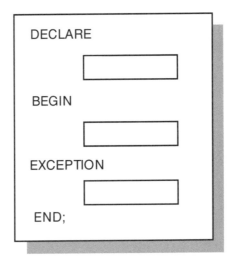

FIGURE B.3   The basic structure for any routine written in PL/SQL

The basic structure for any routine written in PL/SQL is shown in Figure B.3. The block of code between the DECLARE clause and the BEGIN clause is where the programmer defines the variables that will be used in the rest of the program. In short this is where variables are declared. There are various ways to define variables.

Defining Number Variables

```
EXAMPLES

counter              BINARY_INTEGER;
tatal_cost           NUMBER(10,2);
seconds_per_day      CONSTANT NUMBER := 60 * 60 * 24;
final_cost           NUMBER(11,0) :=0;
```

Defining Character Variables

```
EXAMPLES

first_name           VARCHAR2(15) NOT NULL := 'BROWN';
middle_initial       VARCHAR2;
copmpany_name        CONSTANT VARCHAR2(6) := 'IBM';
```

Defining Date Variables

```
EXAMPLES

hire_date            DATE :='01-FEB-96';
raise_date           DATE;
code_complete        DATE :='23-MAR-99';
```

Defining Boolean Variables

```
EXAMPLE

over_weight          BOOLEAN NOT NULL :=TRUE
absent               BOOLEAN := NULL;
```

The section between the BEGIN clause and the EXCEPTION clause is the body of the code. In the body we can use various SQL*PLUS statements to INSERT/UPDATE/SELECT data. Several examples are shown here:

Insert Example

```
DECLARE

curr_sal             NUMBER(9,2)  := 4040.00;
my_name              VARCHAR2(20)    := 'FRED';
hiredate             DATE  := '05-may-94';
```

```
BEGIN
INSERT INTO emp (empno,ename,job,hiredate,sal,deptno)
VALUES (3000,my_name,'PRESIDENT',hiredate,curr_sal,40);

END;
```

Update Example

```
DECLARE

max_value      CONSTANT NUMBER := 3000;
ok_cust        VARCHAR2(8) := 'OK';

BEGIN
UPDATE table_accounts ser credit_limit = max_value
WHERE status = 'EMP' OR status = ok_cust;

END;
```

Delete Example

```
DECLARE

my_year        NUMBER := 1860;

BEGIN

DELETE FROM my_table
where year < my_year;

END;
```

PL/SQL also allows us to code decision clauses into our program based on IF-THEN-ELSE logic. In the following example a test is set up to determine the number of acting jobs a particular actor has had. If the actor has had more than 75 jobs their rating is set to "Waiter" in the table called "actor." Note that the ELSIF clause can be used to specify further testing conditions for the number of jobs the actor has had (num_jobs).

If-Then-Else Example

```
DECLARE

num_jobs      NUMBER(8);
actor_id      NUMBER(4) := 1111;

BEGIN

SELECT COUNT(*) INTO num_jobs FROM auditions
WHERE actorid = actor_id AND called_back = 'YES';

IF num_jobs > 90 THEN

  UPDATE actor SET actor_rating = 'OSCAR winner'
  WHERE actorid=actor_id;

ELSIF num_jobs > 75 THEN

  UPDATE actor SET actor_rating = 'Daytime TV';
ELSE

  UPDATE actor SET actor_rating = 'Dish washer'
  WHERE actorid = actor_id;

END IF;

COMMIT;

END;
```

Simple Loop Example

Simple loops can also be coded using PL/SQL. The statements between the LOOP statement and the END LOOP statement will be executed until the exit condition is reached. The following examples show two different ways to code simple loops.

```
DECLARE

countr   number(4)   := 0;

BEGIN

LOOP
```

```
INSERT INTO my_table
   VALUES (countr, 'THE COUNT IS FINISHED');
    countr = countr + 1;

        IF countr = 66 THEN
            EXIT;
        END IF;

END LOOP;

END;
```

CURSORS

PL/SQL data can be stored in a program structure called a cursor. Therefore the declaration for a cursor must be in the DECLARE section of the code. In the code segment below the cursor name is called c1. The cursor "x" is created from a query against the emp table.

```
DECLARE

g_total             NUMBER(5);
sal_top_limit       CONSTANT NUMBER(5) :=89000;

CURSOR x1 S SELECT ename FROM emp
   WHERE sal > sal_top_limit;

BEGIN
OPEN x1;
 .
 .      ------- program body
 .
CLOSE x1;
END;
```

Notice that before the cursor could be used it must first be opened (in the body of the program). Prior to the END statement all open cursors should be closed.

The cursor is accessed in the body of the program. To access the cursor, we use the instruction "FETCH." In the following examples we access information from our cursor. To exit from the loop we use the PL/SQL functions %NOTFOUND and %FOUND. In the former case, we will exit from the code when all information has been retrieved from the cursor. In the latter example we will continue to FETCH from the cursor as long as there are more rows in the cursor.

```
EXAMPLE 1

LOOP
  FETCH the_cursor INTO my_name, my_comm;
  EXIT WHEN the_cursor%NOTFOUND;
    ---- more program processing
END LOOP;

EXAMPLE 2

FETCH the_cursor INTO my_name, my_sal;
WHILE the_cursor%FOUND LOOP
       ------- more program processing
  FETCH the_cursor INTO my_name, my_sal;
END LOOP;
```

The PL/SQL procedure that follows is used to illustrate how a PL/SQL program can be developed. In this example the purpose of the procedure is to calculate the percentage of space used in the system tablespace. The reader should take note of the following sections in the code.

❏ The DECLARE statement has been replaced with the statement CREATE OR REPLACE PROCEDURE followed by the procedure name.

❏ All variables and cursors are defined in the section between the CREATE OR REPLACE PROCEDURE statement.

❏ The cursors must be opened before they can be used and closed before the program ends.

❏ The program uses a simple loop. The program will break out of the loop when all the rows of data have been "fetched" from the cursor.

❏ The PL/SQL utility DBMS_OUTPUT is used to write output to the screen.

The procedure must first be placed into the database. When the procedure is placed into the database its syntax is checked. If a syntax error occurs the programmer can get debug information by.

❏ Reviewing the source code. The source code for all PL/SQL routines is stored in the table USER_SOURCE. The source can be obtained by issuing the statement: select name, text from user_source;

❏ Reviewing the errors in the code by querying the table USER_ERRORS. All errors generated by PL/SQL routines are stored in the table USER_ERRORS. The following query can be issued to get the errors that occurred when the PL/SQL routine was placed into the database (these are syntax errors not program logic errors).

```
select name,type,line,position,text
from user_erros
where type = 'PROCEDURE' and name = 'PCT_SYSTEM';
```

To execute the procedure the user would enter the following after starting SQL*PLUS (shown in Display B.1).

```
SQLPLUS> set serveroutputon

SQLPLUS> @ pct_system

SQLPLUS> execute pct_system;

SQLPLUS> drop procedure pct_system;
```

DISPLAY B.1

❏ The command set server output on allows SQL*PLUS to send the PL/SQL output to the screen.

❏ The command @pct_system will place the procedure into the database and check its syntax.

❏ The command execute pct_system will run the procedure.

❏ The command drop procedure pct_system will drop/remove the procedure from the database.

```
CREATE OR REPLACE procedure pct_system IS
    free_bytes     number;
    total_free     number := 0;
    total_bytes    number := 0;
    tot_bytes      number;
    pct_used       number(10,4) := 0;
    CURSOR freesp IS
    select bytes from sys.dba_free_space where
  tablespace_name = 'SYSTEM';
    CURSOR totalsp IS
    select bytes from sys.dba_data_files where
  tablespace_name = 'SYSTEM';
BEGIN
    open freesp;
```

```
     open totalsp;
  loop
    fetch freesp into free_bytes;
    exit when freesp%notfound;
    total_free := total_free + free_bytes;
  end loop;
  loop
    fetch totalsp into tot_bytes;
    exit when totalsp%notfound;
    total_bytes := total_bytes + tot_bytes;
  end loop;
    close freesp;
    close totalsp;
    pct_used := ((1-(total_free/total_bytes))*100);
   dbms_output.put_line ('system tablespace total free space
   in BYTES = ' || total_free);
dbms_output.put_line ('system tablespace total size in BYTES
    = ' || total_bytes);
dbms_output.put_line ('percentage of system tablespace stor-
    age used = ' || pct_used);
END pct_system;
```

OBJECT-ORIENTED SQL

Object technology is a way to develop and package software that draws heavily from common experience and the manner in which real-world objects relate to each other. In this book the term object oriented is used to include all software products that support this technology.

The concept of *object* in software development has its origin in the modeling of everyday objects and the way they interact. At the simplest level an object is something that can be identified by a name. An object has certain properties that can be used to describe it, which is referred to as the object's state. Or to put it in object technology terms the object has "state." An object will behave in a given way in response to a given stimulus, therefore it has *behavior*. A software object is the counterpart of one in the real world. It too has state and behavior, expressed in the form of *data* and *procedures*.

Everyday objects communicate with each other by sending and responding to signals or *messages*. Software objects also communicate through the passing of messages. These messages are matched against the objects and procedures involved and the appropriate action is taken.

Human beings group everyday objects into *classes* with similar properties in order to relate one object to another. If we say an object is an envelope, for example, we know a lot about it without knowing exactly what kind of envelope it may be. Software objects that share common properties are also grouped into classes.

Finally, classes of everyday objects are themselves related in a *hierarchy*. They may inherit general features from classes that are above them in the hierarchy, known as *superclass*. A superclass contains other classes, its *subclasses*. Envelopes, for example, are a superclass that includes business envelopes. In the same way, containers form a superclass that includes envelopes, file folders and mailboxes among its subclasses. Software classes may also inherit data and procedures through a class hierarchy.

An object-oriented system (OOS) is defined as one that combines four important features:

1. Data and procedures are combined in software objects
2. Messages are used to communicate with these objects
3. Similar objects are grouped into classes
4. Data and procedures are inherited through a class hierarchy

These features can be implemented in a variety of ways. The main benefit of object technology is its approach to software development rather then the method of implementation.

In Oracle8 objects are organized into types. The Oracle8 type system extends the Oracle7 type system (which consists of scalar built-in types like NUMRER, DATE, VARCHAR) to include two new built-in types REF and LOB, and user-defined types called collections (varray and nested table) and object types. The Oracle8 SQL Data Definition Language (DDL.) has three new statements. They are CREATE TYPE, ALTER TYPE, and DROP TYPE. The CREATE TYPE statement allows users to define named collection types and object types. The ALTER TYPE statement allows users to add methods to and to recompile existing object types. The DROP TYPE statement allows users to delete existing user-defined types that have no data (table) dependency.

The dependency model for types is basically the same as that for PL/SQL procedures with extensions to handle data (i.e., table) dependency and cyclic dependency graphs. The dependency model for types categorizes dependencies into HARD and REF. Mutual referencing types are allowed while cyclic value types are prohibited.

Oracle8 SQL DDE provides new system privileges for user-defined types including CREATE TYPE, CREATE ANY TYPE, ALTER ANY TYPE, DROP ANY TYPE, and EXECUTE ANY TYPE. The EXECUTE ANY PROCEDURE system privilege is applicable to all member subprograms. The EXECUTE object privilege is applicable to types. The Oracle8 GRANT and REVOKE statements allow users to grant and revoke the new system and object privileges for types. Oracle8 allows auditing system privilege options CREATE TYPE, CREATE ANY TYPE, ALTER ANY TYPE, and DROP ANY TYPE, and auditing statement options TYPE and GRANT TYPE.

It is often easier for applications to model their problems using object-oriented models rather than using the relational model. Oracle8 bridges the mismatch between application model and the RDBMS model by extending the RDBMS programmatic interfaces to provide object-oriented programming interfaces. The Oracle8 object model organizes objects into types, and extends the Oracle7 type system to include two new built-in types, namely, REF and LOB, and user-defined types (UDTs), namely, named collection (varray and nested table) and object types.

The Oracte8 SQL DDE provides a new facility for defluing and managing named collection and object types through the CREATE TYPE, ALTER TYPE, and DROP TYPE statements. Oracle8 extends the Oracle7 program-dependency model to handle table dependency on type and cyclic type dependency graphs. The Oracle8 SQL DDL also supports new system and object privileges on types as well as new system privilege and statement auditing options.

THE CREATE TYPE STATEMENT

The CREATE TYPE statement provides users the ability to create new or replace existing UDTs. A UDT can be declared by name as the type of an attribute, a column variable, parameter, and function result.

A REF is a reference to an object. A LOB (Large Object) is a set of contiguous octets (uninterpreted bytes). Both REF and LOB can be declared as types of attributes, columns, variables, parameters, and function results.

An object can also be described as a set of named components, called attributes, and an associated set of operations, called member subprograms (functions and procedures). An attribute consists of a name and a type which can be either a built-in or a user-defined type; furthermore, when the type of an attribute is an object type, the type may be qualified with a REF. A member subprogram is either a PL/SQL function or procedure. The user may define at most one of either a MAP or ORDER member function. This is used by Oracle8 to determine the relative ordering of all instances of the object type.

A varray is a collection of objects that have a variable length and are of the same type; each object in the collection is called an element. The type of a varray element can be either a built-in type, except the LOB type, or an object type any attribute of which must not be a nested table type. Each array element can be selected and assigned by a unique index that is an integer ranging from 1 to N where N is the current number of elements in the varray; there may optionally be a maximum number of varray elements.

A nested table is a relational table that has been extended to be used as variables, parameters, function results, object type attributes, and as columns of other tables.

All types referenced in a UDT (e.g., in attribute declaration) should be previously defined. If a referencing type OT1 contains a reference to a type OT2 that is not yet defined, then Oracle8 issues a warning that type TR must be declared; type OT1 is called an incomplete type. Type TR must be defined some time later in order for type OT1 to ever become valid. Type TR may contain references to type OT1; both types are called mutually referencing types (MRTs). Oracle8 prohibits MRTs whose attributes are all values, that is, type Ti contains an attribute whose type is type TR and type TR contains an attribute whose type is type OT1. Oracle8 allows MRTs at least one of the attributes of REF (e.g., either the type of OT1 attribute is REF TR, or the type of TR attribute is REF OT1).

The CREATE TYPE statement is similar to the CREATE PACKAGE statement. The CREATE TYPE statement specifies the attributes and the signatures for any associated member subprograms of an object type. There is a corresponding CREATE TYPE BODY statement that specifies the definitions or implementations for the member subprograms of the object type; the CREATE TYPE BODY statement also allows replacing existing and adding new member subprograms. For named collection types, the CREATE TYPE statement just specifies the type name of the collection type.

To create or replace a UDT in the user's own schema, the user must have CREATE TYPE or CREATE ANY TYPE system privilege. To create a UDT in another user's schema, the user must have CREATE ANY TYPE system privilege. To replace a UDT in another user's schema, the user must have DROP ANY TYPE system privilege.

CREATE TYPE EXAMPLES

Following are some examples of how to use the CREATE TYPE.

Example 1

The following example creates object type PERSON_T with LOB attributes.

```
CREATE TYPE person_t AS OBJECT
(name CHAR(20),
resume CLOB,
picture BLOB);
```

Example 2

The following example creates two mutually referencing types

```
CREATE TYPE account_t AS OBJECT
(id NUMBER,
customer REF customer_t);

CREATE TYPE customer_t AS OBJECT
(name VARCHAR2(50)
account REF account_t):
```

The type account_t is an incomplete type since it contains a reference to type customer_t which is not yet defined when type account_t is defined.

Example 3

The following statement creates MY_VARRAY as a VARRAY type with 100 elements of type.

```
CHAR(5):

CREATE TYPE my_varray AS VARRAY(100) OF CHAR(5);
```

Example 4

The following example creates a named table type PROJECT_TABLE of object type PROJECT_T.

```
CREATE TYPE project_t AS OBJECT
(pno CHAR(5),
pname CHAR(20),
budgets DEC(7,2));

CREATE TYPE project_table AS TABLE OF project_t;
```

THE ALTER TYPE STATEMENT

The ALTER TYPE statement allows users to add new member subprogram specifications to an existing object type using the REPLACE option, or to explicitly recompile user-defined types' specifications and/or bodies using the COMPILE option. The ALTER TYPE statement with the REPLACE option requires the user to provide all the existing attributes and member subprogram specifications as well as the additional member subprogram specifications.

To alter a UDT in the user's own schema, the user must have CREATE TYPE or CREATE ANY TYPE system privileges. Otherwise, the user must have ALTER ANY TYPE system privilege.

ALTER TYPE EXAMPLES

Following are some examples of how to use the ALTER TYPE statement.

Example 1

In the following example, member function QTR is added to the type definition of DATA_T.

```
CREATE TYPE data_t (derive NUMBER,
MEMBER FUNCTION prod(invent NUMBER,
prodcode CHAR) RETURN NUMBER);

CREATE TYPE BODY data_t
(MEMBER FUNCTION prod(invent NUMBER
prodcode CHAR) RETURN NUMBER IS
BEGIN
RETURN (year + invent);
END;);

ALTER TYPE data_t REPLACE
(derive NUMBER,
MEMBER FUNCTION prod(invent NUMBER,
prodcode CHAR) RETURN NUMBER);
MEMBER FUNCTION qtr(der_qtr DATE) RETURN CHAR;

CREATE OR REPLACE TYPE BODY data_t

(MEMBER FUNCTION prod(invent NUMBER,
prodcode CHAR) RETURN NUMBER IS
BEGIN
RETURN (year + invent);
END;);

(MEMBER FUNCTION qtr(der_qtr DATE) RETURN CHAR IS
BEGIN
RETURN FIRST';
END;);
```

Example 2

```
CREATE TYPE link1 (a NUMBER);

CREATE TYPE link2
(a NUMBER,
 b link1
 MEMBER FUNCTION p(cl NUMBER) RETURN NUMBER);

CREATE TYPE BODY link2
(MEMBER FUNCTION p(cl NUMBER) RETURN NUMBER IS t13 link1;
BEGIN t13 := linkl(13);
dbms~output.pu_line(t13.a); RETURN 5;
END;);
```

The following example recompiles type (both specification and body) LINK2.

```
ALTER TYPE link2 COMPILE;
```

The following example compiles the type specification of LINK2.

```
ALTER TYPE link2 COMPILE SPECIFICATION;
```

The following example compiles the type body of LINK2.

```
ALTER TYPE link2 COMPILE BODY;
```

THE DROP TYPE STATEMENT

The DROP TYPE statement allows users to drop existing UDTs; the FORCE option is required to drop mutually referencing types. The DROP TYPE BODY statement allows users to drop an object type's body.

To drop a UDT in the user's own schema, the user must have CREATE TYPE or CREATE ANY TYPE system privilege. Otherwise, the user must have DROP ANY TYPE system privilege.

Following are some examples of how to use the DROP TYPE statement.

❏ The following statement removes object type (both specification and body) PERSON_T.

```
DROP TYPE person_t
```

The following statement removes object type body LINK2.

```
DROP TYPE BODY link2;
```

THE TYPE DEPENDENCY MODEL

The dependency model for types (i.e., what are the behaviors of dependents on a type when the type's status changes, e.g., when the type is dropped, altered, replaced, or recompiled) is basically the same as that of PL/SQL procedures except for two major differences. Tables can depend on types, and mutually referencing types form cyclic dependency graphs. Oracle8 categorizes type dependencies into data type dependencies and program type dependencies; data type dependencies are dependencies that tables have on types, and program type dependencies are dependencies that programs (i.e., functions, procedures, packages, or views) have on a type. To prevent data from becoming invalid, types with data dependencies cannot be dropped.

In Oracle7, an object (procedure, function, package, etc.) is valid without compilation error only if all objects it depends on are also valid without compilation error. Based on the Oracle7 dependency rule, two mutually referencing types are depending on each other such that it is not possible for both to become valid without compilation error after both entered the invalid states.

To support mutually referencing types, Oracle8 enhances the Oracle7 procedure dependency rule for types as follows. Dependencies are categorized into HARD and REF dependencies. Type Td has a REF dependency on type Tp if type Td references type Tp as "REF Tp" (e.g., type Td has an attribute whose type is "REF Tp") otherwise type Td has a HARD dependency on type Tp. Type Td is called the dependent and type Tp is called the parent. A type becomes valid without compilation error only if all its HARD type parents are valid without compilation error, and only if all its REF type parents already existed (i.e., been defined) regardless of their states (i.e., they may be invalid).

When a type specification Td (HARD or REF) depends on a type specification, Tp is compiled. Type Td is in error (i.e., valid with compilation errors) if type Tp has not been defined. Later, when type Tp is defined, Oracle8 invalidates type Td; this behavior is the same as for procedures in Oracle7. The major difference between Oracle8 and Oracle7 is the invalidation and revalidation rules. When a type Tp is recompiled (through automatic revalidation or explicitly through the ALTER TYPE with COMPILE option) Oracle8 invalidates only HARD type dependents of type Tp and not the REF type dependents of type Tp because the existence status of type Tp has not been changed (even though type T's valid/invalid status might have been changed); similarly, Oracle8 only automatically tries to revalidate HARD type parents of type Tp. When type Tp is dropped, Oracle8 invalidates all direct (HARD and REF) type dependents because type Tp's existence status has changed (Tp no longer exists). When Oracle8 invalidates a type, it also recursively invalidates only indirect HARD type dependents and not the indirect REF dependents since their parents' existence statuses have not changed.

CREATING PRIVILEGES AND AUDITING TYPES

To create, alter, or drop a type, the user must have the required system privileges. Oracle8 extends the GRANT and REVOKE DDL statements to include new system privileges for types. Specifically, the system privilege option for the GRANT and REVOKE statement now includes the CREATE TYPE, CREATE ANY TYPE, ALTER ANY TYPE, DROP ANY TYPE, and EXECUTE ANY TYPE system privileges.

The CREATE TYPE system privilege allows the grantee to create, alter, and drop type specifications and type bodies in his own schema. The CREATE ANY TYPE system privilege allows the grantee to create type specifications and type bodies in any schema as well as alter and drop type specifications and type bodies in his own schema. The ALTER ANY TYPE system privilege allows the grantee to alter any type specification and type body in any schema. The DROP ANY TYPE system privilege allows the grantee to drop any type specification and type body in any schema.

To use a user-defined type in an object (e.g., as the type of an attribute, or the type of a column) in a schema, either the type is in that schema or the owner of the schema has been granted the EXECUTE privilege on the type. Once the EXECUTE object privilege on a type Tl is granted to a grantee, the grantor cannot revoke the EXECUTE object privilege on that type if there are any type or table dependents on type Tl created by the grantee. Oracle8 extends the GRANT and REVOKE DDL statements to include the EXECUTE object privilege on user-defined types.

Following are some examples of how to use the GRANT and REVOKE statements.

❑ The following statement grants the CREATE TYPE system privilege to user Scott.

```
GRANT create type TO scott;
```

❑ The following statement revokes the CREATE TYPE system privilege from user Scott.

```
REVOKE create type FROM scott;
```

❑ The following statement grants the EXECUTE object privilege on type person_t to user scott.

```
GRANT execute ON person_t TO scott;
```

❑ The following statement revokes the EXECUTE object privilege on type person_ t from scott.

```
REVOKE execute ON person t FROM scott;
```

The AUDIT statement has also been extended for types. The TYPE statement option is for choosing the

❏ CREATE TYPE

❏ CREATE TYPE BODY

❏ ALTER TYPE

❏ ALTER TYPE BODY

❏ DROP TYPE

❏ DROP TYPE BODY

Statements for auditing the TYPE option are included in the ALL option. The GRANT TYPE statement option is for choosing the GRANT <privilege> ON <type> and the REVOKE <privilege> ON <type> statements for auditing. The CREATE TYPE, CREATE ANY TYPE, ALTER ANY TYPE, and DROP ANY TYPE system privilege options are for auditing the uses of these statements. For each AUDIT option for type there is a corresponding NOAUDIT option that stops the associated auditing.

DBAWARE REFERENCE

DBAWARE INSTALLATION INSTRUCTIONS

Follow the steps below to install and configure your copy of DBAware 2.0. The install and configuration process should take about 15 minutes.

I. INSTALL DBAWARE (REQUIRED STEP—ALL PLATFORMS)

1. **Refer to the separate section titled "System Requirements," and verify that the target machine meets the minimum requirements.**
2. Start Windows.
3. Insert the DBAware CD-ROM into the appropriate drive.
4. **Note: This step applies to MS-Windows 3.1 platforms only**. If you have not already done so, install WIN32S 1.30a which is included on the DBAware CD-ROM. **WIN32S MUST be installed before you install DBAware.**

   To install WIN32S from the DBAware CD-ROM:

   a. Select Run from the Program Manager File menu
   b. Enter "x:" in the Command Line (where "x" is the letter of the CD-ROM drive)
   c. Select OK.

5. Select Run from the Program Manager File menu. The Run dialog box appears.

6. In the Command Line enter:

   a.   Windows 3.1: "x:", or

   b.   Windows NT, Win95: "x:" (where "x" is the letter of the CD-ROM drive).

7. Select OK. A dialog window gives a brief overview of the installation process.

8. Select Continue. A dialog window appears requesting the name of the directory in which to install the DBAware files. If the pathname you supply is already occupied, be sure to make a backup copy of the old files.

9. Accept the default pathname, or enter another pathname. Click the Continue button. A set of meters show the progress of the installation. The leftmost vertical meter shows the percentage of the current file that has been installed. The center vertical meter shows the percentage of the CD-ROM files that have been installed. The rightmost vertical meter shows the percentage of available disk space on the target drive. The horizontal meter shows the percentage of the total installation that has been done.

Upon completion of the DBAware installation process, DBAware will create either a Program Group (Windows 3.1, NT) or a shortcut entry in the Start->Programs menu (Win95). The working directory will be set to: c:, and the command line will be: "c:.exe—logo:dbaware.bmp c:.im."

II. RDBMS DLL (REQUIRED STEP—ALL PLATFORMS)

In order to access any database, DBAware must call the appropriate DLLs. The directory where these DLLs are stored must be in DBAware's search path. Secondly, the user must designate which DLLs to use. To designate the appropriate DLLs:

1. Start DBAware.

2. Select "File -> Preferences…" to open a window containing a notebook widget. Click on the "RDBMS DLL" tab.

3. Enter the names of the RDBMS DLLs in the appropriate windows.

4. Select "Accept."

III. ARCHIVE DATA (REQUIRED STEP—ALL PLATFORMS)

DBAware archives data into a database. To do this the user must first build two tables and a trigger in the database chosen to hold the archive data. Secondly, the user must "tell" DBAware where to locate the archive data tables. The following steps describe how to accomplish these two steps.

1. Determine which database instance will hold the archive data.
2. Edit the appropriate script, if desired, to alter the amount of archive data stored per DBAware query—the default is 100. Edit..dbaware.ora for an Oracle instance or..dbaware.syb for a Sybase instance.
3. Run the appropriate script for the archive db connection (dbaware1.ora for an Oracle instance or dbaware1.syb for a Sybase instance). Two tables will be created in the archive database: dba_archive_key and dba_archive_data.
4. Start DBAware, if necessary.
5. **Define a database connection object (db connection) to represent the archive database chosen in Step 1.** To define a db connection, click on the first button in DBAware Launcher menu bar—the four green stacked disks.
6. Enter the appropriate information in ALL fields. **Note: DBAware is limited to the permission and resource quotas of the username/password entered in the db connection object.** When done hit enter or click on OK. A symbol representing the database should appear in the DBAware Launcher status area.
7. Test whether DBAware can access the db connection and enter data. Place the cursor **directly** over the db connection symbol. Click **and hold** the right mouse button. A menu will appear under the cursor. Place the cursor over the "Open Ad Hoc Query Tool" menu entry, and release the right mouse button. The Ad Hoc Query Tool window will open, and it will attempt to connect to the database using the information entered in Step 6.
8. Verify that the username/password used by the archive db connection has the necessary permissions to insert and delete rows in the dba_archive_key and dba _archive_data tables. **Hint:** Use the Ad Hoc Query Tool to insert and delete a row in the dba_archive_key table.

IV. TIME ZONE PREFERENCE (REQUIRED STEP—ALL PLATFORMS)

Time plays a very important role in database monitoring. To designate the correct time for DBAware, complete the following steps.

1. Start DBAware, if necessary.
2. Select "File -> Preferences..." to open a window containing a notebook widget. Click the "Time Zones" tab.
3. Select the appropriate time zone settings for you geographical location and time zone.
4. **Verify that time zone settings are correct.** The best way to do this is by examining **all** of the settings on the Time Zone preference page, **and** by examining the time displayed at the bottom of the launcher window.
5. Click on "Accept."

Congratulations! You have successfully installed DBAware 2.0. Start the DBAware tutorial to begin to explore the internals of your database.

TUNING AN ORACLE RDBMS—ONE VIEW

Paul Osborn *Menlo Software*

Although no single database tuning methodology is optimal or complete for every installation, this methodology is designed to work at most sites and with most applications. Its focus is to accomplish the greatest increase in performance with the least amount of effort. Finally, this approach focuses on empirical data to measure performance—not abstract measurements. Note that all query names given below refer to queries described on the Menlo Software web page: http://www.menlosoftware.com.

Tuning a database is an ongoing process, and I would argue that there are at least four distinct phases to tuning:

1. Checking/tuning the init.ora parameters
2. Running and recording benchmarks
3. Monitoring and archiving performance data
4. Optimizing end-user SQL. Most sites don't perform all of the above steps, and, consequently, these sites have an incomplete understanding of their database internals.

Some of the reasons most sites don't regularly tune, benchmark, monitor, and optimize end-user SQL:

1. It's tedious
2. Believe effort will return little result
3. Production constraints (24x7 operation)
4. Other priorities (backup/restore, security, etc.)
5. Don't know how

Each step of tuning a database provides unique benefits. For example, checking/tuning the init.ora parameters is the fastest, easiest—i.e. cheapest—way to boost performance. Running and recording benchmarks enables the DBA to objectively measure the effects of changing the init.ora parameters, develop a record of a db/application's response time, and triage which SQL statements to optimize. Monitoring and archiving performance data is the only way to know what is currently happening in the database, and it improves the DBA's ability to more accurately estimate future resource demands. Tuning the end-user SQL holds the greatest potential performance gains.

CHECKING/TUNING THE INIT.ORA PARAMETERS

Checking the init.ora file consists of periodically checking as many init.ora parameters as practical and tuning the SGA size, the DB Block buffer size, and the Shared Pool size. When performing a check of the init.ora file, the DBA attempts to determine whether any init.ora parameters may be reset to give an immediate boost in database performance.

The determination of how many init.ora parameters to check and how often, is a judgment call made by the DBA. Critical inputs to the judgment include: is the database slow, how often does existing data change, has the size of the database changed significantly, how many people have DBA privileges, has the number of users changed significantly, has the nature of the application changed significantly, etc. Generally, the more dynamic the situation, the more init.ora parameters should be checked and the more frequent the inspections.

The first thing I recommend examining is the size of the SGA—equal to the amount returned by: select sum(value) from v$sga. Generally, make the SGA as large as possible as long as it will still fit in real memory without the operating system swapping or paging parts of the SGA.

The two init.ora parameters that I generally find to have the greatest effect on database performance are: DB_BLOCK_BUFFERS and SHARED_POOL_SIZE. I am not minimizing the importance of correctly setting other init.ora parameters, but often times by tuning these parameters you can realize an immediate impact on the performance of your database.

Before describing exactly how to tune the DB_BLOCK_BUFFERS and SHARED_POOL_SIZE init.ora parameters, I need to define the term: benchmark query. I define a benchmark query as an SQL select statement that returns the amount of time the SQL statement took to execute rather than the result set. The SQL statements I consider the best candidates for benchmark queries are end-user SQL select statements that execute frequently and generate moderate amounts of logical I/O per execution. To capture the SQL statement currently generating the greatest amount of logical I/O per execution, execute the SQL statement

The technique I recommend to tune any init.ora parameter is to:

1. Run a suite of benchmark queries and save the results
2. Change the init.ora parameter
3. Restart the database
4. Rerun the same suit of benchmark queries under the same conditions
5. Was there a significant performance increase?
   Yes: Repeat Steps 1 through 5.
   No: Reset the init.ora parameter to the prior setting and restart the database.

To tune the db block buffer cache, use the benchmark tuning technique and increase the size of the DB_BLOCK_BUFFERS init.ora parameter by 5–25 percent.

The shared pool contains the library cache, the dictionary cache, and some session information if you are using multithreaded servers. Tuning the shared pool involves first tuning the library cache and subsequently tuning the dictionary cache.

Library cache information is stored in the v$librarycache table. The table begins accumulating statistics from scratch every time the database is restarted. The goal is to completely eliminate the number of SQL statement reloads—a SQL statement reparse and reallocation to a new shared SQL area—while your application is running. SQL statements "sharedPoolReloadCount" and "sharedPoolReloadRatio" will measure the SQL statement reloads. If your instance is experiencing reloads increase the SHARED_POOL_SIZE init.ora parameter.

Dictionary cache information is stored in the v$rowcache table, and like the v$librarycache table, it begins accumulating statistics from scratch every time the database is restarted. Only attempt to tune this cache after your application has been running long enough to build meaningful statistics in the v$rowcache table. A data dictionary cache miss should occur less than ten percent of the time under normal circumstances. Also, the percentage of misses should not increase while your application is running. If either of these conditions exist, you should increase the size of the SHARED_POOL_SIZE init.ora parameter.

Queries designed to monitor the efficiency of the server's caches should be grouped and run simultaneously. This provides a more accurate snapshot of the database's internals at a single point in time.

While this is certainly not an exhaustive list of actions one could take to spot check a database's performance, the above steps should be part of any Oracle server optimization process.

RUNNING AND RECORDING BENCHMARKS

As mentioned before, I define a benchmark query as an SQL statement that returns the amount of time it took to execute rather than a result set. The ideal benchmark queries are typical end-user SQL statements that run frequently and generate a moderate amount of logical I/O. Ideally, the benchmarks would run at regular times during every workday.

In addition to objectively measuring the effects of changing the init.ora parameters (described above), running and recording benchmark queries enables a DBA to document a server's performance and establish a baseline. By establishing a server's baseline the DBA can prove how much of a server's "load" is due to a specific application. Also, when a user claims that "the system is slow," the DBA can definitively measure the extent of the performance degradation. To establish a server or application's baseline, run a suite of benchmark queries while no application or only the target application executes and archive the results.

To determine whether to optimize a SQL statement:

1. Run the SQL statement as a benchmark query during a period of high system load—typically during business hours.

2. Run the SQL statement as a benchmark query during a period of nil system load—typically immediately after a cold backup—*without any other application(s) running.*

3. Interpret the results as follows:
   If an SQL statement executes, for example, during business hours in four minutes, but executes during the night in 15 seconds, then this SQL statement is not a good candidate for optimization, as perfect optimization could only save 15 seconds out of four minutes.

CONTINUOUS MONITORING

To be able to accurately predict what may happen within the database in the future, the DBA must monitor the database. Effective database monitoring requires the following 5 elements.

1. Meaningful measurements
2. Accurate measurements
3. At regular intervals
4. Over a period of time
5. Archive the data

The above five elements provide the DBA with a meaningful, accurate body of data—evidence—that can be used to more accurately predict future requirements.

The ideal place to archive the performance data is back into the database. This enables the performance data to be retrieved with SQL, backed up along with the database, and accessible to all IS staff.

The two essential measurements that every DBA should monitor include tablespace free space and extents. Oracle returns an error when a tablespace does not contain enough free space for Oracle to dynamically allocate an extent to a requesting table or index (ORA-1547). For example, if a tablespace contains 10M of free space but a table or index in that tablespace requests an extent with the size greater than 10M, Oracle will return an error to the session attempting to insert a row into that table. The DBA may easily avoid this error as long as the DBA monitors tablespace free space on a regular basis.

Although it is not always practical to do so, tables and indexes should ideally occupy contiguous file space, i.e. one extent. Multiple extents adversely impact I/O, and the DBA should monitor the number of extents used by tables and indexes. If possible, compress tables into one extent via Oracle's Export and Import utilities. Compress indexes, dropping and recreating them with an initial extent of the appropriate size.

By continuously monitoring the database with meaningful and accurate measurements, at regular intervals, over a period of time and archiving the results, the DBA can prevent some database problems from occurring and builds a historical record to make his job easier.

END-USER SQL

Optimizing the end-user's SQL statements requires much time and effort. During this phase of the tuning process, the DBA attempts to verify that the SQL statements actually being run by the end-users are what the application developer anticipated when the application was designed. SQL statements may need restructuring, and indexes may need deletion or construction. Assuming that the DBA does not have the time to optimize every end-user SQL statement, then the DBA must prioritize the end-user SQL statements to optimize. One strategy is to optimize the SQL statement(s) that cause the greatest amount of logical or physical I/O.

To capture the end-user SQL statement causing the most logical or physical I/O per execution:

1. Run the SQL statement "diskReadsLogicalMaxSql" or "diskReadsPhysical-MaxSql" every ten minutes during the time of the day that your system experiences its heaviest load.
2. Archive the results into an Oracle table: Create table sqlTable(sqlText varchar(1000)).

After a week of archiving the end-user SQL statements:

1. Find the statements causing the most disk reads by executing: Select count(distinct) sqlText from sqlTable order by sqlText desc.
2. Benchmark the top five queries.
3. Optimize the top five statements using the Oracle TKPROF and EXPLAIN PLAN utilities (described further in the Oracle Application Developer's Guide).
4. Rerun the benchmarks.
5. Evaluate: was it worth it?

Although this process sounds tedious, and at first it is, I was able to cut the execution time of a batch job to three hours from 15 hours using this technique.

In conclusion then, performance monitoring is an important part of a DBA's responsibilities, and only by accurately measuring a database instance can a DBA know what is happening within that instance. Tuning the init.ora parameters is the easiest and fastest step of the tuning process, but continuously monitoring a database enables a DBA to more accurately predict what will happen within the database. Developing and regularly running a suite of benchmark SQL statements allows the DBA to more efficiently allocate optimization resources. The DBA must first prioritize the SQL statements to be optimized, as optimizing end-user SQL statements requires the most resources during the tuning process.

DBAWARE 2.0 SYSTEM REQUIREMENTS

Thank you for evaluating DBAware! Listed below are the minimum and recommended hardware and software requirements for DBAware 2.0. Please check each item and verify that your system is capable of running DBAware.

I. MINIMUM

Processor: Intel 386, 386SX, 486, or IBM PS/2 Model 70 or 80, and 100 percent compatible computers.

Memory: 640 KB main memory and minimum of **16 MB** of extended memory.

Disk space: Minimum 10 MB free space for the system files, and at least 6.5 MB free space for each user image. Additional disk space is required for archiving data.

Drive (for loading the system): 3.5-inch drive and CD-ROM drive.

Monitor: Any display system having an MS-Windows driver.

Mouse: Any mouse supported by MS-Windows.

Operating System:

> MS-Windows 3.1: MS-DOS 5.0 or greater and **WIN32S**.

> MS-Windows NT: MS-Windows NT 3.51 or 4.0.

> MS-Windows 95: MS-Windows 95.

RDBMS Communication Software:

> Oracle: **SQL*Net 1.1.7.7B or higher**.

> Sybase: **DB-Library 4.2**.

DLL File:

> MS-Windows 3.1, MS-Windows 95: msvcrt40.dll (version: 4.10.6038 or later*) in the...windows subdirectory.

> MS-Windows NT 3.51: msvcrt40.dll (version: 4.10.6038 or later*) in the..winnt subdirectory

> * To check version information:

> a. Locate the msvcrt40.dll file via the search or find commands,

> b. Click on "Properties" and look at the "Product Version" information. You will find the appropriate msvcrt40.dll file in the...directory following installation.

Warning: Use the WIN32 version on Windows NT and 95, and use the WIN32S version in Windows 3.1

II. RECOMMENDED

Processor: Pentium 100mhz+.

Memory: 640 KB main memory *and* **20 MB** of extended memory.

Disk space: Minimum 10 MB free space for the system files, and at least 6.5 MB free space for each user image. Additional disk space is required for archiving data.

Drive (for loading the system): 1.44 MB 3.5-inch drive and CD-ROM drive.

Monitor: A **17+ inch** diagonal display with an MS-Windows driver.

Mouse: A MS-Windows supported mouse with 3 buttons.

Operating System:

MS-Windows 3.1: MS-DOS 5.0 or greater and **WIN32S**.

MS-Windows NT: MS-Windows NT 3.51 or 4.0.

MS-Windows 95: MS-Windows 95.

RDBMS Communication Software:

Oracle: **SQL*Net 1.1.7.7B or higher**.

Sybase: **DB-Library 4.2**.

DBAWARE 2.0 EVALUATION TUTORIAL

Thank you for evaluating DBAware! By following the steps listed below, you will begin to become familiar with DBAware, the most flexible RDBMS monitor available. This tutorial assumes the following:

1. The DBAware installation instructions were completed.
2. DBAware is currently up and running on an MS-Windows client.
3. The client is capable of reaching an RDBMS server via the appropriate RDBMS manufacturer's communications software, e.g. SQL*Net or Open Client.

If a db connection symbol or query name changes color to red in the status area, double-clicking on it will open a window detailing the reason for the error, and advice on how to correct the error. If at any time during this tutorial that occurs, double-click on the query or db connection, correct the error listed, and continue with the tutorial.

The following tutorial assumes an Oracle RDBMS. If you are running another RDBMS, you will still be able to follow the examples.

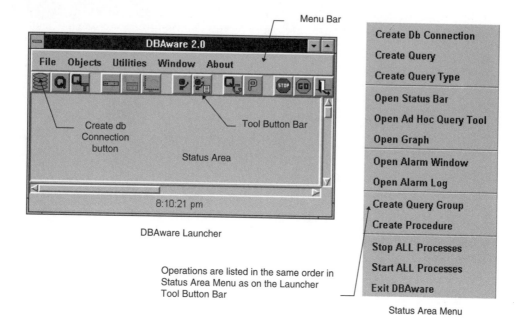

Menu Bar

DBAware Launcher

Create db Connection button

Tool Button Bar

Status Area

Create Db Connection
Create Query
Create Query Type
Open Status Bar
Open Ad Hoc Query Tool
Open Graph
Open Alarm Window
Open Alarm Log
Create Query Group
Create Procedure
Stop ALL Processes
Start ALL Processes
Exit DBAware

Status Area Menu

Operations are listed in the same order in Status Area Menu as on the Launcher Tool Button Bar

CREATING A DB CONNECTION

For DBAware to access an RDBMS, the appropriate username, password, and connect string information must be entered. To create an object to represent an RDBMS server, position the cursor in the Status Area of the DBAware Launcher window and click **and hold** the right mouse button. The Status Area Menu will appear.

While continuing to hold the right mouse button down, position the cursor directly over the first entry—Create Db Connection. The DB Connection—Add window will appear.

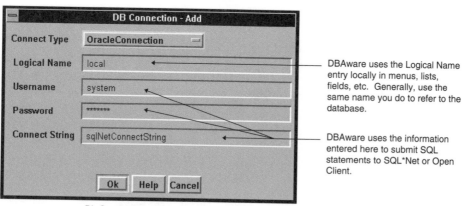

DBAware uses the Logical Name entry locally in menus, lists, fields, etc. Generally, use the same name you do to refer to the database.

DBAware uses the information entered here to submit SQL statements to SQL*Net or Open Client.

Db Connection - Add Window

Enter the appropriate information, i.e. select the appropriate Connect Type, enter a name to represent the database, a correct username/password combination and a correct connect string for SQL*Net or Open Client.

Click on OK, and a symbol representing the db connection will appear in the status area of the DBAware Launcher.

CREATING A QUERY

Place the cursor directly over the blue database symbol, and click and hold the right mouse button. A menu listing common operations will appear directly under the cursor.

Create Query
Open Ad Hoc Query Tool
Querying OFF
Querying ON
Archiving OFF
Archiving ON
Alarm Log Entries
Edit DB Connection
Delete DB Connection

Db Connection Menu

The db connection menu will open. The db connection menu allows you to perform operations associated with the underlying db connection object. Briefly, the menu allows you to set the querying or archiving for all queries associated with the db connection off or on. Also, you can open a window to view all associated alarm log entries. Finally, you can edit the db connection or delete it and all associated queries.

Continue to hold the right mouse button down, position the cursor over the Create Query menu item, and release the mouse button. A Query—Add window will appear.

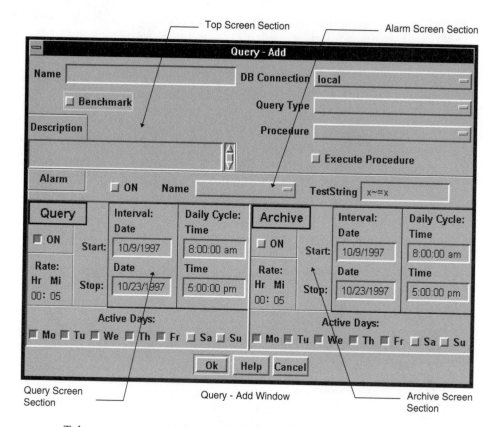

Query - Add Window

Take a moment to look over the Query—Add window. The Query—Add window is organized into four sections: Top, Alarm, Query, and Archive.

In the Top Screen Section, position the cursor over the Query Type menu button, and click and hold the left mouse button. A list of all Query Types—SQL statements—will appear. While continuing to hold the right mouse button down, position the cursor over the third entry—dataDictionaryEfficiency—and release the right mouse button.

The controls in the Query Screen Section allow you to determine when a Query should run against the database. Examining that section now, you can see that the query is turned on and set to run every five minutes over a two-week interval, from 8am to 5pm, Monday through Friday.

Note: One of DBAware's strengths is that it archives data into a single database. If you haven't already done so, please complete the steps found on page three of your installation guide.

The Archive Screen Section controls determine when the data returned by the query is to be archived to the archive database. The restrictions are: the Archive Rate must be a multiple of the Query Rate, and the Archive Interval, Archive Daily Cycle, and Archive Active Days be subsets of their counterparts. For example, if

the query executes every five minutes—Query Rate of five minutes—then the
query may archive the data every 5, 10, 15... minutes. Similarly, if the query only
executes 8am till 5pm it may only archive data during that time.

Click on the Archive On button to start archiving.

If you have the time, click on the Help button and examine the function of the
other widgets—particularly the Benchmark Query Button (a powerful feature).

Sybase users

Use the Help button to examine the functionality provided by the Procedure menu
button and the Procedure button. Also, read._inst.txt now if you have not already
done so.

Click on Ok to save the query.

The Launcher window will update:

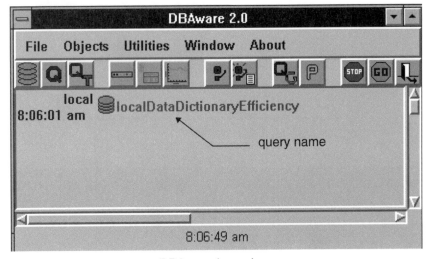

DBAware Launcher

QUERY OPERATIONS

Position the cursor over the query name in the Status Area, and click and hold the
right mouse button. A Query Menu will appear

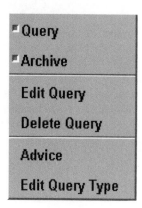

Query Menu

The first two selections allow you to toggle the query and archiving on or off. Edit Query allows you to change the query's parameters. Delete Query will delete the query. Advice opens a window with information from the associated Query Type. Edit Query Type allows you to edit the SQL of the associated Query Type.

Release the mouse button without selecting any options.

Position the cursor over the query name, and double-click on it. A graph window will appear:

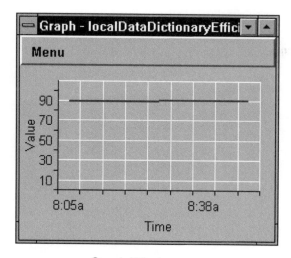

Graph Window

Clicking on the Menu command will open the following menu.

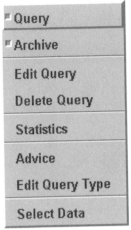

Graph Window Menu

Most of the commands should be familiar to you from the discussion regarding the Query Menu above. The Statistics menu item opens a window that will display statistics on the graph, and the Select Data menu item allows you to have the graph display data from other queries.

DRILL DOWN REPORTS

Position the cursor over the db connection symbol in the Status Area and double-click on it. A drill down reports window will open.

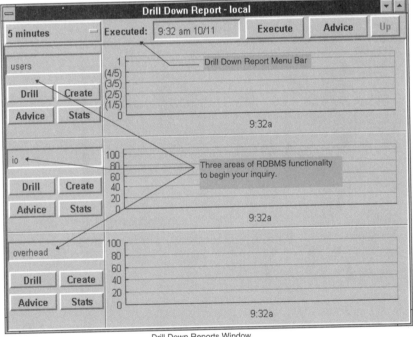

Drill Down Reports Window

The Drill Down Report window allows you to drill down into the different areas of RDBMS functionality. The controls in the Drill Down Report Menu Bar allow you to: set the frequency of the queries, execute the queries immediately, see advice associated with this level of the drill down report, and navigate up to a higher level in the Drill Down Report.

For example, click on the Drill button in the user's area of functionality. The drill down report window will update with new queries all returning information about users.

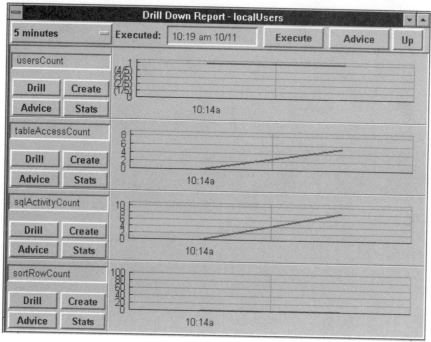

Drill Down Window

Refer back to the buttons located on the left side of the window. The Create buttons will create a query that will operate independently of the Drill Down Report. The Advice buttons will open a window displaying advice for the associated query, and the Stats button will open a window that will display statistics for the associated query.

If you have time now, continue to explore the Drill Down Report.

Close the Drill Down Report window.

AD HOC QUERY TOOL

DBAware contains another tool to facilitate inquiry into your RDBMS internals—the Ad Hoc Query Tool. To open it, position the cursor over the db connection symbol in the Launcher, click and hold the right mouse button, and the db connection menu will appear. Position the cursor over the second menu item, Open Ad Hoc Query Tool, and release the right mouse button.

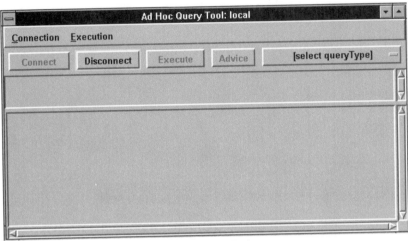

Ad Hoc Query Tool

The Ad Hoc Query Tool window will open with the tool already connected to the database. You can enter you own SQL statements into the middle window and click on the execute button, or you can select one of DBAware's query types by pressing and holding the far right button. For now, use the far right button to select the usersCount query type.

The middle window will populate with the SQL code, and the Ad Hoc Query Tool will immediately execute it.

Leave the window open for now.

CREATING YOUR OWN QUERIES

One other powerful feature of DBAware is the ability to create your own SQL statement. For example, the usersCount query type returned the total number of users logged into this RDBMS. However if you're only interested in the number of users associated with your application or department you need to alter the underlying SQL statement.

To create a new metric, position the cursor immediately before the first letter of the SQL statement in the middle window. Click once, and the entire SQL statement will be highlighted. Now, click and hold the right mouse button to bring up the edit menu.

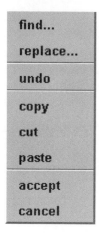

Edit Menu

The edit menu facilitates common operations on text. You can call it up in most, if not all, input and text DBAware fields.

Select copy or cut to move the text into the paste buffer.

Again, leave the Ad Hoc Query Tool window open. Return to the Launcher window, and click on the third button in the Launcher tool bar—the one with a QT. A Query Type—Add window will appear.

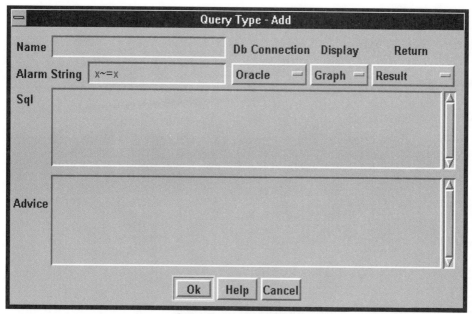

Query Type - Add Window

Place the cursor in the SQL text area and bring up the edit menu again by clicking and holding on the right mouse button. Select paste and release the mouse button. The SQL statement will paste into the SQL text area. Modify the SQL so that it returns the users you are interested in, and type in a unique entry in the Name field. Click on the Ok button to save your work.

Return to the Ad Hoc Query Tool, and click and hold on the query type menu button. You will find your query type listed amongst the others.

Although this concludes the abbreviated tutorial, DBAware contains more functionality—including alarming, reconnection, RDBMS error trapping, etc. If you like, you may download the complete DBAware tutorial from our web site: http:\www.menlosoftware.com Again, thank you for evaluating DBAware 2.0.

PRODUCT SUMMARY

Oracle Corporation offers a wide range of products for reporting, decision support, and application development. The various products interface with the Oracle database management system. The combination of the Oracle RDFBMS with its supporting applications is the reason for the Oracle Corporation's continued dominance in the information technology market.

ORACLE DEVELOPMENT TOOLS

PL/SQL This procedural language extends the standard SQL database language. PL/SQL is tightly integrated with the Oracle Database server. PL/SQL allows for the implementation of looping and branching, in addition to the SQL's capabilities to insert, delete, update and retrieve. Oracle has embedded PL/SQL in all its development products.

Oracle Precompilers The Oracle for UNIX precompilers allows users of standard programming languages to embed native SQL statements within procedural programs. Oracle supports C/C++, COBOL, FORTRAN, And ADA through its precompilers Pro*C/C++, Pro*COBOL, Pro*FORTRAN, Pro*ADA, respectively.

Developer/2000 Oracle Developer is Oracle's development environment for building enterprise class database applications for client/server and the Web. It provides a set of integrated and productive builders that allow developers to construct sophisticated and multilingual database forms, reports, and charts. These components use powerful declarative capabilities to create applications from database definitions without writing a single line of code.

Developer/2000 offers a complete solution when Oracle clients need to design, program, implement, and maintain systems.

Oracle Forms Oracle Forms is a feature-rich application building tool that produces production-quality screens utilizing data stored in the database. The features also include embedding graphics, sound, video, word processing documents and spreadsheets through the use of OLE2.

Oracle Reports Oracle Report is a feature-rich reporting tool that produces production quality output using data sources such as the Oracle database. Developers are able to embed graphics, sound, video and a wide assortment of visual aids in screen and hard-copy (printed) output.

Oracle Graphics Oracle Graphics is an on-line graphical analysis tool. It integrates graphics with relational database technology and provides the user with the ability to easily generate a wide variety of charts. Oracle Graphics includes a runtime module that allows users to create database driven graphical reports.

SQL*Plus SQL*Plus provides an interactive programming interface to the Oracle RDBMS for ad hoc queries, formatting facilities and database creation and manipulation. SQL*Plus is used in the application development process to define database tables, to test SQL statements, and to develop reports.

SQL*Net SQL*Net's sophisticated layered architecture allows standard applications to run transparently over any type of network by simply installing the appropriate Oracle Protocol Adapter.

Designer/2000 Oracle Designer/2000 is a toolset for recording definitions of user needs and automating the rapid construction of flexible, graphical, client/server applications. Integrated with Oracle's Developer/2000, Designer/2000 provides a solution for developing second generation enterprise client/server systems.

CASE*Designer CASE*Designer is a multiwindowed, multitasking graphical development tool. CASE*Designer allows simultaneous access to Oracle's business modeling software.

CASE*Dictionary The Oracle CASE*Dictionary is a distributed, shared, multiuser database, that records all the information and functional needs of the organization, including the design decisions and implementation details.

CASE*Generator The Oracle CASE*Generator creates advanced, working applications using the application development tool SQL*FORMS.

ORACLE APPLICATIONS

Oracle Applications provide for process automation and information access not only for the traditional realm of ERP applications manufacturing and supply chain, financial accounting, and human resources but also for the customer-facing business with integrated applications for Front Office manager.

ORACLE FINANCIALS

Oracle Financials, is a complete finance, accounting, management and human resource application. Oracle Financials consist of several applications including:

Oracle General Ledger Oracle General Ledger is a full-function financial management and accounting application.

Oracle Payables Oracle Payables is an account payables and accounting application.

Oracle Purchasing Oracle Purchasing is a purchasing and accounting application that helps you negotiate bigger discounts, eliminates paper flow, increases your financial control and increases productivity.

Oracle Assets Oracle Assets is an accounting solution that lets you manage your property and equipment by maintaining an accurate asset inventory, select the best tax and accounting strategies for your asset base, compare the adequacy of insurance coverage, and control capital spending.

Oracle Projects Oracle Projects provides a central repository of validated costs, revenue, billing and performance data associated with business activities or projects, facilitating top-line revenue growth and increased bottom-line profitability.

Oracle Manufacturing Oracle Manufacturing is tightly integrated with all Oracle Financial products. Some of the products under Oracle Manufacturing includes Oracle Bill of Materials, Oracle Capacity, Oracle Cost Management, Oracle Work in Process, Oracle MasterScheduling/MRP.

ORACLE HUMAN RESOURCE MANAGEMENT SYSTEM

Oracle HRMS provides the power to maximize the potential of your workforce through effective recruitment, staffing, training, compensation, benefits and planning. Each module is part of a comprehensive suite that provides a unified picture of the HR capital within the enterprise.

Some of the applications include:

Oracle Human Resources Oracle Human Resources is a proactive management solution that helps you control costs while developing and supporting various enterprise organizations.

Oracle Training Administration Oracle Training Administration is designed to support the full range of business activities associated with training and development. Its purpose is to improve the abilities of the employees or external students to meet current and future objectives in a cost-effective and targeted way. Tightly integrated with Career Management functions within the Human Resources applications, Oracle Training Administration is also integrated with the Oracle Financials applications to administer the financial aspects of the training business.

Oracle Payroll Oracle Payroll is a high-performance, graphical, rules-based payroll management system designed to keep pace with the changing needs of the enterprise and the workforce.

BIBLIOGRAPHY

The following manuals and papers where used as reference material.

1. *SQL*Plus. User's Guide and Reference*, Release 3.3 © 1998 Oracle Corporation Part No. A42562-1

2. *Oracle8 Administrators Guide,* © 1998 Oracle Corporation Part No. A58397

3. *Oracle8 Concepts Guide*, Volume 1 and Volume 2 © 1998 Oracle Corporation Part No. A58424

4. *Norther California Oracle Users Group Journal*, Volume 10, Number 3 August 1997.

5. *Inside Windows NT*, Helen Custer © 1993 Microsoft Press ISBN 1-55615-481-X.

6. *Oracle8 Design Tips*, Dave Ensor and Ian Stevenson © 1997 O'Reilly & Associates ISBN 1-56592-361-8.

7. *Oracle Network Products Getting Started*, Deborah Steiner © 1997 Oracle Corporation part number A48747-1.

8. *Oracle Server Space Management*. An Oracle Services Advanced Technologies Research Paper. (part number A00000-0 Revision 1.3 (95/10/03).

9. *Object Technology Sourcebook*, Judith Jeffcoate and Alison Templeton © 1991 Ovum Ltd. ISBN 0 903969 59 9

10. *Oracle8 DBA Handbook*. Kevin Loney © 1998 Osborne/McGraw-Hill ISBN 0-07-8822406-0.

11. *Troubleshooting Internetworking Systems* (© 1993 CISCO SYSTEMS).

INDEX

CBT SOFTWARE LICENSE AGREEMENT

**IF YOU DO NOT AGREE WITH THESE TERMS AND CONDITIONS,
DO NOT INSTALL THE SOFTWARE.**

This is a legal agreement you and CBT System Ltd. ("Licensor"). The licensor ("Licensor") from whom you have licensed the CBT Group PLC courseware (the "Software"). By installing, copying or otherwise using the Software, you agree to be bound by the terms of this Agreement License Agreement (the "License"). If you do not agree to the terms of this License, the Licensor is unwilling to license the Software to you. In such event, you may not use or copy the Software, and you should promptly contact the Licensor for instructions on the return of the unused Software.

1. **Use.** Licensor grants to you a non-exclusive, nontransferable license to use Licensor's software product (the "Software") the Software and accompanying documentation in accordance with the terms and conditions of this license agreement ("License") License and as specified in your agreement with Licensor (the "Governing Agreement"). In the event of any conflict between this License and the Governing Agreement, the Governing Agreement shall control.

You may:

a. (if specified as a "personal use" version) install the Software on a single stand-alone computer or a single network node from which node the Software cannot be accessed by another computer, provided that such Software shall be used by only one individual; or

b. (if specified as a "workstation" version) install the Software on a single stand-alone computer or a single network node from which node the Software cannot be accessed by another computer, provided that such Software shall be used by only one individual; or

c. (if specified as a "LAN" version) install the Software on a local area network server that provides access to multiple computers, up to the maximum number of computers or users specified in your Governing Agreement, provided that such Software shall be used only by employees of your organization; or

d. (if specified as an "enterprise" version) install the Software or copies of the Software on multiple local or wide area network servers, intranet servers, stand-alone computers and network nodes (and to make copies of the Software for such purpose) at one or more sites, which servers provide access to a multiple number of users, up to the maximum number of users specified in your Governing Agreement, provided that such Software shall be used only by employees of your organization.

This License is not a sale. Title and copyrights to the Software, accompanying documentation and any copy made by you remain with Licensor or its suppliers or licensors.

2. **Intellectual Property.** The Software is owned by Licensor or its licensors and is protected by United States and other jurisdictions' copyright laws and international treaty provisions. Therefore, you may not use, copy, or distribute the Software without the express written authorization of CBT Group PLC. This License authorizes you to use the Software for the internal training needs of your employees only, and to make one copy of the Software solely for backup or archival purposes. You may not print copies of any user documentation provided in "online" or electronic form. Licensor retains all rights not expressly granted.

3. **Restrictions.** You may not transfer, rent, lease, loan or time-share the Software or accompanying documentation. You may not reverse engineer, decompile, or disassemble the Software, except to the extent the foregoing restriction is expressly prohibited by applicable law. You may not modify, or create derivative works based upon the Software in whole or in part.

1. **Confidentiality**. The Software contains confidential trade secret information belonging to Licensor, and you may use the software only pursuant to the terms of your Governing Agreement, if any, and the license set forth herein. In addition, you may not disclose the Software to any third party.

2. **Limited Liability**. IN NO EVENT WILL THE Licensor's LIABILITY UNDER, ARISING OUT OF OR RELATING TO THIS AGREEMENT EXCEED THE AMOUNT PAID TO LICENSOR FOR THE SOFTWARE. LICENSOR SHALL NOT BE LIABLE FOR ANY SPECIAL, INCIDENTAL, INDIRECT OR CONSEQUENTIAL DAMAGES, HOWEVER CAUSED AND ON ANY THEORY OF LIABILITY., REGARDLESS OR WHETHER LICENSOR HAS BEEN ADVISED OF THE POSSIBILITY OF SUCH DAMAGES. WITHOUT LIMITING THE FOREGOING, LICENSOR WILL NOT BE LIABLE FOR LOST PROFITS, LOSS OF DATA, OR COSTS OF COVER.

3. **Limited Warranty**. LICENSOR WARRANTS THAT SOFTWARE WILL BE FREE FROM DEFECTS IN MATERIALS AND WORKMANSHIP UNDER NORMAL USE FOR A PERIOD OF THIRTY (30) DAYS FROM THE DATE OF RECEIPT. THIS LIMITED WARRANTY IS VOID IF FAILURE OF THE SOFTWARE HAS RESULTED FROM ABUSE OR MISAPPLICATION. ANY REPLACEMENT SOFTWARE WILL BE WARRANTED FOR A PERIOD OF THIRTY (30) DAYS FROM THE DATE OF RECEIPT OF SUCH REPLACEMENT SOFTWARE. THE SOFTWARE AND DOCUMENTATION ARE PROVIDED "AS IS". LICENSOR HEREBY DISCLAIMS ALL OTHER WARRANTIES, EXPRESS, IMPLIED, OR STATUTORY, INCLUDING WITHOUT LIMITATION, THE IMPLIED WARRANTIES OF MERCHANTABILITY AND FITNESS FOR A PARTICULAR PURPOSE.

4. **Exceptions**. SOME STATES DO NOT ALLOW THE LIMITATION OF INCIDENTAL DAMAGES OR LIMITATIONS ON HOW LONG AN IMPLIED WARRANTY LASTS, SO THE ABOVE LIMITATIONS OR EXCLUSIONS MAY NOT APPLY TO YOU. This agreement gives you specific legal rights, and you may also have other rights which vary from state to state.

5. **U.S. Government-Restricted Rights**. The Software and accompanying documentation are deemed to be "commercial computer Software" and "commercial computer Software documentation," respectively, pursuant to FAR Section 227.7202 and FAR Section 12.212, as applicable. Any use, modification, reproduction release, performance, display or disclosure of the Software and accompanying documentation by the U.S. Government shall be governed solely by the terms of this Agreement and shall be prohibited except to the extent expressly permitted by the terms of this Agreement.

6. **Export Restrictions**. You may not download, export, or re-export the Software (a) into, or to a national or resident of, Cuba, Iraq, Libya, Yugoslavia, North Korea, Iran, Syria or any other country to which the United States has embargoed goods, or (b) to anyone on the United States Treasury Department's list of Specially Designated Nations or the U.S. Commerce Department's Table of Deny Orders. By installing or using the Software, you are representing and warranting that you are not located in, under the control of, or a national resident of any such country or on any such list.

7. **General**. This License is governed by the laws of the United States and the State of California, without reference to conflict of laws principles. The parties agree that the United Nations Convention on Contracts for the International Sale of Goods shall not apply to this License. If any provision of this Agreement is held invalid, the remainder of this License shall continue in full force and effect.

8. **More Information**. Should you have any questions concerning this Agreement, or if you desire to contact Licensor for any reason, please contact: CBT Systems USA Ltd., 1005 Hamilton Court, Menlo Park, California 94025, Attn: Chief Legal Officer.

IF YOU DO NOT AGREE WITH THE ABOVE TERMS AND CONDITIONS, SO NOT INSTALL THE SOFTWARE AND RETURN IT TO THE LICENSOR.

LICENSE AGREEMENT AND LIMITED WARRANTY

READ THE FOLLOWING TERMS AND CONDITIONS CAREFULLY BEFORE OPENING THIS CD PACKAGE. THIS LEGAL DOCUMENT IS AN AGREEMENT BETWEEN YOU AND PRENTICE-HALL, INC. (THE "COMPANY"). BY OPENING THIS SEALED CD PACKAGE, YOU ARE AGREEING TO BE BOUND BY THESE TERMS AND CONDITIONS. IF YOU DO NOT AGREE WITH THESE TERMS AND CONDITIONS, DO NOT OPEN THE CD PACKAGE. PROMPTLY RETURN THE UNOPENED CD PACKAGE AND ALL ACCOMPANYING ITEMS TO THE PLACE YOU OBTAINED THEM FOR A FULL REFUND OF ANY SUMS YOU HAVE PAID.

1.   **GRANT OF LICENSE:** In consideration of your purchase of this book, and your agreement to abide by the terms and conditions of this Agreement, the Company grants to you a nonexclusive right to use and display the copy of the enclosed software program (hereinafter the "SOFTWARE") on a single computer (i.e., with a single CPU) at a single location so long as you comply with the terms of this Agreement. The Company reserves all rights not expressly granted to you under this Agreement.

2.   **OWNERSHIP OF SOFTWARE:** You own only the magnetic or physical media (the enclosed CD) on which the SOFTWARE is recorded or fixed, but the Company and the software developers retain all the rights, title, and ownership to the SOFTWARE recorded on the original CD copy(ies) and all subsequent copies of the SOFTWARE, regardless of the form or media on which the original or other copies may exist. This license is not a sale of the original SOFTWARE or any copy to you.

3.   **COPY RESTRICTIONS:** This SOFTWARE and the accompanying printed materials and user manual (the "Documentation") are the subject of copyright. The individual programs on the CD are copyrighted by the authors of each program. Some of the programs on the CD include separate licensing agreements. If you intend to use one of these programs, you must read and follow its accompanying license agreement. You may not copy the Documentation or the SOFTWARE, except that you may make a single copy of the SOFTWARE for backup or archival purposes only. You may be held legally responsible for any copying or copyright infringement which is caused or encouraged by your failure to abide by the terms of this restriction.

4.   **USE RESTRICTIONS:** You may not network the SOFTWARE or otherwise use it on more than one computer or computer terminal at the same time. You may physically transfer the SOFTWARE from one computer to another provided that the SOFTWARE is used on only one computer at a time. You may not distribute copies of the SOFTWARE or Documentation to others. You may not reverse engineer, disassemble, decompile, modify, adapt, translate, or create derivative works based on the SOFTWARE or the Documentation without the prior written consent of the Company.

5.   **TRANSFER RESTRICTIONS:** The enclosed SOFTWARE is licensed only to you and may not be transferred to any one else without the prior written consent of the Company. Any unauthorized transfer of the SOFTWARE shall result in the immediate termination of this Agreement.

6.   **TERMINATION:** This license is effective until terminated. This license will terminate automatically without notice from the Company and become null and void if you fail to comply with any provisions or limitations of this license. Upon termination, you shall destroy the Documentation and all copies of the SOFTWARE. All provisions of this Agreement as to warranties, limitation of liability, remedies or damages, and our ownership rights shall survive termination.

7.   **MISCELLANEOUS:** This Agreement shall be construed in accordance with the laws of the United States of America and the State of New York and shall benefit the Company, its affiliates, and assignees.

8.   **LIMITED WARRANTY AND DISCLAIMER OF WARRANTY:** The Company warrants that the SOFTWARE, when properly used in accordance with the Documentation, will operate in substantial conformity with the description of the SOFTWARE set forth in the Documentation. The Company does not warrant that the SOFTWARE will meet your requirements or that the operation

of the SOFTWARE will be uninterrupted or error-free. The Company warrants that the media on which the SOFTWARE is delivered shall be free from defects in materials and workmanship under normal use for a period of thirty (30) days from the date of your purchase. Your only remedy and the Company's only obligation under these limited warranties is, at the Company's option, return of the warranted item for a refund of any amounts paid by you or replacement of the item. Any replacement of SOFTWARE or media under the warranties shall not extend the original warranty period. The limited warranty set forth above shall not apply to any SOFTWARE which the Company determines in good faith has been subject to misuse, neglect, improper installation, repair, alteration, or damage by you. EXCEPT FOR THE EXPRESSED WARRANTIES SET FORTH ABOVE, THE COMPANY DISCLAIMS ALL WARRANTIES, EXPRESS OR IMPLIED, INCLUDING WITHOUT LIMITATION, THE IMPLIED WARRANTIES OF MERCHANTABILITY AND FITNESS FOR A PARTICULAR PURPOSE. EXCEPT FOR THE EXPRESS WARRANTY SET FORTH ABOVE, THE COMPANY DOES NOT WARRANT, GUARANTEE, OR MAKE ANY REPRESENTATION REGARDING THE USE OR THE RESULTS OF THE USE OF THE SOFTWARE IN TERMS OF ITS CORRECTNESS, ACCURACY, RELIABILITY, CURRENTNESS, OR OTHERWISE.

IN NO EVENT, SHALL THE COMPANY OR ITS EMPLOYEES, AGENTS, SUPPLIERS, OR CONTRACTORS BE LIABLE FOR ANY INCIDENTAL, INDIRECT, SPECIAL, OR CONSEQUENTIAL DAMAGES ARISING OUT OF OR IN CONNECTION WITH THE LICENSE GRANTED UNDER THIS AGREEMENT, OR FOR LOSS OF USE, LOSS OF DATA, LOSS OF INCOME OR PROFIT, OR OTHER LOSSES, SUSTAINED AS A RESULT OF INJURY TO ANY PERSON, OR LOSS OF OR DAMAGE TO PROPERTY, OR CLAIMS OF THIRD PARTIES, EVEN IF THE COMPANY OR AN AUTHORIZED REPRESENTATIVE OF THE COMPANY HAS BEEN ADVISED OF THE POSSIBILITY OF SUCH DAMAGES. IN NO EVENT SHALL LIABILITY OF THE COMPANY FOR DAMAGES WITH RESPECT TO THE SOFTWARE EXCEED THE AMOUNTS ACTUALLY PAID BY YOU, IF ANY, FOR THE SOFTWARE.

SOME JURISDICTIONS DO NOT ALLOW THE LIMITATION OF IMPLIED WARRANTIES OR LIABILITY FOR INCIDENTAL, INDIRECT, SPECIAL, OR CONSEQUENTIAL DAMAGES, SO THE ABOVE LIMITATIONS MAY NOT ALWAYS APPLY. THE WARRANTIES IN THIS AGREEMENT GIVE YOU SPECIFIC LEGAL RIGHTS AND YOU MAY ALSO HAVE OTHER RIGHTS WHICH VARY IN ACCORDANCE WITH LOCAL LAW.

ACKNOWLEDGMENT

YOU ACKNOWLEDGE THAT YOU HAVE READ THIS AGREEMENT, UNDERSTAND IT, AND AGREE TO BE BOUND BY ITS TERMS AND CONDITIONS. YOU ALSO AGREE THAT THIS AGREEMENT IS THE COMPLETE AND EXCLUSIVE STATEMENT OF THE AGREEMENT BETWEEN YOU AND THE COMPANY AND SUPERSEDES ALL PROPOSALS OR PRIOR AGREEMENTS, ORAL, OR WRITTEN, AND ANY OTHER COMMUNICATIONS BETWEEN YOU AND THE COMPANY OR ANY REPRESENTATIVE OF THE COMPANY RELATING TO THE SUBJECT MATTER OF THIS AGREEMENT.

Should you have any questions concerning this Agreement or if you wish to contact the Company for any reason, please contact in writing at the address below.

Robin Short

Prentice Hall PTR

One Lake Street

Upper Saddle River, New Jersey 07458

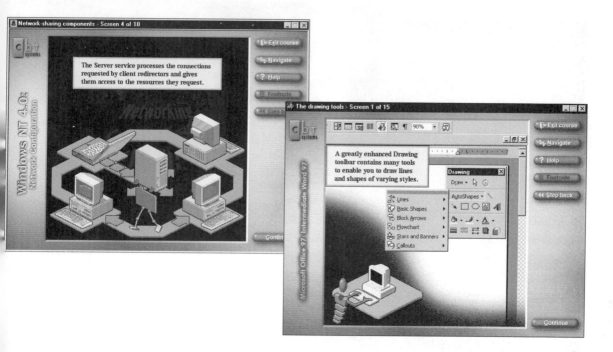

Other curricula available from CBT Systems:

- Cisco
- Informix
- Java
- Marimba
- Microsoft
- Netscape
- Novell

- Oracle
- SAP
- Sybase
- C/C++
- Centura
- Information Technology/ Core Concepts

- Internet and Intranet Skills
- Internetworking
- UNIX

To order additional CBT Systems courseware today call 800.789.8590 or visit www.clbooks.com/training/cbt.htm

Oracle SQL
HIGH-PERFORMANCE TUNING

Guy Harrison

1997, 500pp, paper,
0-13-614231-1

A BOOK/CD-ROM PACKAGE

The first guide to Oracle
performance that focuses on tuning
SQL code rather than the server.

Oracle8 & UNIX®
Performance Tuning

Ahmed Alomari

1999, paper, 0-13-907676-X

A BOOK/CD-ROM PACKAGE

Detailed coverage of maximizing
Oracle server performance by
tuning both the database and
the underlying UNIX system. Covers both
Oracle8 and Oracle7.

Oracle Database
Administration
ON UNIX® SYSTEMS

Lynnwood Brown

1997, 352pp, paper,
0-13-244666-9

A BOOK/CD-ROM PACKAGE

Focuses exclusively on Oracle
database administration in UNIX
environments.

Data Warehousing
with Oracle
AN ADMINISTRATOR'S
HANDBOOK

Sima Yazdani and Shirley Wong

1997, 400pp, paper,
0-13-570557-6

World-class Oracle experts show
exactly how to understand, plan,
implement and administer an
enterprise data warehouse application
using Oracle.

Inside Oracle
Designer/2000

Albert Lulushi

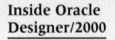

1998, 992pp, paper, 0-13-849753-2

The most comprehensive
guide to date on using
Designer/2000 Version 2.

Building Intelligent
Databases with
Oracle PL/SQL
Triggers, and
Stored Procedures,
SECOND EDITION

Kevin T. Owens

1998, 450pp, paper,
0-13-794314-8

Focuses on how to develop procedural
constraints through triggers and stored
procedures.

| Back | Forward | Home | Reload | Images | Open | Print | Find | Stop |

http://www.phptr.com/

| What's New? | What's Cool? | Destinations | Net Search | People | Software |

PRENTICE HALL
Professional Technical Reference
Tomorrow's Solutions for Today's Professionals.

Keep Up-to-Date with
PH PTR Online!

We strive to stay on the cutting-edge of what's happening in professional computer science and engineering. Here's a bit of what you'll find when you stop by **www.phptr.com**:

@ Special interest areas offering our latest books, book series, software, features of the month, related links and other useful information to help you get the job done.

Deals, deals, deals! Come to our promotions section for the latest bargains offered to you exclusively from our retailers.

$ Need to find a bookstore? Chances are, there's a bookseller near you that carries a broad selection of PTR titles. Locate a Magnet bookstore near you at www.phptr.com.

! What's New at PH PTR? We don't just publish books for the professional community, we're a part of it. Check out our convention schedule, join an author chat, get the latest reviews and press releases on topics of interest to you.

✉ Subscribe Today! **Join PH PTR's monthly email newsletter!**

Want to be kept up-to-date on your area of interest? Choose a targeted category on our website, and we'll keep you informed of the latest PH PTR products, author events, reviews and conferences in your interest area.

Visit our mailroom to subscribe today! **http://www.phptr.com/mail_lists**

ABOUT THE CD

The enclosed CD-ROM contains the following computer-based training (CBT) course module from CBT Systems:

Oracle8 New Features: Object Technology & Other New Features.

The CD can be used on Windows NT

DBAware 2.0

Listed below are the minimum and recommended hardware and software requirements for DBAware 2.0. Please check each item and verify that your system is capable of running DBAware.

I. Minimum

Processor: Intel 386, 386SX, 486, or IBM PS/2 Model 70 or 80, and 100 percent compatible computers.

Memory: 640 KB main memory and minimum of **16 MB** of extended memory.

Disk space: Minimum 10 MB free space for the system files, and at least 6.5 MB free space for each user image. Additional disk space is required for archiving data.

Drive (for loading the system): 3.5-inch drive and CD-ROM drive.

Monitor: Any display system having an MS-Windows driver.

Mouse: Any mouse supported by MS-Windows.

Operating System:

    MS-Windows 3.1: MS-DOS 5.0 or greater and **WIN32S**.

    MS-Windows NT: MS-Windows NT 3.51 or 4.0.

    MS-Windows 95: MS-Windows 95.

RDBMS Communication Software:

    Oracle: **SQL*Net 1.1.7.7B or higher**.

    Sybase: **DB-Library 4.2**.

DLL File:

MS-Windows 3.1, MS-Windows 95: msvcrt40.dll (version: 4.10.6038 or later*) in the...windows subdirectory.

MS-Windows NT 3.51: msvcrt40.dll (version: 4.10.6038 or later*) in the..winnt subdirectory

Warning: Use the WIN32 version on Windows NT and 95, and use the WIN32S version in Windows 3.1

Technical Support

If you have a problem with the CBT software, please contact CBT Technical Support. In the US call 1 (800) 938-3247. If you are outside the US call 3531-283-0380.

Prentice Hall does not offer technical support for this software. However, if there is a problem with the media, you may obtain a replacement copy by e-mailing us with your problem at: disc_exchange@prenhall.com